Charles Dickens

Works of Charles Dickens

Charles Dickens

Works of Charles Dickens

ISBN/EAN: 9783741191985

Manufactured in Europe, USA, Canada, Australia, Japa

Cover: Foto ©Andreas Hilbeck / pixelio.de

Manufactured and distributed by brebook publishing software (www.brebook.com)

Charles Dickens

Works of Charles Dickens

OF

CHARLES DICKENS.

HOUSEHOLD EDITION.

ILLUSTRATED FROM DRAWINGS BY F. O. C. DARLEY
AND JOHN GILBERT.

BLEAK HOUSE.
VOL. II.

NEW YORK:
SHELDON AND COMPANY.
335 BROADWAY, COR. WORTH ST.
1863.

Entered according to Act of Congress, in the year 1863, by
HENRY O. HOUGHTON,
in the Clerk's Office of the District Court of the District of Massachusetts.

RIVERSIDE, CAMBRIDGE:
STEREOTYPED AND PRINTED BY H. O. HOUGHTON.

BLEAK HOUSE.

CONTENTS OF VOLUME II.

CHAPTER XVI.
Tom-all-alone's	PAGE 7

CHAPTER XVII.
Esther's Narrative 19

CHAPTER XVIII.
Lady Dedlock 39

CHAPTER XIX.
Moving on 63

CHAPTER XX.
A New Lodger 83

CHAPTER XXI.
The Smallweed Family 104

CHAPTER XXII.
Mr. Bucket 129

CHAPTER XXIII.
Esther's Narrative 148

CHAPTER XXIV.
An Appeal Case 173

CONTENTS.

CHAPTER XXV.
Mrs. Snagsby sees it all 198

CHAPTER XXVI.
Sharpshooters 211

CHAPTER XXVII.
More Old Soldiers than one 230

CHAPTER XXVIII.
The Ironmaster 248

CHAPTER XXIX.
The Young Man 264

CHAPTER XXX.
Esther's Narrative 278

CHAPTER XXXI.
Nurse and Patient 300

BLEAK HOUSE.

CHAPTER XVI.

TOM-ALL-ALONE'S.

My Lady Dedlock is restless, very restless. The astonished fashionable intelligence hardly knows where to have her. To-day she is at Chesney Wold; yesterday she was at her house in town; to-morrow she may be abroad, for anything the fashionable intelligence can with confidence predict. Even Sir Leicester's gallantry has some trouble to keep pace with her. It would have more, but that his other faithful ally, for better and for worse — the gout — darts into the old oak bed-chamber at Chesney Wold, and grips him by both legs.

Sir Leicester receives the gout as a troublesome demon, but still a demon of the patrician order. All the Dedlocks, in the direct male line, through a course of time during and beyond which the memory of man goeth not to the contrary, have had the gout. It can be proved, sir. Other men's fathers may have died of the rheumatism, or may have taken base contagion from the tainted blood of the sick vulgar, but the Dedlock family have communicated something exclusive, even to the levelling process of dying, by dying of their own family gout. It has come down, through the illustrious line, like the plate, or the pictures, or the place in Lincolnshire. It is among their dignities. Sir Leicester is, perhaps, not wholly without an impression, though he has never resolved it into words, that the angel of death in the discharge of his necessary duties may observe to the shades of the aristocracy, "My lords and gentlemen, I have the honor to present to you another Dedlock certified to have arrived per the family gout."

Hence, Sir Leicester yields up his family legs to the family disorder, as if he held his name and fortune on that feudal tenure. He feels, that for a Dedlock to be laid upon his back and spasmodically twitched and stabbed in his extremities, is a liberty taken somewhere; but, he thinks, "We have all yielded to this; it belongs to us; it has, for some hundreds of years, been understood that we are not to make the vaults in the park interesting on more ignoble terms; and I submit myself to the compromise."

And a goodly show he makes, lying in a flush of crimson and gold, in the midst of the great drawing-room, before his favorite picture of my Lady, with broad strips of sunlight shining in, down the long perspective, through the long line of windows, and alternating with soft reliefs of shadow. Outside, the stately oaks, rooted for ages in the green ground which has never known ploughshare, but was still a Chase when kings rode to battle with sword and shield, and rode a-hunting with bow and arrow, — bear witness to his greatness. Inside, his forefathers, looking on him from the walls, say, "Each of us was a passing reality here, and left this colored shadow of himself, and melted into remembrance as dreamy as the distant voices of the rooks now lulling you to rest;" and bear their testimony to his greatness, too. And he is very great, this day. And woe to Boythorn, or other daring wight, who shall presumptuously contest an inch with him!

My Lady is at present represented, near Sir Leicester, by her portrait. She has flitted away to town, with no intention of remaining there, and will soon flit hither again, to the confusion of the fashionable intelligence. The house in town is not prepared for her reception. It is muffled and dreary. Only one Mercury in powder gapes disconsolate at the hall-window; and he mentioned last night to another Mercury of his acquaintance, also accustomed to good society, that if that sort of thing was to last — which it couldn't, for a man of his spirits couldn't bear it, and a man of his figure couldn't be expected to bear it — there would be no resource for him, upon his honor, but to cut his throat!

What connection can there be, between the place in Lincolnshire, the house in town, the Mercury in powder, and the whereabout of Jo the outlaw with the broom, who had that distant ray of light upon him when he swept the churchyard-step? What connection can there have been between many people in the innumerable histories of this world, who, from opposite sides of great gulfs, have, nevertheless, been very curiously brought together!

Jo sweeps his crossing all day long, unconscious of the link, if any link there be. He sums up his mental condition, when asked a question, by replying that he "don't know nothink." He knows that it's hard to keep the mud off the crossing in dirty weather, and harder still to live by doing it. Nobody taught him, even that much; he found it out.

Jo lives — that is to say, Jo has not yet died — in a ruinous place, known to the like of him by the name of

Tom-all-alone's. It is a black, dilapidated street, avoided by all decent people; where the crazy houses were seized upon, when their decay was far advanced, by some bold vagrants, who, after establishing their own possession, took to letting them out in lodgings. Now, these tumbling tenements contain, by night, a swarm of misery. As, on the ruined human wretch, vermin parasites appear, so, these ruined shelters have bred a crowd of foul existence that crawls in and out of gaps in walls and boards; and coils itself to sleep, in maggot numbers, where the rain drips in; and comes and goes, fetching and carrying fever, and sowing more evil in its every footprint, than Lord Coodle, and Sir Thomas Doodle, and the Duke of Foodle, and all the fine gentlemen in office, down to Zoodle, shall set right in five hundred years — though born expressly to do it.

Twice, lately, there has been a crash and a cloud of dust, like the springing of a mine, in Tom-all-alone's; and, each time, a house has fallen. These accidents have made a paragraph in the newspapers, and have filled a bed or two in the nearest hospital. The gaps remain, and there are not unpopular lodgings among the rubbish. As several more houses are nearly ready to go, the next crash in Tom-all-alone's may be expected to be a good one.

This desirable property is in Chancery, of course. It would be an insult to the discernment of any man with half an eye, to tell him so. Whether "Tom" is the popular representative of the original plaintiff or defendant in Jarndyce and Jarndyce; or, whether Tom lived here when the suit had laid the street waste, all alone, until other settlers came to join him; or, whether the traditional title is a comprehensive name for a retreat cut off from honest company and put out of the pale of hope; perhaps nobody knows. Certainly, Jo don't know.

" For *I* don't," says Jo, " *I* don't know nothink."

It must be a strange state to be like Jo! To shuffle through the streets, unfamiliar with the shapes, and in utter darkness as to the meaning, of those mysterious symbols, so abundant over the shops, and at the corners of streets, and on the doors, and in the windows! To see people read, and to see people write, and to see the postmen deliver letters, and not to have the least idea of all that language — to be, to every scrap of it, stone blind and dumb! It must be very puzzling to see the good company going to the churches on Sundays, with their books in their hands, and to think (for perhaps Jo *does* think, at odd times) what does it all mean, and if it means anything to anybody, how comes it that it means nothing to me? To be hustled, and jostled, and moved on; and really to feel that it would appear to be perfectly true that I have no business, here, or there, or anywhere; and yet to be perplexed by the consideration that I *am* here somehow, too, and everybody overlooked me until I became the creature that I am! It must be a strange state, not merely to be told that I am scarcely human (as in the case of my offering myself for a witness), but to feel it of my own knowledge all my life! To see the horses, dogs, and cattle, go by me, and to know that in ignorance I belong to them, and not to the superior beings in my shape, whose delicacy I offend! Jo's ideas of a Criminal Trial, or a Judge, or a Bishop, or a Government, or that inestimable jewel to him (if he only knew it) the Constitution, should be strange! His whole material and immaterial life is wonderfully strange; his death, the strangest thing of all.

Jo comes out of Tom-all-alone's, meeting the tardy morning which is always late in getting down there, and munches his dirty bit of bread as he comes along. His way lying through many streets, and the houses not yet being open, he sits down to breakfast on the door-step of the Society for the Propagation of the Gospel in Foreign Parts, and gives it a brush when he has finished, as an acknowledgment of the accommodation. He admires the size of the edifice, and wonders what it's all about. He has no idea, poor wretch, of the spiritual destitution of a coral reef in the Pacific, or what it costs to look up the precious souls among the cocoa-nuts and bread-fruit.

He goes to his crossing, and begins to lay it out for the day. The town awakes; the great tee-totum is set up for its daily spin and whirl; all that unaccountable reading and writing, which has been suspended for a few hours, recommences. Jo, and the other lower animals, get on in the unintelligible mess as they can. It is market-day. The blinded oxen, over-goaded, over-driven, never-guided, run into wrong places and are beaten out; and plunge, red-eyed and foaming, at stone walls; and often sorely hurt the innocent, and often sorely hurt themselves. Very like Jo and his order; very, very like!

A band of music comes and plays. Jo listens to it. So does a dog — a drover's dog, waiting for his master outside a butcher's shop, and evidently thinking about those sheep he has had upon his mind for some hours, and is happily rid of. He seems perplexed respecting three or four; can't remember where he left them; looks up and down the street, as half expecting to see them astray; suddenly pricks up his ears and remembers all about it. A thoroughly vagabond dog, accustomed to low company and public-houses; a terrific dog to sheep; ready at a whistle to scamper over their backs, and tear out mouthfuls of their wool; but an educated, improved, developed dog, who has been taught his duties and knows how to discharge them. He and Jo listen to the music, probably with much the same amount of animal satisfaction; likewise, as to awakened association, aspiration, or regret, melancholy or joyful reference to things beyond the senses, they are probably upon a par. But, otherwise, how far above the human listener is the brute!

Turn that dog's descendants wild, like Jo, and in a very few years they will so degenerate that they will lose even their bark — but not their bite.

The day changes as it wears itself away, and becomes dark and drizzly. Jo fights it out, at his crossing, among the mud and wheels, the horses, whips, and umbrellas, and gets but a scanty sum to pay for the unsavory shelter of Tom-all-alone's. Twilight comes on; gas begins to start up in the shops; the lamplighter, with his ladder, runs along the margin of the pavement. A wretched evening is beginning to close in.

In his chambers, Mr. Tulkinghorn sits meditating an application to the nearest magistrate to-morrow morning for a warrant. Gridley, a disappointed suitor, has been here to-day, and has been alarming. We are not to be put in bodily fear, and that ill-conditioned fellow shall be held to bail again. From the ceiling, foreshortened Allegory, in the person of one impossible Roman upsidedown, points with the arm of Samson (out of joint, and an odd one) obtrusively toward the window. Why should Mr. Tulkinghorn, for such no reason, look out of window? Is the hand not always pointing there? So he does not look out of window.

And if he did, what would it be to see a woman going by? There are women enough in the world, Mr. Tulkinghorn thinks — too many; they are at the bottom of all that goes wrong in it, though, for the matter of that, they create business for lawyers. What would it be to see a woman going by, even though she were going secretly? They are all secret. Mr. Tulkinghorn knows that, very well.

But they are not all like the woman who now leaves him and his house behind; between whose plain dress, and her refined manner, there is something exceedingly inconsistent. She should be an upper servant by her attire, yet, in her air and step, though both are hurried and assumed — as far as she can assume in the muddy streets, which she treads with an unaccustomed foot — she is a lady. Her face is veiled, and still she sufficiently betrays herself to make more than one of those who pass her look round sharply.

She never turns her head. Lady or servant, she has a purpose in her, and can follow it. She never turns her head, until she comes to the crossing where Jo plies with his broom. He crosses with her, and begs. Still, she does not turn her head until she has landed on the other side. Then, she slightly beckons to him, and says, "Come here!"

Jo follows her, a pace or two, into a quiet court.

"Are you the boy I have read of in the papers?" she asked behind her veil.

"I don't know," says Jo, staring moodily at the veil, "nothink about no papers. I don't know nothink about nothink at all."

"Were you examined at an Inquest?"

"I don't know nothink about no — where I was took

by the beadle, do you mean?" says Jo. "Was the boy's name at the Inkwhich, Jo?"

"Yes."

"That's me!" says Jo.

"Come farther up."

"You mean about the man?" says Jo, following. "Him as wos dead?"

"Hush! Speak in a whisper! Yes. Did he look, when he was living, so very ill and poor?"

"Oh, jist!" says Jo.

"Did he look like — not like *you*?" says the woman, with abhorrence.

"Oh, not so bad as me," says Jo. "I'm a reg'lar one *I* am! You didn't know him, did you?"

"How dare you ask me if I knew him?"

"No offence, my lady," says Jo, with much humility; for even he has got at the suspicion of her being a lady.

"I am not a lady. I am a servant."

"You are a jolly servant!" says Jo, without the least idea of saying anything offensive; merely as a tribute of admiration.

"Listen and be silent. Don't talk to me, and stand farther from me! Can you show me all those places that were spoken of in the account I read? The place he wrote for, the place he died at, the place where you were taken to, and the place where he was buried? Do you know the place where he was buried?"

Jo answers with a nod; having also nodded as each other place was mentioned.

"Go before me, and show me all those dreadful places. Stop opposite to each, and don't speak to me unless I speak to you. Don't look back. Do what I want, and I will pay you well."

Jo attends closely while the words are being spoken; tells them off on his broom-handle, finding them rather hard; pauses to consider their meaning; considers it satisfactory, and nods his ragged head.

"I am fly," says Jo. "But fen larks, you know. Stow hooking it!"

"What does the horrible creature mean?" exclaims the servant, recoiling from him.

"Stow cutting away, you know!" says Jo.

"I don't understand you. Go on before! I will give you more money than you ever had in your life."

Jo screws up his mouth into a whistle, gives his ragged head a rub, takes his broom under his arm, and leads the way; passing deftly, with his bare feet, over the hard stones, and through the mud and mire.

Cook's Court. Jo stops. A pause.

"Who lives here?"

"Him wot give him his writing, and give me half a bull," says Jo, in a whisper, without looking over his shoulder.

"Go on to the next."

Krook's house. Jo stops again. A longer pause.

"Who lives here?"

"*He* lived here." Joe answers as before.

After a silence, he is asked, "In which room?"

"In the back room up there. You can see the winder from this corner. Up there! That's where I see him stritched out. This is the public 'ouse where I was took to."

"Go on to the next!"

It is a longer walk to the next; but, Jo, relieved of his first suspicions, sticks to the terms imposed upon him, and does not look round. By many devious ways reeking with offence of many kinds, they come to the little tunnel of a court, and to the gas-lamp (lighted now), and to the iron gate.

"He was put there," says Jo, holding to the bars and looking in.

"Where? Oh, what a scene of horror!"

"There!" says Jo, pointing. "Over yinder. Among them piles of bones, and close to that there kitchin winder! They put him wery nigh the top. They was obliged to stamp upon it to git it in. I could unkiver it for you with my broom, if the gate was open. That's why they locks it, I s'pose," giving it a shake. "It's always locked. Look at the rat!" cries Jo, excited. "Hi! Look! There he goes! Ho! Into the ground!"

The servant shrinks into a corner — into a corner of that hideous archway, with its deadly stains contaminating her dress; and putting out her two hands, and passionately telling him to keep away from her, for he is loathsome to her, so remains for some moments. Jo stands staring, and is still staring when she recovers herself.

"Is this place of abomination consecrated ground?"

"I don't know nothink of consequential ground," says Jo, still staring.

"Is it blessed!"

"WHICH?" says Jo, in the last degree amazed.

"Is it blessed?"

"I'm blest if I know," says Jo, staring more than ever; "but I shouldn't think it warn't. Blest?" repeats Jo, something troubled in his mind. "It a'n't done it much good if it is. Blest? I should think it was t'othered myself. But *I* don't know nothink!"

The servant takes as little heed of what he says, as

she seems to take of what she has said herself. She draws off her glove, to get some money from her purse. Jo silently notices how white and small her hand is, and what a jolly servant she must be to wear such sparkling rings.

She drops a piece of money in his hand, without touching it, and shuddering as their hands approach. " Now," she adds, " show me the spot again ! "

Jo thrusts the handle of his broom between the bars of the gate, and with his utmost power of elaboration, points it out. At length, looking aside to see if he has made himself intelligible, he finds that he is alone.

His first proceeding is, to hold the piece of money to the gas-light, and to be overpowered at finding that it is yellow — gold. His next is, to give it a one-sided bite at the edge, as a test of its quality. His next, to put it in his mouth for safety, and to sweep the step and passage with great care. His job done, he sets off for Tom-all-alone's ; stopping in the light of innumerable gas-lamps to produce the piece of gold, and give it another one-sided bite, as a reassurance of its being genuine.

The Mercury in powder is in no want of society to-night, for my Lady goes to a grand dinner, and three or four balls. Sir Leicester is fidgety, down at Chesney Wold, with no better company than the gout ; he complains to Mrs. Rouncewell that the rain makes such a monotonous pattering on the terrace, that he can't read the paper, even by the fireside in his own snug dressing-room.

" Sir Leicester would have done better to try the other side of the house, my dear," says Mrs. Rouncewell to Rosa. " His dressing-room is on my Lady's side. And in all these years I never heard the step upon the Ghost's Walk, more distinct than it is to-night ! "

CHAPTER XVII.

ESTHER'S NARRATIVE.

RICHARD very often came to see us while we remained in London (though he soon failed in his letter-writing), and with his quick abilities, his good spirits, his good temper, his gayety and freshness, was always delightful. But, though I liked him more and more, the better I knew him, I still felt more and more, how much it was to be regretted that he had been educated in no habits of application and concentration. The system which had addressed him in exactly the same manner as it had addressed hundreds of other boys, all varying in character and capacity, had enabled him to dash through his tasks, always with fair credit, and often with distinction; but in a fitful, dazzling way that had confirmed his reliance on those very qualities in himself, which it had been most desirable to direct and train. They were great qualities, without which no high place can be meritoriously won; but, like fire and water, though excellent servants, they were very bad masters. If they had been under Richard's direction, they would have been his friends; but Richard being under their direction, they became his enemies.

I write down these opinions, not because I believe that this or any other thing was so, because I thought so; but only because I did think so, and I want to be quite candid about all I thought and did. These were my thoughts about Richard. I thought I often observed besides, how right my Guardian was in what he had said; and that the uncertainties and delays of the Chancery suit had imparted to his nature something of the careless spirit of a gamester, who felt that he was part of a great gaming system.

Mr. and Mrs. Bayham Badger coming one afternoon, when my Guardian was not at home, in the course of conversation I naturally inquired after Richard.

"Why, Mr. Carstone," said Mrs. Badger, "is very well, and is, I assure you, a great acquisition to our society. Captain Swosser used to say of me that I was always better than land a-head and a breeze a-starn to the midshipmen's mess when the purser's junk had become as tough as the fore-topsel weather earrings. It was his naval way of mentioning generally that I was an acquisition to any society. I may render the same tribute, I am sure, to Mr. Carstone. But I — you won't think me premature if I mention it?"

I said no, as Mrs. Badger's insinuating tone seemed to require such an answer.

"Nor Miss Clare?" said Mrs. Bayham Badger, sweetly.

Ada said no, too, and looked uneasy.

"Why, you see, my dears," said Mrs. Badger — "you'll excuse me calling you my dears?"

We entreated Mrs. Badger not to mention it.

"Because you really are, if I may take the liberty of saying so," pursued Mrs. Badger, "so perfectly charming. You see, my dears, that although I am still young — or Mr. Bayham Badger pays me the compliment of saying so — "

"No," Mr. Badger called out, like some one contradicting at a public meeting. "Not at all!"

"Very well," smiled Mrs. Badger, "we will say still young."

("Undoubtedly," said Mr. Badger.)

"My dears, though still young, I have had many opportunities of observing young men. There were many such on board the dear old Crippler, I assure you. After that, when I was with Captain Swosser in the Mediterranean, I embraced every opportunity of knowing and befriending the midshipmen under Captain Swosser's command. *You* never heard them called the young gentlemen, my dears, and probably would not understand allusions to their pipe-claying their weekly accounts; but it is otherwise with me, for blue water has been a second home to me, and I have been quite a sailor. Again, with Professor Dingo."

("A man of European reputation," murmured Mr. Badger.)

"When I lost my dear first, and became the wife of my dear second," said Mrs. Badger, speaking of her former husbands as if they were parts of a charade, "I still enjoyed opportunities of observing youth. The class attendant on Professor Dingo's lectures was a large one, and it became my pride, as the wife of an eminent scientific man seeking herself in science the utmost consolation it could impart, to throw our house open to the students, as a kind of Scientific Exchange. Every Tuesday evening there was lemonade and a mixed biscuit, for all who chose to partake of those refreshments. And there was science to an unlimited extent."

("Remarkable assemblies those, Miss Summerson," said Mr. Badger, reverentially. "There must have been great intellectual friction going on there, under the auspices of such a man!")

"And now," pursued Mrs. Badger, "now that I am the wife of my dear third, Mr. Badger, I still pursue those habits of observation which were formed during the lifetime of Captain Swosser, and adapted to new and unexpected purposes during the lifetime of Professor Dingo. I therefore have not come to the consideration of Mr. Carstone as a Neophyte. And yet I am very much of the opinion, my dears, that he has not chosen his profession advisedly."

Ada looked so very anxious now, that I asked Mrs. Badger on what she founded her supposition?

"My dear Miss Summerson," she replied, "on Mr. Carstone's character and conduct. He is of such a very easy disposition, that probably he would never think it worth while to mention how he really feels; but, he feels languid about the profession. He has not that positive interest in it which makes it his vocation. If he has any decided impression in reference to it, I should say it was that it is a tiresome pursuit. Now, this is not promising. Young men, like Mr. Allan Woodcourt, who take it from a strong interest in all that it can do, will find some reward in it through a great deal of work for a very little money, and through years of considerable endurance and disappointment. But I am quite convinced that this would never be the case with Mr. Carstone."

"Does Mr. Badger think so too?" asked Ada, timidly.

"Why," said Mr. Badger, "to tell the truth, Miss Clare, this view of the matter had not occurred to me until Mrs. Badger mentioned it. But, when Mrs. Badger put it in that light, I naturally gave great consideration to it; knowing that Mrs. Badger's mind, in addition to its natural advantages, has had the rare advantage of being formed by two such very distinguished (I will even say illustrious) public men as Captain Swosser of the Royal Navy and Professor Dingo. The conclusion at which I have arrived is — in short, is Mrs. Badger's conclusion."

"It was a maxim of Captain Swosser's," said Mrs. Badger, "speaking in his figurative, naval manner, that when you make pitch hot, you cannot make it too hot; and that if you only have to swab a plank, you should swab it as if Davy Jones were after you. It appears to me that this maxim is applicable to the medical, as well as to the nautical profession."

"To all professions," observed Mr. Badger. "It was admirably said by Captain Swosser. Beautifully said."

"People objected to Professor Dingo, when we were staying in the North of Devon, after our marriage," said Mrs. Badger, "that he disfigured some of the houses and other buildings, by chipping off fragments of those edifices with his little geological hammer. But the Professor replied, that he knew of no building, save the Temple of Science. The principle is the same, I think?"

"Precisely the same," said Mr. Badger. "Finely expressed! The Professor made the same remark, Miss Summerson, in his last illness; when (his mind wandering) he insisted on keeping his little hammer under the pillow, and chipping at the countenances of the attendants. The ruling passion!"

Although we could have dispensed with the length at which Mr. and Mrs. Badger pursued the conversation, we both felt that it was disinterested in them to express the opinion they had communicated to us, and that there was a great probability of its being sound. We agreed to say nothing to Mr. Jarndyce until we had spoken to Richard; and, as he was coming next evening, we resolved to have a very serious talk with him.

So, after he had been a little while with Ada, I went in and found my darling (as I knew she would be) prepared to consider him thoroughly right in whatever he said.

"And how do you get on, Richard?" said I. I always sat down on the other side of him. He made quite a sister of me.

"Oh! well enough!" said Richard.

"He can't say better than that, Esther, can he?" cried my pet, triumphantly.

I tried to look at my pet in the wisest manner, but of course I couldn't.

"Well enough?" I repeated.

"Yes," said Richard, "well enough. It's rather jog-trotty and humdrum. But it'll do as well as anything else!"

"Oh! my dear Richard!" I remonstrated.

"What's the matter?" said Richard.

"Do as well as anything else!"

"I don't think there's any harm in that, Dame Durden," said Ada, looking so confidingly at me across him! "Because if it will do as well as anything else, it will do very well, I hope."

"Oh, yes, I hope so," returned Richard, carelessly tossing his hair from his forehead. "After all, it may be only a kind of probation till our suit is — I forgot though. I am not to mention the suit. Forbidden ground! Oh, yes, it's all right enough. Let us talk about something else."

Ada would have done so, willingly, and with a full persuasion that we had brought the question to a most satisfactory state. But I thought it would be useless to stop there, so I began again.

"No, but Richard," said I, "and my dear Ada! Consider how important it is to you both, and what a point of honor it is towards your cousin, that you, Richard, should be quite in earnest without any reservation. I think we had better talk about this, really, Ada. It will be too late, very soon."

"Oh, yes! We must talk about it!" said Ada. "But I think Richard is right."

What was the use of my trying to look wise, when she was so pretty, and so engaging, and so fond of him!

"Mr. and Mrs. Badger were here yesterday, Richard," said I, "and they seemed disposed to think that you had no great liking for the profession."

"Did they though?" said Richard. "Oh! Well, that rather alters the case, because I had no idea that they thought so, and I should not have liked to disappoint or inconvenience them. The fact is, I don't care much about it. But oh, it don't matter! It'll do as well as anything else!"

"You hear him, Ada!" said I.

"The fact is," Richard proceeded, half thoughtfully and half jocosely, "it is not quite in my way. I don't take to it. And I get too much of Mrs. Bayham Badger's first and second."

"I am sure *that's* very natural!" cried Ada, quite delighted. "The very thing we both said yesterday, Esther!"

"Then," pursued Richard, "it's monotonous, and to-day is too like yesterday, and to-morrow is too like to-day."

"But I am afraid," said I, "this is an objection to all kinds of application — to life itself, except under some very uncommon circumstances."

"Do you think so?" returned Richard, still considering. "Perhaps! Ha! Why, then, you know," he added, suddenly becoming gay again, "we travel outside a circle, to what I said just now. It'll do as well as anything else. Oh, it's all right enough! Let us talk about something else."

But, even Ada, with her loving face — and if it had seemed innocent and trusting, when I first saw it in that memorable November fog, how much more so did it seem now, when I knew her innocent and trusting heart — even Ada shook her head at this, and looked serious. So I thought it a good opportunity to hint to Richard, that if he were sometimes a little careless of himself, I was sure he never meant to be careless of Ada; and that it was a part of his affectionate consideration for her, not to slight the importance of a step that might influence both their lives. This made him almost grave.

"My dear Mother Hubbard," he said, "that's the very thing! I have thought of that, several times; and have been quite angry with myself for meaning to be so much in earnest, and — somehow — not exactly being so. I don't know how it is; I seem to want something or other to stand by. Even you have no idea how fond I am of Ada (my darling cousin, I love you, so much!) but I don't settle down to constancy in other things. It's such uphill work, and it takes such a time!" said Richard, with an air of vexation.

"That may be," I suggested, "because you don't like what you have chosen."

"Poor fellow!" said Ada. "I am sure I don't wonder at it!"

No. It was not of the least use my trying to look wise. I tried again; but how could I do it, or how could it have any effect if I could, while Ada rested her clasped hands upon his shoulder, and while he looked at her tender blue eyes, and while they looked at him!

"You see, my precious girl," said Richard, passing her golden curls through and through his hand, "I was a little hasty, perhaps; or I misunderstood my own inclinations, perhaps. They don't seem to lie in that direction. I couldn't tell, till I tried. Now, the question is, whether it's worth while to undo all that has been done. It seems like making a great disturbance about nothing particular."

"My dear Richard," said I, "how *can* you say about nothing particular?"

"I don't mean absolutely that," he returned. "I mean that it *may* be nothing particular, because I may never want it."

Both Ada and I urged, in reply, not only that it was decidedly worth while to undo what had been done, but that it must be undone. I then asked Richard whether he had thought of any more congenial pursuit?

"There, my dear Mrs. Shipton," said Richard, "you touch me home. Yes, I have. I have been thinking that the law is the boy for me."

"The law!" repeated Ada, as if she were afraid of the name.

"If I went into Kenge's office," said Richard, "and if I were placed under articles to Kenge, I should have my eye on the — hum! — the forbidden ground — and should be able to study it, and master it, and to satisfy myself that it was not neglected, and was being properly conducted. I should be able to look after Ada's interests, and my own interests (the same thing); and I should peg away at Blackstone and all those fellows with the most tremendous ardor."

I was not by any means so sure of that; and I saw how his hankering after the vague things yet to come of those long-deferred hopes, cast a shade on Ada's face. But I thought it best to encourage him in any project of continuous exertion, and only advised him to be quite sure that his mind was made up now.

"My dear Minerva," said Richard, "I am as steady as you are. I made a mistake; we are all liable to mistakes; I won't do so any more, and I'll become such a lawyer as is not often seen. That is, you know," said Richard, relapsing into doubt, "if it really is worth while, after all, to make such a disturbance about nothing particular!"

This led to our saying again, with a great deal of gravity, all that we had said already, and to our coming to much the same conclusion afterwards. But, we so strongly advised Richard to be frank and open with Mr. Jarndyce, without a moment's delay, — and his disposition was naturally so opposed to concealment, — that he sought him out at once (taking us with him), and made a full avowal. "Rick," said my Guardian, after hearing him attentively, "we can retreat with honor, and we will. But we must be careful — for our cousin's sake — Rick, for our cousin's sake — that we make no more such mistakes. Therefore, in the matter of the law, we will have a good trial before we decide. We will look before we leap, and take plenty of time about it."

Richard's energy was of such an impatient and fitful kind, that he would have liked nothing better than to have gone to Mr. Kenge's office in that hour, and to have entered into articles with him on the spot. Submitting, however, with a good grace to the caution that we had shown to be so necessary, he contented himself with sitting down among us in his lightest spirits, and talking as if his one unvarying purpose in life from childhood had been that one which now held possession of him. My Guardian was very kind and cordial with him, but rather grave; enough so to cause Ada, when he had departed and we were going up-stairs to bed, to say:

"Cousin John, I hope you don't think the worse of Richard?"

"No, my love," said he.

"Because it was very natural that Richard should be mistaken in such a difficult case. It is not uncommon."

"No, no, my love," said he. "Don't look unhappy."

"Oh, I am not unhappy, cousin John!" said Ada, smiling cheerfully, with her hand upon his shoulder, where she had put it in bidding him good-night. "But I should be a little so, if you thought at all the worse of Richard."

"My dear," said Mr. Jarndyce, "I should think the worse of him only if you were ever in the least unhappy through his means. I should be more disposed to quarrel with myself, even then, than with poor Rick, for I brought you together. But, tut, all this is nothing! He has time before him, and the race to run. *I* think the worse of him? Not I, my loving cousin! And not you, I swear!"

"No, indeed, cousin John," said Ada, "I am sure I could not — I am sure I would not — think any ill of Richard, if the whole world did. I could, and I would, think better of him then, than at any other time!"

So quietly and honestly she said it, with her hands

upon his shoulders — both hands now — and looking up into his face, like the picture of Truth!

"I think," said my Guardian, thoughtfully regarding her, "I think it must be somewhere written that the virtues of the mothers shall, occasionally, be visited on the children, as well as the sins of the fathers. Good-night, my rosebud. Good-night, little woman. Pleasant slumbers! Happy dreams!"

This was the first time I ever saw him follow Ada with his eyes, with something of a shadow on their benevolent expression. I well remember the look with which he had contemplated her and Richard, when she was singing in the fire-light; it was but a very little while since he had watched them passing down the room in which the sun was shining, and away into the shade; but his glance was changed, and even the silent look of confidence in me which now followed it once more, was not quite so hopeful and untroubled as it had originally been.

Ada praised Richard more to me, that night, than ever she had praised him yet. She went to sleep, with a little bracelet he had given her clasped upon her arm. I fancied she was dreaming of him when I kissed her cheek after she had slept an hour, and saw how tranquil and happy she looked.

For I was so little inclined to sleep, myself, that night, that I sat up working. It would not be worth mentioning for its own sake, but I was wakeful and rather low-spirited. I don't know why. At least, I don't think I know why. At least, perhaps I do, but I don't think it matters.

At any rate, I made up my mind to be so dreadfully industrious, that I would leave myself not a moment's leisure to be low-spirited. For, I naturally said, "Esther! You to be low-spirited. *You!*" And it really was time to say so, for I — yes, I really did see myself in the glass, almost crying. "As if you had anything to make you unhappy, instead of everything to make you happy, you ungrateful heart!" said I.

If I could have made myself go to sleep, I would have done it directly; but, not being able to do that, I took out of my basket some ornamental work for our house (I mean Bleak House) that I was busy with at that time, and sat down to it with great determination. It was necessary to count all the stitches in that work, and I resolved to go on with it until I couldn't keep my eyes open, and then to go to bed.

I soon found myself very busy. But I had left some silk down-stairs in a work-table drawer in the temporary Growlery; and coming to a stop for want of it, I took my candle and went softly down to get it. To my great surprise, on going in, I found my Guardian still there, and sitting looking at the ashes. He was lost in thought, his book lay unheeded by his side, his silvered iron-gray hair was scattered confusedly upon his forehead as though his hand had been wandering among it while his thoughts were elsewhere, and his face looked worn. Almost frightened by coming upon him so unexpectedly, I stood still for a moment; and should have retired without speaking, had he not, in again passing his hand abstractedly through his hair, seen me and started.

"Esther!"

I told him what I had come for.

"At work so late, my dear?"

"I am working late to-night," said I, "because I couldn't sleep, and wished to tire myself. But, dear

Guardian, you are late too, and look weary. You have no trouble, I hope, to keep you waking?"

"None, little woman, that *you* would readily understand," said he.

He spoke in a regretful tone so new to me, that I inwardly repeated, as if that would help me to his meaning, "That *I* could readily understand!"

"Remain a moment, Esther," said he. "You were in my thoughts."

"I hope I was not the trouble, Guardian?"

He slightly waved his hand, and fell into his usual manner. The change was so remarkable, and he appeared to make it by dint of so much self-command, that I found myself again inwardly repeating, "None that *I* could understand!"

"Little woman," said my Guardian, "I was thinking — that is, I have been thinking since I have been sitting here — that you ought to know, of your own history, all I know. It is very little. Next to nothing."

"Dear Guardian," I replied, "when you spoke to me before on that subject"—

"But since then," he gravely interposed, anticipating what I meant to say, "I have reflected that your having anything to ask me, and my having anything to tell you, are different considerations, Esther. It is perhaps my duty to impart to you the little I know."

"If you think so, Guardian, it is right."

"I think so," he returned, very gently, and kindly, and very distinctly. "My dear, I think so now. If any real disadvantage can attach to your position, in the mind of any man or woman worth a thought, it is right that you, at least, of all the world, should not magnify it to yourself, by having vague impressions of its nature."

I sat down; and said, after a little effort to be as calm as I ought to be, "One of my earliest remembrances, Guardian, is of these words. 'Your mother, Esther, is your disgrace, and you were hers. The time will come, and soon enough, when you will understand this better, and will feel it too, as no one save a woman can.'" I had covered my face with my hands, in repeating the words; but I took them away now with a better kind of shame, I hope, and told him, that to him I owed the blessing that I had from my childhood to that hour never, never, never felt it. He put up his hand as if to stop me. I well knew that he was never to be thanked, and said no more.

"Nine years, my dear," he said, after thinking for a little while, "have passed since I received a letter from a lady living in seclusion, written with a stern passion and power that rendered it unlike all other letters I have ever read. It was written to me (as it told me in so many words), perhaps, because it was the writer's idiosyncrasy to put that trust in me: perhaps because it was mine to justify it. It told me of a child, an orphan girl then twelve years old, in some such cruel words as those which live in your remembrance. It told me that the writer had bred her in secrecy from her birth, had blotted out all trace of her existence, and that if the writer were to die before the child became a woman, she would be left entirely friendless, nameless, and unknown. It asked me to consider if I would, in that case, finish what the writer had begun?"

I listened in silence, and looked attentively at him.

"Your early recollection, my dear, will supply the gloomy medium through which all this was seen and expressed by the writer, and the distorted religion which clouded her mind with impressions of the need there was for the child to expiate an offence of which she was quite innocent. I felt concerned for the little creature, in her darkened life; and replied to the letter."

I took his hand and kissed it.

"It laid the injunction on me that I should never propose to see the writer, who had long been estranged from all intercourse with the world, but who would see a confidential agent if I would appoint one. I accredited Mr. Kenge. The lady said, of her own accord, and not of his seeking, that her name was an assumed one. That she was, if there were any ties of blood in such a case, the child's aunt. That more than this she would never (and he was well persuaded of the steadfastness of her resolution), for any human consideration, disclose. My dear, I have told you all."

I held his hand for a little while in mine.

"I saw my ward oftener than she saw me," he added, cheerily making light of it, "and I always knew she was beloved, useful, and happy. She repays me twenty-thousand-fold, and twenty more to that, every hour in every day!"

"And oftener still," said I, "she blesses the Guardian who is a Father to her!"

At the word Father, I saw his former trouble come into his face. He subdued it as before, and it was gone in an instant; but, it had been there, and it had come so swiftly upon my words that I felt as if they had given him a shock. I again inwardly repeated, wondering, "That *I* could readily understand. None that *I* could readily understand!" No, it was true. I did not understand it. Not for many and many a day.

"Take a fatherly good-night, my dear," said he, kissing

me on the forehead, "and so to rest. These are late hours for working and thinking. You do that for all of us, all day long, little housekeeper!"

I neither worked nor thought any more that night. I opened my grateful heart to Heaven in thankfulness for its providence to me and its care of me, and fell asleep.

We had a visitor next day. Mr. Allan Woodcourt came. He came to take leave of us; he had settled to do so beforehand. He was going to China, and to India, as a surgeon on board ship. He was to be away a long, long time.

I believe — at least I know — that he was not rich. All his widowed mother could spare had been spent in qualifying him for his profession. It was not lucrative to a young practitioner, with very little influence in London; and although he was, night and day, at the service of numbers of poor people, and did wonders of gentleness and skill for them, he gained very little by it in money. He was seven years older than I. Not that I need mention it, for it hardly seems to belong to anything.

I think — I mean, he told us — that he had been in practice three or four years, and that if he could have hoped to contend through three or four more he would not have made the voyage on which he was bound. But he had no fortune or private means, and so he was going away. He had been to see us several times altogether. We thought it a pity he should go away. Because he was distinguished in his art among those who knew it best, and some of the greatest men belonging to it had a high opinion of him.

When he came to bid us good-by, he brought his mother with him for the first time. She was a pretty old lady, with bright black eyes, but she seemed proud. She came from Wales; and had had, a long time ago, an eminent person for an ancestor, of the name of Morgan ap-Kerrig — of some place that sounded like Gimlet — who was the most illustrious person that ever was known, and all of whose relations were a sort of Royal Family. He appeared to have passed his life in always getting up into mountains, and fighting somebody; and a Bard whose name sounded like Crumlinwallinwer had sung his praises, in a piece which was called, as nearly as I could catch it, Mewlinnwillinwodd.

Mrs. Woodcourt, after expatiating to us on the fame of her great kinsman, said that, no doubt, wherever her son Allan went, he would remember his pedigree, and would on no account form an alliance below it. She told him that there were many handsome English ladies in India who went out on speculation, and that there were some to be picked up with property; but, that neither charms nor wealth would suffice for the descendant from such a line, without birth: which must ever be the first consideration. She talked so much about birth that, for a moment, I half fancied, and with pain — but, what an idle fancy to suppose that she could think or care what *mine* was!

Mr. Woodcourt seemed a little distressed by her prolixity, but he was too considerate to let her see it, and contrived delicately to bring the conversation round to making his acknowledgments to my Guardian for his hospitality, and for the very happy hours — he called them the very happy hours — he had passed with us. The recollection of them, he said, would go with him wherever he went, and would be always treasured. And so we gave him our hands, one after another — at least, they did — and I did; and so he put his lips to Ada's hand —

and to mine; and so he went away upon his long, long voyage!

I was very busy indeed, all day, and wrote directions home to the servants, and wrote notes for my Guardian, and dusted his books and papers, and jingled my house-keeping keys a good deal, one way and another. I was still busy between the lights, singing and working by the window, when who should come in but Caddy, whom I had no expectation of seeing!

"Why, Caddy, my dear," said I, "what beautiful flowers!"

She had such an exquisite little nosegay in her hand.

"Indeed, I think so, Esther," replied Caddy. "They are the loveliest I ever saw."

"Prince, my dear?" said I, in a whisper.

"No," answered Caddy, shaking her head, and holding them to me to smell. "Not Prince."

"Well, to be sure, Caddy!" said I. "You must have two lovers!"

"What? Do they look like that sort of thing?" said Caddy.

"Do they look like that sort of thing?" I repeated, pinching her cheek.

Caddy only laughed in return; and telling me that she had come for half-an-hour, at the expiration of which time Prince would be waiting for her at the corner, sat chatting with me and Ada in the window; every now and then handing me the flowers again, or trying how they looked against my hair. At last, when she was going, she took me into my room and put them in my dress.

"For me?" said I, surprised.

"For you," said Caddy, with a kiss. They were left behind by Somebody.

"Left behind?"

"At poor Miss Flite's," said Caddy. "Somebody who has been very good to her, was hurrying away an hour ago, to join a ship, and left these flowers behind. No, no! Don't take them out. Let the pretty little things lie here!" said Caddy, adjusting them with a careful hand, "because I was present myself, and I shouldn't wonder if Somebody left them on purpose!"

"Do they look like that sort of thing?" said Ada, coming laughingly behind me, and clasping me merrily round the waist. "Oh, yes, indeed they do, Dame Durden! They look very, very like that sort of thing. Oh, very like it, indeed, my dear!"

CHAPTER XVIII.

LADY DEDLOCK.

It was not so easy as it had appeared at first, to arrange for Richard's making a trial of Mr. Kenge's office. Richard himself was the chief impediment. As soon as he had it in his power to leave Mr. Badger at any moment, he began to doubt whether he wanted to leave him at all. He didn't know, he said, really. It wasn't a bad profession; he couldn't assert that he disliked it; perhaps he liked it as well as he liked any other — suppose he gave it one more chance! Upon that, he shut himself up, for a few weeks, with some books and some bones, and seemed to acquire a considerable fund of information with great rapidity. His fervor, after lasting about a month, began to cool; and when it was quite cooled, began to grow warm again. His vacillations between law and medicine lasted so long, that Midsummer arrived before he finally separated from Mr. Badger, and entered on an experimental course of Messrs. Kenge and Carboy. For all his waywardness, he took great credit to himself as being determined to be in earnest "this time." And he was so good-natured throughout, and in such high spirits, and so fond of Ada, that it was very difficult indeed to be otherwise than pleased with him.

"As to Mr. Jarndyce," who, I may mention, found the wind much given, during this period, to stick in the east;

"As to Mr. Jarndyce," Richard would say to me, "he is the finest fellow in the world, Esther! I must be particularly careful, if it were only for his satisfaction, to take myself well to task, and have a regular wind-up of this business now."

The idea of his taking himself well to task, with that laughing face and heedless manner, and with a fancy that everything could catch and nothing could hold, was ludicrously anomalous. However, he told us between-whiles, that he was doing it to such an extent, that he wondered his hair didn't turn gray. His regular wind-up of the business was (as I have said), that he went to Mr. Kenge's about Midsummer, to try how he liked it.

All this time he was, in money affairs, what I have described him in a former illustration : generous, profuse, wildly careless, but fully persuaded that he was rather calculating and prudent. I happened to say to Ada, in his presence, half jestingly, half seriously, about the time of his going to Mr. Kenge's, that he needed to have Fortunatus's purse, he made so light of money, which he answered in this way, —

"My jewel of a dear cousin, you hear this old woman! Why does she say that? Because I gave eight pounds odd (or whatever it was) for a certain neat waistcoat and buttons a few days ago. Now, if I had stayed at Badger's I should have been obliged to spend twelve pounds at a blow, for some heart-breaking lecture-fees. So I make four pounds — in a lump — by the transaction!"

It was a question much discussed between him and my Guardian what arrangements should be made for his living in London, while he experimented on the law ; for, we had long since gone back to Bleak House, and it was too far off to admit of his coming there oftener than once a week. My Guardian told me that if Richard were to settle down at Mr. Kenge's, he would take some apartments or chambers, where we, too, could occasionally stay for a few days at a time; "but, little woman," he added, rubbing his head very significantly, "he hasn't settled down there yet!" The discussions ended in our hiring for him, by the month, a neat little furnished lodging in a quiet old house near Queen Square. He immediately began to spend all the money he had, in buying the oddest little ornaments and luxuries for this lodging; and as often as Ada and I dissuaded him from making any purchase that he had in contemplation which was particularly unnecessary and expensive, he took credit for what it would have cost, and made out that to spend anything less on something else was to save the difference.

While these affairs were in abeyance, our visit to Mr. Boythorn's was postponed. At length, Richard having taken possession of his lodging, there was nothing to prevent our departure. He could have gone with us at that time of the year, very well; but, he was in the full novelty of his new position, and was making most energetic attempts to unravel the mysteries of the fatal suit. Consequently we went without him; and my darling was delighted to praise him for being so busy.

We made a pleasant journey down into Lincolnshire by the coach, and had an entertaining companion in Mr. Skimpole. His furniture had been all cleared off, it appeared, by the person who took possession of it on his blue-eyed daughter's birthday; but he seemed quite relieved to think that it was gone. Chairs and tables, he said, were wearisome objects; they were monotonous ideas, they had no variety of expression, they looked you out of countenance, and you looked them out of countenance. How pleasant, then, to be bound to no particular chairs and tables, but to sport like a butterfly among all the furniture on hire, and to flit from rosewood to mahogany, and from mahogany to walnut, and from this shape to that, as the humor took one!

"The oddity of the thing is," said Mr. Skimpole, with a quickened sense of the ludicrous, "that my chairs and tables were not paid for, and yet my landlord walks off with them as composedly as possible. Now, that seems droll! There is something grotesque in it. The chair and table merchant never engaged to pay my landlord my rent. Why should my landlord quarrel with *him*? If I have a pimple on my nose which is disagreeable to my landlord's peculiar ideas of beauty, my landlord has no business to scratch my chair and table merchant's nose, which has no pimple on it. His reasoning seems defective!"

"Well," said my Guardian, good-humoredly, "it's pretty clear that whoever became security for those chairs and tables will have to pay for them."

"Exactly!" returned Mr. Skimpole. "That's the crowning point of unreason in the business! I said to my landlord, 'My good man, you are not aware that my excellent friend Jarndyce will have to pay for those things that you are sweeping off in that indelicate manner. Have you no consideration for *his* property?' He hadn't the least."

"And refused all proposals," said my Guardian.

"Refused all proposals," returned Mr. Skimpole. "I made him business proposals. I had him into my room, I said, 'You are a man of business, I believe?' He replied, 'I am.' 'Very well,' said I, 'now let us be business-like. Here is an inkstand, here are pens and paper, here are wafers. What do you want? I have occupied your house for a considerable period, I believe to our mutual satisfaction until this unpleasant misunderstanding arose; let us be at once friendly and business-like. What do you want?' In reply to this, he made use of the figurative expression — which has something Eastern about it — that he had never seen the color of my money. 'My amiable friend,' said I, 'I never have any money. I never know anything about money.' 'Well, sir,' said he, 'what do you offer, if I give you time?' 'My good fellow,' said I, 'I have no idea of time; but, you say you are a man of business, and whatever you can suggest to be done in a business-like way with pen, and ink, and paper — and wafers — I am ready to do. Don't pay yourself at another man's expense (which is foolish), but be business-like!' However, he wouldn't be, and there was an end of it."

If these were some of the inconveniences of Mr. Skimpole's childhood, it assuredly possessed its advantages too. On the journey he had a very good appetite for such refreshment as came in our way (including a basket of choice hot-house peaches), but never thought of paying for anything. So when the coachman came round for his fee, he pleasantly asked him what he considered a very good fee indeed, now — a liberal one — and, on his replying, half-a-crown for a single passenger, said it was little enough too, all things considered; and left Mr. Jarndyce to give it him.

It was delightful weather. The green corn waved so beautifully, the larks sang so joyfully, the hedges were so full of wild flowers, the trees were so thickly out in leaf, the bean-fields, with a light wind blowing over them, filled the air with such a delicious fragrance! Late in the afternoon we came to the market-town where we were to alight from the coach — a dull little town, with a church-spire, and a market-place, and a market-cross, and one intensely sunny street, and a pond with an old horse cooling his legs in it, and a very few men sleepily lying and standing about in narrow little bits of shade. After the rustling of the leaves and the waving of the corn all along the road, it looked as still, as hot, as motionless a little town as England could produce.

At the inn, we found Mr. Boythorn on horseback, waiting with an open carriage to take us to his house, which was a few miles off. He was overjoyed to see us, and dismounted with great alacrity.

"By Heaven!" said he, after giving us a courteous greeting, "this is a most infamous coach. It is the most flagrant example of an abominable public vehicle that ever encumbered the face of the earth. It is twenty-five minutes after its time, this afternoon. The coachman ought to be put to death!"

"*Is* he after his time?" said Mr. Skimpole, to whom he happened to address himself. "You know my infirmity."

"Twenty-five minutes! Twenty-six minutes!" replied Mr. Boythorn, referring to his watch. "With two ladies in the coach, this scoundrel has deliberately delayed his arrival six-and-twenty minutes. Deliberately! It is impossible that it can be accidental! But his father — and his uncle — were the most profligate coachmen that ever sat upon a box."

While he said this in tones of the greatest indignation, he handed us into the little phaeton with the utmost gentleness, and was all smiles and pleasure.

"I am sorry, ladies," he said, standing bareheaded at the carriage-door, when all was ready, "that I am obliged to conduct you nearly two miles out of the way. But our direct road lies through Sir Leicester Dedlock's park; and, in that fellow's property, I have sworn never to set foot of mine, or horse's foot of mine, pending the present relations between us, while I breathe the breath of life!" And here, catching my Guardian's eye, he broke into one of his tremendous laughs, which seemed to shake even the motionless little market-town.

"Are the Dedlocks down here, Lawrence?" said my Guardian as we drove along, and Mr. Boythorn trotted on the green turf by the roadside.

"Sir Arrogant Numskull is here," replied Mr. Boythorn. "Ha, ha, ha! Sir Arrogant is here, and I am glad to say, has been laid by the heels here. My Lady," in naming whom he always made a courtly gesture as if particularly to exclude her from any part in the quarrel, "is expected, I believe, daily. I am not in the least surprised that she postpones her appearance as long as possible. Whatever can have induced that transcendent woman to marry that effigy and figure-head of a baronet, is one of the most impenetrable mysteries that ever baffled human inquiry. Ha, ha, ha, ha!"

"I suppose," said my Guardian, laughing, "*we* may set foot in the park while we are here? The prohibition does not extend to us, does it?"

"I can lay no prohibition on my guests," he said, bending his head to Ada and me, with a smiling politeness which sat so gracefully upon him, "except in the matter of their departure. I am only sorry that I cannot have the happiness of being their escort about Chesney Wold, which is a very fine place! But, by the light of this summer day, Jarndyce, if you call upon the owner, while you stay with me, you are likely to have but a cool reception. He carries himself like an eight-day clock at all times; like one of a race of eight-day clocks in gorgeous cases that never go and never went — ha, ha, ha! — but he will have some extra stiffness, I can promise you, for the friends of his friend and neighbor Boythorn!"

"I shall not put him to the proof," said my Guardian. "He is as indifferent to the honor of knowing me, I dare say, as I am to the honor of knowing him. The air of the grounds, and perhaps such a view of the house as any other sight-seer might get, are quite enough for me."

"Well!" said Mr. Boythorn, "I am glad of it on the whole. It's in better keeping. I am looked upon, about here, as a second Ajax defying the lightning. Ha, ha, ha, ha! When I go into our little church on a Sunday, a considerable part of the inconsiderable congregation expect to see me drop, scorched and withered, on the pavement under the Dedlock displeasure. Ha, ha, ha, ha! I have no doubt he is surprised that I don't. For he is, by Heaven! the most self-satisfied, and the shallowest, and the most coxcomical and utterly brainless ass!"

Our coming to the ridge of a hill we had been ascending, enabled our friend to point out Chesney Wold itself to us, and diverted his attention from its master.

It was a picturesque old house, in a fine park richly wooded. Among the trees, and not far from the residence, he pointed out the spire of the little church of which he had spoken. Oh, the solemn woods over which the light and shadow travelled swiftly, as if Heavenly wings were sweeping on benignant errands through the summer air; the smooth green slopes, the glittering water, the garden where the flowers were so symmetrically arranged in clusters of the richest colors, how beautiful they looked! The house, with gable and chimney, and tower, and turret, and dark doorway, and broad terrace-walk, twining among the balustrades of which, and lying heaped upon the vases, there was one great flush of roses, seemed scarcely real in its light solidity, and in the serene and peaceful hush that rested all around it. To Ada and to me that, above all, appeared the pervading influence. On everything, house, garden, terrace, green slopes, water, old oaks, fern, moss, woods again, and far away across the openings in the prospect, to the distance lying wide before us with a purple bloom upon it, there seemed to be such undisturbed repose.

When we came into the little village, and passed a small inn with the sign of the Dedlock Arms swinging over the road in front, Mr. Boythorn interchanged greetings with a young gentleman sitting on a bench outside the inn-door, who had some fishing-tackle lying beside him.

"That's the housekeeper's grandson, Mr. Rouncewell by name," said he; "and he is in love with a pretty girl up at the House. Lady Dedlock has taken a fancy to the pretty girl, and is going to keep her about her own fair person — an honor which my young friend himself does not at all appreciate. However, he can't marry just yet, even if his Rosebud were willing; so he is fain to make the best of it. In the meanwhile, he comes here pretty often, for a day or two at a time, to — fish. Ha, ha, ha, ha!"

"Are he and the pretty girl engaged, Mr. Boythorn?" asked Ada.

"Why, my dear Miss Clare," he returned, "I think they may perhaps understand each other; but you will see them soon, I dare say, and I must learn from you on such a point — not you from me."

Ada blushed; and Mr. Boythorn, trotting forward on his comely gray horse, dismounted at his own door, and stood ready, with extended arm and uncovered head, to welcome us when we arrived.

He lived in a pretty house, formerly the Parsonage-house, with a lawn in front, a bright flower-gardèn at the side, and a well-stocked orchard and kitchen-garden in the rear, enclosed with a venerable wall that had of itself a ripened ruddy look. But, indeed, everything about the place wore an aspect of maturity and abundance. The old lime-tree walk was like green cloisters, the very shadows of the cherry-trees and apple-trees were heavy with fruit, the gooseberry-bushes were so laden that their branches arched and rested on the earth, the strawberries and raspberries grew in like profusion, and the peaches basked by the hundred on the wall. Tumbled about among the spread nets and the glass frames sparkling and winking in the sun, there were such heaps of drooping pods, and marrows, and cucumbers, that every foot of ground appeared a vegetable treasury, while the smell of sweet herbs and all kinds of wholesome growth (to say nothing of the neighboring meadows where the hay was carrying) made the whole air a great nosegay. Such stillness and composure reigned within the orderly precincts of the old red wall, that even the feathers hung in garlands to scare the birds hardly stirred; and the wall had such a ripening influence that where, here and there high up, a disused nail and scrap of list still clung to it, it was easier to fancy that they had mellowed with the changing seasons, than that they had rusted and decayed according to the common fate.

The house, though a little disorderly in comparison with the garden, was a real old house, with settles in the chimney of the brick-floored kitchen, and great beams across the ceilings. On one side of it was the terrible piece of ground in dispute, where Mr. Boythorn maintained a sentry in a smock-frock, day and night, whose duty was supposed to be, in case of aggression, immediately to ring a large bell hung up there for the purpose, to unchain a great bull-dog established in a kennel as his ally, and generally to deal destruction on the enemy. Not content with these precautions, Mr. Boythorn had himself composed and posted there, on painted boards to which his name was attached in large letters, the following solemn warnings: "Beware of the Bull-dog. He is most ferocious. Lawrence Boythorn." "The blunderbuss is loaded with slugs. Lawrence Boythorn." "Mantraps and spring-guns are set here at all times of the day and night. Lawrence Boythorn." "Take notice. That any person or persons audaciously presuming to trespass on this property, will be punished with the utmost severity of private chastisement, and prosecuted with the utmost rigor of the law. Lawrence Boythorn." These he showed us, from the drawing-room widow, while his bird was hopping about his head; and he laughed, "Ha, ha, ha, ha! Ha, ha, ha, ha!" to that extent as he pointed them out, that I really thought he would have hurt himself.

"But, this is taking a good deal of trouble," said Mr. Skimpole in his light way, "when you are not in earnest after all?"

"Not in earnest!" returned Mr. Boythorn, with unspeakable warmth. "Not in earnest! If I could have hoped to train him, I would have bought a Lion instead of that dog, and would have turned him loose upon the first intolerable robber who should dare to make an encroachment on my rights. Let Sir Leicester Dedlock consent to come out and decide this question by single combat, and I will meet him with any weapon known to mankind in any age or country. I am that much in earnest. Not more!"

We arrived at his house on a Saturday. On the Sunday morning we all set forth to walk to the little church in the park. Entering the park, almost immediately by the disputed ground, we pursued a pleasant footpath winding among the verdant turf and the beautiful trees, until it brought us to the church porch.

The congregation was extremely small and quite a rustic one, with the exception of a large muster of servants from the House, some of whom were already in their seats, while others were yet dropping in. There were some stately footmen; and there was a perfect picture of an old coachman, who looked as if he were the official representative of all the pomps and vanities that had ever been put into his coach. There was a very pretty show of young women; and above them, the handsome old face and fine responsible portly figure of the housekeeper, towered preëminent. The pretty girl, of whom Mr. Boythorn had told us, was close by her. She was so very pretty, that I might have known her by her beauty, even if I had not seen how blushingly conscious she was of the eyes of the young fisherman, whom I discovered not far off. One face, and not an agreeable one, though it was handsome, seemed maliciously watchful of this pretty girl, and indeed of everyone and everything there. It was a Frenchwoman's.

As the bell was yet ringing and the great people were not yet come, I had leisure to glance over the church, which smelt as earthy as a grave, and to think what a shady, ancient, solemn little church it was. The windows, heavily shaded by trees, admitted a subdued light that made the faces around me pale, and darkened the old brasses in the pavement, and the time and damp-worn monuments, and rendered the sunshine in the little porch, where a monotonous ringer was working at the bell, inestimably bright. But a stir in that direction, a gathering of reverential awe in the rustic faces, and a blandly-ferocious assumption on the part of Mr. Boythorn of being resolutely unconscious of somebody's existence, forewarned me that the great people were come, and that the service was going to begin.

"'Enter not into judgment with thy servant, O Lord, for in thy sight — '"

Shall I ever forget the rapid beating of my heart, occasioned by the look I met, as I stood up! Shall I ever forget the manner in which those handsome proud eyes seemed to spring out of their languor, and to hold mine! It was only a moment before I cast mine down — released again, if I may say so — on my book; but, I knew the beautiful face quite well, in that short space of time.

And, very strangely, there was something quickened within me, associated with the lonely days at my godmother's; yes, away even to the days when I had stood on tiptoe to dress myself at my little glass, after dressing my doll. And this, although I had never seen this lady's face before in all my life — I was quite sure of it — absolutely certain.

It was easy to know that the ceremonious, gouty, gray-haired gentleman, the only other occupant of the great pew, was Sir Leicester Dedlock; and that the lady was Lady Dedlock. But why her face should be, in a confused way, like a broken glass to me, in which I saw scraps of old remembrances; and why I should be so fluttered and troubled (for I was still), by having casually met her eyes; I could not think.

I felt it to be an unmeaning weakness in me, and I tried to overcome it by attending to the words I heard. Then, very strangely, I seemed to hear them, not in the reader's voice, but in the well-remembered voice of my godmother. This made me think, did Lady Dedlock's face accidentally resemble my godmother's? It might be that it did, a little; but, the expression was so different, and the stern decision which had worn into my godmother's face, like weather into rocks, was so completely wanting in the face before me, that it could not be that resemblance which had struck me. Neither did I know the loftiness and haughtiness of Lady Dedlock's face, at all, in any one. And yet *I — I*, little Esther Summerson, the child who lived a life apart, and on whose birthday there was no rejoicing — seemed to arise before my own eyes, evoked out of the past by some power in this fashionable lady, whom I not only entertained no fancy that I had ever seen, but whom I perfectly well knew I had never seen until that hour.

It made me tremble so, to be thrown into this unaccountable agitation, that I was conscious of being distressed even by the observation of the French maid, though I knew she had been looking watchfully here, and there, and everywhere, from the moment of her coming into the church. By degrees, though very slowly, I at last overcame my strange emotion. After a long time, I looked towards Lady Dedlock again. It was while they were preparing to sing, before the sermon. She took no heed of me, and the beating at my heart was gone. Neither did it revive for more than a few moments, when she once or twice afterwards glanced at Ada or at me through her glass.

The service being concluded, Sir Leicester gave his arm with much state and gallantry to Lady Dedlock — though he was obliged to walk by the help of a thick stick — and escorted her out of church to the pony carriage in which they had come. The servants then dispersed, and so did the congregation: whom Sir Leicester had contemplated all along (Mr. Skimpole said to Mr. Boythorn's infinite delight), as if he were a considerable landed proprietor in Heaven.

"He believes he is!" said Mr. Boythorn. "He firmly believes it. So did his father, and his grandfather, and his great-grandfather!"

"Do you know," pursued Mr. Skimpole, very unexpectedly to Mr. Boythorn, "it's agreeable to me to see a man of that sort."

"*Is* it!" said Mr. Boythorn.

"Say that he wants to patronize me," pursued Mr. Skimpole. "Very well! I don't object."

"*I* do," said Mr. Boythorn, with great vigor.

"Do you really?" returned Mr. Skimpole, in his easy light vein. "But, that's taking trouble, surely. And why should you take trouble? Here am I, content to receive things childishly, as they fall out: and I never take trouble! I come down here for instance, and I find a mighty potentate, exacting homage. Very well! I say 'Mighty potentate, here *is* my homage! It's easier to give it, than to withhold it. Here it is. If you have anything of an agreeable nature to show me, I shall be happy to see it; if you have anything of an agreeable nature to give me, I shall be happy to accept it.' Mighty potentate replies in effect, 'This is a sensible fellow. I find him accord with my digestion and my bilious system. He doesn't impose upon me the necessity of rolling myself up like a hedgehog with my points outward. I expand, I open, I turn my silver lining outward like Milton's cloud, and it's more agreeable to both of us.' That's my view of such things: speaking as a child!"

"But suppose you went down somewhere else to-morrow," said Mr. Boythorn, "where there was the opposite of that fellow — or of this fellow. How then?"

"How then?" said Mr. Skimpole, with an appearance of the utmost simplicity and candor. "Just the same, then! I should say, 'My esteemed Boythorn'— to make you the personification of our imaginary friend — 'my esteemed Boythorn, you object to the mighty potentate? Very good. So do I. I take it that my business in the social system is to be agreeable; I take it that everybody's business in the social system is to be agreeable. It's a system of harmony, in short. Therefore, if you object, I object. Now, excellent Boythorn, let us go to dinner!'"

"But, excellent Boythorn might say," returned our host, swelling and growing very red, "I'll be ——"

"I understand," said Mr. Skimpole. "Very likely he would."

"—— if I *will* go to dinner!" cried Mr. Boythorn, in a violent burst, and stopping to strike his stick upon the ground. "And he would probably add, 'Is there such a thing as principle, Mr. Harold Skimpole?'"

"To which Harold Skimpole would reply, you know," he returned in his gayest manner, and with his most ingenuous smile, "'Upon my life I have not the least idea! I don't know what it is you call by that name, or where it is, or who possesses it. If you possess it, and find it comfortable, I am quite delighted, and congratulate you heartily. But I know nothing about it, I assure you; for I am a mere child, and I lay no claim to it, and I don't want it!' So, you see, excellent Boythorn and I would go to dinner after all!"

This was one of many little dialogues between them, which I always expected to end, and which I dare say would have ended under other circumstances, in some violent explosion on the part of our host. But he had so high a sense of his hospitable and responsible position as our entertainer, and my Guardian laughed so sincerely at and with Mr. Skimpole, as a child who blew bubbles and broke them all day long, that matters never went beyond this point. Mr. Skimpole, who always seemed quite unconscious of having been on delicate ground, then betook himself to beginning some sketch in the park which he never finished, or to playing fragments of airs on the piano, or to singing scraps of songs, or to lying down on his back under a tree, and looking at the sky — which he couldn't help thinking, he said, was what he was meant for; it suited him so exactly.

"Enterprise and effort," he would say to us (on his back), "are delightful to me. I believe I am truly cosmopolitan. I have the deepest sympathy with them. I lie in a shady place like this, and think of adventurous spirits going to the North Pole, or penetrating to the heart of the Torrid Zone, with admiration. Mercenary creatures ask, 'What is the use of a man's going to the North Pole? What good does it do?' I can't say; but, for anything I *can* say, he may go for the purpose — though he don't know it — of employing my thoughts as I lie here. Take an extreme case. Take the case of the Slaves on American plantations. I dare say they are worked hard, I dare say they don't altogether like it, I dare say theirs is an unpleasant experience on the whole; but, they people the landscape for me, they give it a poetry for me, and perhaps that is one of the pleasanter objects of their existence. I am very sensible of it, if it be, and I shouldn't wonder if it were!"

I always wondered on these occasions whether he ever thought of Mrs. Skimpole and the children, and in what point of view they presented themselves to his cosmopolitan mind. So far as I could understand, they rarely presented themselves at all.

The week had gone round to the Saturday following that beating of my heart in the church; and every day had been so bright and blue, that to ramble in the woods, and to see the light striking down among the transparent leaves, and sparkling in the beautiful interlacings of the shadows of the trees, while the birds poured out their songs, and the air was drowsy with the hum of insects, had been most delightful. We had one favorite spot, deep in moss and last year's leaves, where there were some felled trees from which the bark was all stripped off. Seated among these, we looked through a green vista supported by thousands of natural columns, the whitened stems of trees, upon a distant prospect made so radiant by its contrast with the shade in which we sat, and made so precious by the arched perspective through which we saw it, that it was like a glimpse of the better land. Upon the Saturday we sat here, Mr. Jarndyce, Ada, and I, until we heard thunder muttering in the distance, and felt the large raindrops rattle through the leaves.

The weather had been all the week extremely sultry; but, the storm broke so suddenly — upon us, at least, in that sheltered spot — that before we reached the outskirts of the wood, the thunder and lightning were frequent, and the rain came plunging through the leaves, as if every drop were a great leaden bead. As it was not a time for standing among trees, we ran out of the wood, and up and down the moss-grown steps which crossed the plantation-fence like two broad-staved ladders placed back to back, and made for a keeper's lodge which was close at hand. We had often noticed the dark beauty of this lodge standing in a deep twilight of trees, and how the ivy clustered over it, and how there was a steep hollow near, where we had once seen the keeper's dog dive down into the fern as if it were water.

The lodge was so dark within, now the sky was overcast, that we only clearly saw the man who came to the door when we took shelter there, and put two chairs for Ada and me. The lattice-windows were all thrown open, and we sat, just within the doorway, watching the storm. It was grand to see how the wind awoke, and bent the trees, and drove the rain before it like a cloud of smoke; and to hear the solemn thunder, and to see the lightning; and while thinking with awe of the tremendous powers by which our little lives are encompassed, to consider how beneficent they are, and how upon the smallest flower and leaf there was already a freshness poured from all this seeming rage, which seemed to make creation new again.

"Is it not dangerous to sit in so exposed a place?"

"Oh, no, Esther dear!" said Ada, quietly.

Ada said it to me; but, *I* had not spoken.

The beating at my heart came back again. I had never heard the voice, as I had never seen the face, but it affected me in the same strange way. Again, in a moment, there arose before my mind innumerable pictures of myself.

Lady Dedlock had taken shelter in the lodge, before our arrival there, and had come out of the gloom within. She stood behind my chair, with her hand upon it. I saw her with her hand close to my shoulder, when I turned my head.

"I have frightened you?" she said.

No. It was not fright. Why should I be frightened!

"I believe," said Lady Dedlock to my Guardian, "I have the pleasure of speaking to Mr. Jarndyce."

"Your remembrance does me more honor than I had supposed it would, Lady Dedlock," he returned.

"I recognized you in church on Sunday. I am sorry that any local disputes of Sir Leicester's — they are not of his seeking, however, I believe — should render it a matter of some absurd difficulty to show you any attention here."

"I am aware of the circumstances," returned my Guardian, with a smile, "and am sufficiently obliged."

She had given him her hand, in an indifferent way that seemed habitual to her, and spoke in a correspondingly indifferent manner, though in a very pleasant voice. She was as graceful as she was beautiful; perfectly self-possessed; and had the air, I thought, of being able to attract and interest any one, if she had thought it worth her while. The keeper had brought her a chair, on which she sat, in the middle of the porch between us.

"Is the young gentleman disposed of, whom you wrote to Sir Leicester about, and whose wishes Sir Leicester was sorry not to have it in his power to advance in any way?" she said, over her shoulder, to my Guardian.

"I hope so," said he.

She seemed to respect him, and even to wish to conciliate him. There was something very winning in her haughty manner; and it became more familiar — I was going to say more easy, but that could hardly be — as she spoke to him over her shoulder.

"I presume this is your other ward, Miss Clare?"

He presented Ada, in form.

"You will lose the disinterested part of your Don Quixote character," said Lady Dedlock to Mr. Jarndyce, over her shoulder again, "if you only redress the wrongs of beauty like this. But present me," and she turned full upon me, "to this young lady too!"

"Miss Summerson really is my ward," said Mr. Jarndyce. "I am responsible to no Lord Chancellor in her case."

"Has Miss Summerson lost both her parents?" said my Lady.

"Yes."

"She is very fortunate in her Guardian."

Lady Dedlock looked at me, and I looked at her, and said I was indeed. All at once she turned from me with a hasty air, almost expressive of displeasure or dislike, and spoke to him over her shoulder again.

"Ages have passed since we were in the habit of meeting, Mr. Jarndyce."

"A long time. At least I thought it was a long time, until I saw you last Sunday," he returned.

"What! Even you are a courtier, or think it necessary to become one to me!" she said, with some disdain. "I have achieved that reputation, I suppose."

"You have achieved so much, Lady Dedlock," said my Guardian, "that you pay some little penalty, I dare say. But none to me."

"So much!" she repeated, slightly laughing. "Yes!"

With her air of superiority, and power, and fascination, and I know not what, she seemed to regard Ada and me as little more than children. So, as she slightly laughed, and afterwards sat looking at the rain, she was as self-possessed, and as free to occupy herself with her own thoughts, as if she had been alone.

"I think you knew my sister, when we were abroad together, better than you knew me?" she said, looking at him again.

"Yes, we happened to meet oftener," he returned.

"We went our several ways," said Lady Dedlock, "and had little in common even before we agreed to differ. It is to be regretted, I suppose, but it could not be helped."

Lady Dedlock again sat looking at the rain. The storm soon began to pass upon its way. The shower greatly abated, the lightning ceased, the thunder rolled among the distant hills, and the sun began to glisten on the wet leaves and the falling rain. As we sat there, silently, we saw a little pony phaeton coming towards us at a merry pace.

"The messenger is coming back, my Lady," said the keeper, "with the carriage."

As it drove up, we saw that there were two people inside. There alighted from it, with some cloaks and wrappers, first the Frenchwoman whom I had seen in church, and secondly the pretty girl; the Frenchwoman with a defiant confidence; the pretty girl confused and hesitating.

"What now?" said Lady Dedlock. "Two!"

"I am your maid, my Lady, at the present," said the Frenchwoman. "The message was for the attendant."

"I was afraid you might mean me, my Lady," said the pretty girl.

"I did mean you, child," replied her mistress, calmly. "Put that shawl on me."

She slightly stooped her shoulders to receive it, and the pretty girl lightly dropped it in its place. The Frenchwoman stood unnoticed, looking on with her lips very tightly set.

"I am sorry," said Lady Dedlock to Mr. Jarndyce, "that we are not likely to renew our former acquaintance. You will allow me to send the carriage back for your two wards. It shall be here directly."

But as he would on no account accept this offer, she took a graceful leave of Ada — none of me — and put her hand upon his proffered arm, and got into the carriage; which was a little, low, park carriage, with a hood.

"Come in, child!" she said to the pretty girl, "I shall want you. Go on!"

The carriage rolled away; and the Frenchwoman, with the wrappers she had brought hanging over her arm, remained standing where she had alighted.

I suppose there is nothing Pride can so little bear with, as Pride itself, and that she was punished for her imperious manner. Her retaliation was the most singular I could have imagined. She remained perfectly still until the carriage had turned into the drive, and then, without the least discomposure of countenance, slipped off her shoes, left them on the ground, and walked deliberately in the same direction, through the wettest of the wet grass.

"Is that young woman mad?" said my Guardian.

"Oh, no, sir!" said the keeper, who, with his wife,

was looking after her. "Hortense is not one of that sort. She has as good a headpiece as the best. But she's mortal high and passionate — powerful high and passionate; and what with having notice to leave, and having others put above her, she don't take kindly to it."

"But why should she walk shoeless, through all that water?" said my Guardian.

"Why, indeed, sir, unless it is to cool her down!" said the man.

"Or unless she fancies it's blood," said the woman. "She'd as soon walk through that as anything else, I think, when her own's up!"

We passed not far from the House, a few minutes afterwards. Peaceful as it had looked when we first saw it, it looked even more so now, with a diamond spray glittering all about it, a light wind blowing, the birds no longer hushed but singing strongly, everything refreshed by the late rain, and the little carriage shining at the doorway like a fairy carriage made of silver. Still, very steadfastly and quietly walking towards it, a peaceful figure too in the landscape, went Mademoiselle Hortense, shoeless, through the wet grass.

CHAPTER XIX.

MOVING ON.

IT is the long vacation in the regions of Chancery Lane. The good ships Law and Equity, those teak-built, copper-bottomed, iron-fastened, brazen-faced, and not by any means fast-sailing Clippers, are laid up in ordinary. The Flying Dutchman, with a crew of ghostly clients imploring all whom they may encounter to peruse their papers, has drifted, for the time being, Heaven knows where. The Courts are all shut up; the public offices lie in a hot sleep; Westminster Hall itself is a shady solitude where nightingales might sing, and a tenderer class of suitors than is usually found there, walk.

The Temple, Chancery Lane, Serjeants' Inn, and Lincoln's Inn even unto the Fields, are like tidal harbors at low water; where stranded proceedings, offices at anchor, idle clerks lounging on lop-sided stools that will not recover their perpendicular until the current of Term sets in, lie high and dry upon the ooze of the long vacation. Outer doors of chambers are shut up by the score, messages and parcels are to be left at the Porter's Lodge by the bushel. A crop of grass would grow in the chinks of the stone pavement outside Lincoln's Inn Hall, but that the ticket-porters, who have nothing to do beyond sitting in the shade there, with their white aprons over their heads to keep the flies off, grub it up and eat it thoughtfully.

There is only one Judge in town. Even he only comes twice a-week to sit in chambers. If the country folks of those assize towns on his circuit could see him now! No full-bottomed wig, no red petticoats, no fur, no javelin-men, no white wands. Merely a close-shaved gentleman in white trousers and a white hat, with sea-bronze on the judicial countenance, and a strip of bark peeled by the solar rays from the judicial nose, who calls in at the shell-fish shop as he comes along, and drinks iced ginger-beer!

The bar of England is scattered over the face of the earth. How England can get on through four long summer months without its bar — which is its acknowledged refuge in adversity, and its only legitimate triumph in prosperity — is beside the question; assuredly that shield and buckler of Britannia are not in present wear. The learned gentleman who is always so tremendously indignant at the unprecedented outrage committed on the feelings of his client by the opposite party, that he never seems likely to recover it, is doing infinitely better than might be expected, in Switzerland. The learned gentleman who does the withering business, and who blights all opponents with his gloomy sarcasm, is as merry as a grig at a French watering-place. The learned gentleman who weeps by the pint on the smallest provocation, has not shed a tear these six weeks. The very learned gentleman who has cooled the natural heat of his gingery complexion in pools and fountains of law, until he has become great in knotty arguments for Term-time, when he poses the drowsy Bench with legal "chaff," inexplicable to the uninitiated and to most of the initiated too, is roaming, with a characteristic delight in aridity and dust, about Constantinople. Other dispersed fragments of the same great Palladium are to be found on the canals of Venice, at the second cataract of the Nile, in the baths of Germany, and sprinkled on the sea-sand all over the English coast. Scarcely one is to be encountered in the deserted region of Chancery Lane. If such a lonely member of the bar do flit across the waste, and come upon a prowling suitor who is unable to leave off haunting the scenes of his anxiety, they frighten one another, and retreat into opposite shades.

It is the hottest long vacation known for many years. All the young clerks are madly in love, and, according to their various degrees, pine for bliss with the beloved object, at Margate, Ramsgate, or Gravesend. All the middle-aged clerks think their families too large. All the unowned dogs who stray into the Inns of Court, and pant about staircases and other dry places, seeking water, give short howls of aggravation. All the blind men's dogs in the streets draw their masters against pumps, or trip them over buckets. A shop with a sun-blind, and a watered pavement, and a bowl of gold and silver fish in the window, is a sanctuary. Temple Bar gets so hot, that it is, to the adjacent Strand and Fleet Street, what a heater is in an urn, and keeps them simmering all night.

There are offices about the Inns of Court in which a man might be cool, if any coolness were worth purchasing at such a price in dulness; but, the little thoroughfares immediately outside those retirements seem to blaze. In Mr. Krook's court, it is so hot that the people turn their houses inside out, and sit in chairs upon the pavement — Mr. Krook included, who there pursues his studies, with his cat (who never is too hot) by his side.

The Sol's Arms has discontinued the harmonic meetings for the season, and Little Swills is engaged at the Pastoral Gardens down the river, where he comes out in quite an innocent manner, and sings comic ditties of a juvenile complexion, calculated (as the bill says) not to wound the feelings of the most fastidious mind.

Over all the legal neighborhood, there hangs, like some great veil of rust, or gigantic cobweb, the idleness and pensiveness of the long vacation. Mr. Snagsby, the law-stationer of Cook's Court, Cursitor Street, is sensible of the influence; not only in his mind as a sympathetic and contemplative man, but also in his business as a law-stationer aforesaid. He has more leisure for musing in Staple Inn and in the Rolls Yard, during the long vacation, than at other seasons; and he says to the two 'prentices, what a thing it is in such hot weather to think that you live in an island, with the sea a-rolling and a-bowling right round you.

Guster is busy in the little drawing-room, on this present afternoon in the long vacation, when Mr. and Mrs. Snagsby have it in contemplation to receive company. The expected guests are rather select than numerous, being Mr. and Mrs. Chadband, and no more. From Mr. Chadband's being much given to describe himself, both verbally and in writing, as a vessel, he is occasionally mistaken by strangers for a gentleman connected with navigation; but, he is, as he expresses it, "in the ministry." Mr. Chadband is attached to no particular denomination; and is considered by his persecutors to have nothing so very remarkable to say on the greatest of subjects as to render his volunteering, on his own account, at all incumbent on his conscience; but, he has his followers, and Mrs. Snagsby is of the number. Mrs.

Snagsby has but recently taken a passage upward by the vessel, Chadband; and her attention was attracted to that Bark A 1, when she was something flushed by the hot weather.

"My little woman," says Mr. Snagsby to the sparrows in Staple Inn, "likes to have her religion rather sharp, you see!"

So, Guster, much impressed by regarding herself for the time as the handmaid of Chadband, whom she knows to be endowed with the gift of holding forth for four hours at a stretch, prepares the little drawing-room for tea. All the furniture is shaken and dusted, the portraits of Mr. and Mrs. Snagsby are touched up with a wet cloth, the best tea-service is set forth, and there is excellent provision made of dainty new bread, crusty twists, cool fresh butter, thin slices of ham, tongue and German sausage, and delicate little rows of anchovies nestling in parsley; not to mention new-laid eggs, to be brought up warm in a napkin, and hot buttered toast. For, Chadband is rather a consuming vessel — the persecutors say a gorging vessel; and can wield such weapons of the flesh as a knife and fork, remarkably well.

Mr. Snagsby in his best coat, looking at all the preparations when they are completed, and coughing his cough of deference behind his hand, says to Mrs. Snagsby, "At what time did you expect Mr. and Mrs. Chadband, my love?"

"At six," says Mrs. Snagsby.

Mr. Snagsby observes in a mild and casual way, that "it's gone that."

"Perhaps you'd like to begin without them," is Mrs. Snagsby's reproachful remark.

Mr. Snagsby does look as if he would like it very

much, but he says, with his cough of mildness, "No, my dear, no. I merely named the time."

"What's time," says Mrs. Snagsby, "to eternity?"

"Very true, my dear," says Mr. Snagsby. "Only when a person lays in victuals for tea, a person does it with a view — perhaps — more to time. And when a time is named for having tea, it's better to come up to it."

"To come up to it!" Mrs. Snagsby repeats with severity. "Up to it! As if Mr. Chadband was a fighter!"

"Not at all, my dear," says Mr. Snagsby.

Here, Guster, who had been looking out of the bedroom window, comes rustling and scratching down the little staircase like a popular ghost, and, falling flushed into the drawing-room, announces that Mr. and Mrs. Chadband have appeared in the court. The bell at the inner door in the passage immediately thereafter tinkling, she is admonished by Mrs. Snagsby, on pain of instant reconsignment to her patron saint, not to omit the ceremony of announcement. Much discomposed in her nerves (which were previously in the best order) by this threat, she so fearfully mutilates that point of state as to announce "Mr. and Mrs. Cheeseming, least which, Imeantersay, whatsername!" and retires conscience-stricken from the presence.

Mr. Chadband is a large yellow man, with a fat smile, and a general appearance of having a good deal of train oil in his system. Mrs. Chadband is a stern, severe-looking, silent woman. Mr. Chadband moves softly and cumbrously, not unlike a bear who has been taught to walk upright. He is very much embarrassed about the arms, as if they were inconvenient to him, and he wanted to grovel; is very much in a perspiration about the head; and never speaks without first putting up his great hand, as delivering a token to his hearers that he is going to edify them.

"My friends," says Mr. Chadband, " Peace be on this house! On the master thereof, on the mistress thereof, on the young maidens, and on the young men! My friends, why do I wish for peace? What is peace? Is it war? No. Is it strife? No. Is it lovely, and gentle, and beautiful, and pleasant, and serene, and joyful? Oh, yes! Therefore, my friends, I wish for peace, upon you and upon yours."

In consequence of Mrs. Snagsby looking deeply edified, Mr. Snagsby thinks it expedient on the whole to say Amen, which is well received.

"Now, my friends," proceeds Mr. Chadband, "since I am upon this theme"—

Guster presents herself. Mrs. Snagsby, in a spectral bass voice, and without removing her eyes from Chadband, says, with dread distinctness, " Go away!"

" Now, my friends," says Chadband, " since I am upon this theme, and in my lowly path improving it"—

Guster is heard unaccountably to murmur "one thousing seven hundred and eighty-two." The spectral voice repeats more solemnly, " Go away!"

" Now, my friends," says Mr. Chadband, "we will inquire in a spirit of love"—

Still Guster reiterates, " one thousing seven hundred and eighty-two."

Mr. Chadband, pausing with the resignation of a man accustomed to be persecuted, and languidly folding up his chin into his fat smile, says, " Let us hear the maiden! Speak, maiden!"

"One thousing seven hundred and eighty-two, if you please, sir. Which he wish to know what the shilling ware for," says Guster, breathless.

"For?" returns Mrs. Chadband. "For his fare!"

Guster replied that "he insists on one and eightpence, or on summonsizzing the party." Mrs. Snagsby and Mrs. Chadband are proceeding to grow shrill in indignation, when Mr. Chadband quiets the tumult by lifting up his hand.

"My friends," says he, "I remember a duty unfulfilled yesterday. It is right that I should be chastened in some penalty. I ought not to murmur. Rachel, pay the eightpence!"

While Mrs. Snagsby, drawing her breath, looks hard at Mr. Snagsby, as who should say, "you hear this apostle!" and while Mr. Chadband glows with humility and train oil, Mrs. Chadband pays the money. It is Mr. Chadband's habit — it is the head and front of his pretensions indeed — to keep this sort of debtor and creditor account in the smallest items, and to post it publicly on the most trivial occasions.

"My friends," says Chadband, "eightpence is not much; it might justly have been one-and-fourpence; it might justly have been half-a-crown. Oh, let us be joyful, joyful! Oh, let us be joyful!"

With which remark, which appears from its sound to be an extract in verse, Mr. Chadband stalks to the table, and, before taking a chair, lifts up his admonitory hand.

"My friends," says he, "what is this which we now behold as being spread before us? Refreshment. Do we need refreshment then, my friends? We do. And why do we need refreshment, my friends? Because we are but mortal, because we are but sinful, because we are but of the earth, because we are not of the air. Can we fly, my friends? We cannot. Why can we not fly, my friends?"

Mr. Snagsby, presuming on the success of his last point, ventures to observe in a cheerful and rather knowing tone, "No wings." But is immediately frowned down by Mrs. Snagsby.

"I say, my friends," pursues Mr. Chadband, utterly rejecting and obliterating Mr. Snagsby's suggestion, "why can we not fly? Is it because we are calculated to walk? It is. Could we walk, my friends, without strength? We could not. What should we do without strength, my friends? Our legs would refuse to bear us, our knees would double up, our ankles would turn over, and we should come to the ground. Then from whence, my friends, in a human point of view, do we derive the strength that is necessary to our limbs? Is it," says Chadband, glancing over the table, " from bread in various forms, from butter which is churned from the milk which is yielded untoe us by the cow, from the eggs which are laid by the fowl, from ham, from tongue, from sausage, and from such like? It is. Then let us partake of the good things which are set before us!"

The persecutors denied that there was any particular gift in Mr. Chadband's piling verbose flights of stairs, one upon another, after this fashion. But this can only be received as a proof of their determination to persecute, since it must be within everybody's experience, that the Chadband style of oratory is widely received and much admired.

Mr. Chadband, however, having concluded for the present, sits down at Mrs. Snagsby's table, and lays about him prodigiously. The conversion of nutriment of any sort into oil of the quality already mentioned, appears to be a process so inseparable from the constitution of this exemplary vessel, that in beginning to eat and drink, he may be described as always becoming a kind of considerable Oil Mills, or other large factory for the production of that article on a wholesome scale. On the present evening of the long vacation, in Cook's Court, Cursitor Street, he does such a powerful stroke of business, that the warehouse appears to be quite full when the works cease.

At this period of the entertainment, Guster, who has never recovered her first failure, but has neglected no possible or impossible means of bringing the establishment and herself into contempt — among which may be briefly enumerated her unexpectedly performing clashing military music on Mr. Chadband's head with plates, and afterwards crowning that gentleman with muffins — at which period of the entertainment, Guster whispers Mr. Snagsby that he is wanted.

"And being wanted in the — not to put too fine a point upon it — in the shop!" says Mr. Snagsby, rising, "perhaps this good company will excuse me for half a minute."

Mr. Snagsby descends, and finds the two 'prentices intently contemplating a police constable, who holds a ragged boy by the arm.

"Why, bless my heart," says Mr. Snagsby, "what's the matter!"

"This boy," says the constable, "although he's repeatedly told to, won't move on" —

"I'm always a-moving on, sir," cries the boy, wiping away his grimy tears with his arm. "I've always been a-moving and a-moving on, ever since I was born.

Where can I possible move to, sir, more nor I do move!"

"He won't move on," says the constable, calmly, with a slight professional hitch of his neck involving its better settlement in his stiff stock, "although he has been repeatedly cautioned, and therefore I am obliged to take him into custody. He's as obstinate a young gonoph as I know. He won't move on."

"Oh, my eye! Where can I move to!" cries the boy, clutching quite desperately at his hair, and beating his bare feet upon the floor of Mr. Snagsby's passage.

"Don't you come none of that, or I shall make blessed short work of you!" says the constable, giving him a passionless shake. "My instructions are, that you are to move on. I have told you so five hundred times."

"But where?" cries the boy.

"Well! Really, constable, you know," says Mr. Snagsby, wistfully, and coughing behind his hand his cough of great perplexity and doubt; "really that does seem a question. Where, you know?"

"My instructions don't go to that," replies the constable. "My instructions are that this boy is to move on."

Do you hear, Jo? It is nothing to you or to any one else, that the great lights of the parliamentary sky have failed for some few years, in this business, to set you the example of moving on. The one grand recipe remains for you — the profound philosophical prescription — the be-all and the end-all of your strange existence upon earth. Move on! You are by no means to move off, Jo, for the great lights can't at all agree about that. Move on!

Mr. Snagsby says nothing to this effect; says nothing

at all, indeed; but coughs his forlornest cough, expressive of no thoroughfare in any direction. By this time, Mr. and Mrs. Chadband, and Mrs. Snagsby, hearing the altercation, have appeared upon the stairs. Guster having never left the end of the passage, the whole household are assembled.

"The simple question is, sir," says the constable, "whether you know this boy. He says you do."

Mrs. Snagsby, from her elevation, instantly cries out, "No he don't!"

"My lit-tle woman!" says Mr. Snagsby, looking up the staircase. "My love, permit me! Pray have a moment's patience, my dear. I do know something of this lad, and in what I know of him, I can't say that there's any harm; perhaps on the contrary, constable." To whom the law-stationer relates his Joful and woful experience, suppressing the half-crown fact.

"Well!" says the constable, "so far, it seems, he had grounds for what he said. When I took him into custody up in Holborn, he said you knew him. Upon that, a young man who was in the crowd said he was acquainted with you, and you were a respectable housekeeper, and if I'd call and make the inquiry he'd appear. The young man don't seem inclined to keep his word, but— Oh! Here *is* the young man!"

Enter Mr. Guppy, who nods to Mr. Snagsby, and touches his hat with the chivalry of clerkship to the ladies on the stairs.

"I was strolling away from the office just now, when I found this row going on," says Mr. Guppy to the law-stationer; "and as your name was mentioned, I thought it was right the thing should be looked into."

"It was very good-natured of you, sir," says Mr.

Snagsby, "and I am obliged to you." And Mr. Snagsby again relates his experience, again suppressing the half-crown fact.

"Now, I know where you live," says the constable, then, to Jo. "You live down in Tom-all-alone's. That's a nice innocent place to live in, a'n't it?"

"I can't go and live in no nicer place, sir," replies Jo. "They wouldn't have nothink to say to me if I was to go to a nice innocent place fur to live. Who ud go and let a nice innocent lodging to such a reg'lar one as me!"

"You are very poor, a'n't you?" says the constable.

"Yes, I am indeed, sir, wery poor in gin'ral," replies Jo.

"I leave you to judge now! I shook these two half-crowns out of him," says the constable, producing them to the company, "in only putting my hand upon him!"

"They're wot's left, Mr. Snagsby," says Jo, "out of a sov'ring as wos give me by a lady in a wale as sed she wos a servant and as come to my crossin one night and asked to be showd this 'ere ouse and the ouse wot him as you giv the writin to died at, and the berrin ground wot he's berrid in. She ses to me she ses 'are you the boy at the Inkwhich?' she ses. I ses 'yes' I ses. She ses to me she ses 'can you show me all them places?' I ses 'yes I can' I ses. And she ses to me 'do it' and I dun it and she giv me a sov'ring and hooked it. And I a'n't had much of the sov'ring neither," says Jo, with dirty tears, "fur I had to pay five bob, down in Tom-all-alone's, afore they'd square it fur to giv me change, and then a young man he thieved another five while I was asleep and another boy he thieved ninepence and the landlord he stood drains round with a lot more on it."

"You don't expect anybody to believe this, about the lady and the sovereign, do you?" says the constable, eying him aside with ineffable disdain.

"I don't know as I do, sir," replies Jo. "I don't expect nothink at all, sir, much, but that's the true hist'ry on it."

"You see what he is!" the constable observes to the audience. "Well, Mr. Snagsby, if I don't lock him up this time, will you engage for his moving on?"

"No!" cries Mrs. Snagsby from the stairs.

"My little woman!" pleads her husband. "Constable, I have no doubt he'll move on. You know you really must do it," says Mr. Snagsby.

"I'm everyways agreeable, sir," says the hapless Jo.

"Do it, then," observes the constable. "You know what you have got to do. Do it! And recollect you won't get off so easy next time. Catch hold of your money. Now, the sooner you're five mile off, the better for all parties."

With this farewell hint, and pointing generally to the setting sun, as a likely place to move on to, the constable bids his auditors good afternoon; and makes the echoes of Cook's Court perform slow music for him as he walks away on the shady side, carrying his iron-bound hat in his hand for a little ventilation.

Now, Jo's improbable story concerning the lady and the sovereign has awakened more or less the curiosity of all the company. Mr. Guppy, who has an inquiring mind in matters of evidence, and who has been suffering severely from the lassitude of the long vacation, takes that interest in the case, that he enters on a regular cross-examination of the witness, which is found so interesting by the ladies that Mrs. Snagsby politely invites him to step up-stairs, and drink a cup of tea, if he will excuse the disarranged state of the tea-table, consequent on their previous exertions. Mr. Guppy yielding his assent to this proposal, Jo is requested to follow into the drawing-room doorway, where Mr. Guppy takes him in hand as a witness, patting him into this shape, that shape, and the other shape, like a butterman dealing with so much butter, and worrying him according to the best models. Nor is the examination unlike many such model displays, both in respect of its eliciting nothing, and of its being lengthy; for, Mr. Guppy is sensible of his talent, and Mrs. Snagsby feels, not only that it gratifies her inquisitive disposition, but that it lifts her husband's establishment higher up in the law. During the progress of this keen encounter, the vessel Chadband, being merely engaged in the oil trade, gets aground, and waits to be floated off.

"Well!" says Mr. Guppy, "either this boy sticks to it like cobbler's wax, or there is something out of the common here that beats anything that ever came into my way at Kenge and Carboy's."

Mrs. Chadband whispers Mrs. Snagsby, who exclaims, "You don't say so!"

"For years!" replies Mrs. Chadband.

"Has known Kenge and Carboy's office for years," Mrs. Snagsby triumphantly explains to Mr. Guppy. "Mrs. Chadband — this gentleman's wife — Reverend Mr. Chadband."

"Oh, indeed!" says Mr. Guppy.

"Before I married my present husband," says Mrs. Chadband.

"Was you a party in anything, ma'am?" says Mr. Guppy, transferring his cross-examination.

"No."

"*Not* a party in anything, ma'am?" says Mr. Guppy. Mrs. Chadband shakes her head.

"Perhaps you were acquainted with somebody who was a party in something, ma'am?" says Mr. Guppy, who likes nothing better than to model his conversation on forensic principles.

"Not exactly that, either!" replies Mrs. Chadband, humoring the joke with a hard-favored smile.

"Not exactly that, either!" repeats Mr. Guppy. "Very good. Pray, ma'am was it a lady of your acquaintance who had some transactions (we will not at present say what transactions) with Kenge and Carboy's office, or was it a gentleman of your acquaintance? Take time, ma'am. We shall come to it presently. Man or woman, ma'am?"

"Neither," says Mrs. Chadband, as before.

"Oh! A child!" says Mr. Guppy, throwing on the admiring Mrs. Snagsby the regular acute professional eye which is thrown on British jurymen. "Now, ma'am, perhaps you'll have the kindness to tell us *what* child."

"You have got it at last, sir," says Mrs. Chadband, with another hard-favored smile. "Well, sir, it was before your time, most likely, judging from your appearance. I was left in charge of a child named Esther Summerson, who was put out in life by Messrs. Kenge and Carboy."

"Miss Summerson, ma'am!" cries Mr. Guppy, excited.

"*I* call her Esther Summerson," says Mrs. Chadband,

with austerity. "There was no Miss-ing of the girl in my time. It was Esther. 'Esther, do this! Esther, do that!' and she was made to do it."

"My dear ma'am," returns Mr. Guppy, moving across the small apartment, "the humble individual who now addresses you received that young lady in London, when she first came here from the establishment to which you have alluded. Allow me to have the pleasure of taking you by the hand."

Mr. Chadband, at last seeing his opportunity, makes his accustomed signal, and rises with a smoking head, which he dabs with his pocket-handkerchief. Mrs. Snagsby whispers "Hush!"

"My friends," says Chadband, "we have partaken, in moderation" (which was certainly not the case so far as he was concerned), "of the comforts which have been provided for us. May this house live upon the fatness of the land; may corn and wine be plentiful therein; may it grow, may it thrive, may it prosper, may it advance, may it proceed, may it press forward! But, my friends, have we partaken of anything else? We have. My friends, of what else have we partaken? Of spiritual profit? Yes. From whence have we derived that spiritual profit? My young friend, stand forth!"

Jo, thus apostrophized, gives a slouch backward, and another slouch forward, and another slouch to each side, and confronts the eloquent Chadband, with evident doubts of his intentions.

"My young friend," says Chadband, "you are to us a pearl, you are to us a diamond, you are to us a gem, you are to us a jewel. And why, my young friend?"

"*I* don't know," replies Jo. "I don't know nothink."

"My young friend," says Chadband, "it is because you

know nothing that you are to us a gem and jewel. For what are you, my young friend? Are you a beast of the field? No. A bird of the air? No. A fish of the sea or river? No. You are a human boy, my young friend. A human boy. Oh, glorious to be a human boy! And why glorious, my young friend? Because you are capable of receiving the lessons of wisdom, because you are capable of profiting by this discourse which I now deliver for your good, because you are not a stick, or a staff, or a stock, or a stone, or a post, or a pillar.

>O running stream of sparkling joy
>To be a soaring human boy!

And do you cool yourself in that stream now, my young friend? No. Why do you not cool yourself in that stream now? Because you are in a state of darkness, because you are in a state of obscurity, because you are in a state of sinfulness, because you are in a state of bondage. My young friend, what *is* bondage? Let us, in a spirit of love, inquire."

At this threatening stage of the discourse, Jo, who seems to have been gradually going out of his mind, smears his right arm over his face, and gives a terrible yawn. Mrs. Snagsby indignantly expresses her belief that he is a limb of the arch-fiend.

"My friends," says Mr. Chadband, with his persecuted chin folding itself into its fat smile again as he looks round, "it is right that I should be humbled, it is right that I should be tried, it is right that I should be mortified, it is right that I should be corrected. I stumbled, on Sabbath last, when I thought with pride of my three hours' improving. The account is now favorably balanced: my creditor has accepted a composition. Oh, let us be joyful, joyful! Oh, let us be joyful!"

Great sensation on the part of Mrs. Snagsby.

"My friends," says Chadband, looking round him in conclusion, "I will not proceed with my young friend now. Will you come to-morrow, my young friend, and inquire of this good lady where I am to be found to deliver a discourse untoe you, and will you come like the thirsty swallow upon the next day, and upon the day after that, and upon the day after that, and upon many pleasant days, to hear discourses?" (This, with a cow-like lightness.)

Jo, whose immediate object seems to be to get away on any terms, gives a shuffling nod. Mr. Guppy then throws him a penny, and Mrs. Snagsby calls to Guster to see him safely out of the house. But, before he goes down-stairs Mr. Snagsby loads him with some broken meats from the table, which he carries away, hugging in his arms.

So, Mr. Chadband — of whom the persecutors say that it is no wonder he should go on for any length of time uttering such abominable nonsense, but that the wonder rather is that he should ever leave off, having once the audacity to begin — retires into private life until he invests a little capital of supper in the oil-trade. Jo moves on, through the long vacation, down to Blackfriars Bridge, where he finds a baking stony corner, wherein to settle to his repast.

And there he sits, munching and gnawing, and looking up at the great Cross on the summit of St. Paul's Cathedral, glittering above a red and violet-tinted cloud of smoke. From the boy's face one might suppose that sacred emblem to be, in his eyes, the crowning confusion of the great, confused city; so golden, so high up, so far out of his reach. There he sits, the sun going down, the river running fast, the crowd flowing by him in two streams — everything moving on to some purpose and to one end — until he is stirred up, and told to "move on" too.

CHAPTER XX.

A NEW LODGER.

THE long vacation saunters on towards term-time, like an idle river very leisurely strolling down a flat country to the sea. Mr. Guppy saunters along with it congenially. He has blunted the blade of his penknife, and broken the point off, by sticking that instrument into his desk in every direction. Not that he bears the desk any ill-will, but he must do something, and it must be something of an unexciting nature, which will lay neither his physical nor his intellectual energies under too heavy contribution. He finds that nothing agrees with him so well, as to make little gyrations on one leg of his stool, and stab his desk, and gape.

Kenge and Carboy are out of town, and the articled clerk has taken out a shooting-license, and gone down to his father's, and Mr. Guppy's two fellow-stipendiaries are away on leave. Mr. Guppy, and Mr. Richard Carstone, divide the dignity of the office. But Mr. Carstone is for the time being established in Kenge's room, whereat Mr. Guppy chafes. So exceedingly, that he with bitter sarcasm informs his mother, in the confidential moments when he sups with her off a lobster and lettuce, in the Old Street Road, that he is afraid the office is hardly good enough for swells, and that if he had known there was a swell coming, he would have got it painted.

Mr. Guppy suspects everybody who enters on the occupation of a stool in Kenge and Carboy's office, of entertaining, as a matter of course, sinister designs upon him. He is clear that every such person wants to depose him. If he be ever asked how, why, when, or wherefore, he shuts up one eye and shakes his head. On the strength of these profound views, he in the most ingenious manner takes infinite pains to counterplot, when there is no plot; and plays the deepest games of chess without any adversary.

It is a source of much gratification to Mr. Guppy, therefore, to find the new-comer constantly poring over the papers in Jarndyce and Jarndyce; for he well knows that nothing but confusion and failure can come of that. His satisfaction communicates itself to a third saunterer through the long vacation in Kenge and Carboy's office; to wit, Young Smallweed.

Whether Young Smallweed (metaphorically called Small and eke Chick Weed, as it were jocularly to express a fledgling) was ever a boy, is much doubted in Lincoln's Inn. He is now something under fifteen, and an old limb of the law. He is facetiously understood to entertain a passion for a lady at a cigar-shop, in the neighborhood of Chancery Lane, and for her sake to have broken off a contract with another lady, to whom he had been engaged some years. He is a town-made article, of small stature and weazen features; but may be perceived from a considerable distance by means of his very tall hat. To become a Guppy is the object of his ambition. He dresses at that gentleman (by whom he is patronized), talks at him, walks at him, founds himself entirely on him. He is honored with Mr. Guppy's particular confidence, and occasionally advises him, from the deep wells of his experience, on difficult points in private life.

Mr. Guppy has been lolling out of window all the morning, after trying all the stools in succession and finding none of them easy, and after several times putting his head into the iron safe with a notion of cooling it. Mr. Smallweed has been twice despatched for effervescent drinks, and has twice mixed them in the two official tumblers and stirred them up with the ruler. Mr. Guppy propounds, for Mr. Smallweed's consideration, the paradox that the more you drink the thirstier you are; and reclines his head upon the window-sill in a state of hopeless languor.

While thus looking out into the shade of Old Square, Lincoln's Inn, surveying the intolerable bricks and mortar, Mr. Guppy becomes conscious of a manly whisker emerging from the cloistered walk below, and turning itself up in the direction of his face. At the same time, a low whistle is wafted through the Inn, and a suppressed voice cries, "Hip! Gup-py!"

"Why, you don't mean it?" says Mr. Guppy, aroused. "Small! Here's Jobling!" Small's head looks out of window too, and nods to Jobling.

"Where have you sprung up from?" inquires Mr. Guppy.

"From the market-gardens down by Deptford. I can't stand it any longer. I must enlist. I say! I wish you'd lend me half-a-crown. Upon my soul, I'm hungry."

Jobling looks hungry, and also has the appearance of having run to seed in the market-gardens down by Deptford.

"I say! Just throw out half-a-crown, if you have got one to spare. I want to get some dinner."

"Will you come and dine with me?" says Mr. Guppy, throwing out the coin, which Mr. Jobling catches neatly.

"How long should I have to hold out?" says Jobling.

"Not half an hour. I am only waiting here till the enemy goes," returns Mr. Guppy, butting inward with his head.

"What enemy?"

"A new one. Going to be articled. Will you wait?"

"Can you give a fellow anything to read in the meantime?" says Mr. Jobling.

Smallweed suggests the Law List. But Mr. Jobling declares, with much earnestness, that he "can't stand it."

"You shall have the paper," says Mr. Guppy. "He shall bring it down. But you had better not be seen about here. Sit on our staircase and read. It's a quiet place."

Jobling nods intelligence and acquiescence. The sagacious Smallweed supplies him with the newspaper, and occasionally drops his eye upon him from the landing as a precaution against his becoming disgusted with waiting, and making an untimely departure. At last the enemy retreats, and then Smallweed fetches Mr. Jobling up.

"Well, and how are you?" says Mr. Guppy, shaking hands with him.

"So, so. How are you?"

Mr. Guppy replying that he is not much to boast of, Mr. Jobling ventures on the question, "How is *she*?" This Mr. Guppy resents as a liberty; retorting, "Jobling, there *are* chords in the human mind —" Jobling begs pardon.

"Any subject but that!" says Mr. Guppy, with a

gloomy enjoyment of his injury. "For there *are* chords, Jobling—"

Mr. Jobling begs pardon again.

During this short colloquy, the active Smallweed, who is of the dinner-party, has written in legal characters on a slip of paper, " Return immediately." This notification to all whom it may concern, he inserts in the letter-box; and then putting on the tall hat, at the angle of inclination at which Mr. Guppy wears his, informs his patron that they may now make themselves scarce.

Accordingly they betake themselves to a neighboring dining-house, of the class known among its frequenters by the denomination Slap-Bang, where the waitress, a bouncing young female of forty, is supposed to have made some impression on the susceptible Smallweed; of whom it may be remarked that he is a weird changeling, to whom years are nothing. He stands precociously possessed of centuries of owlish wisdom. If he ever lay in a cradle, it seems as if he must have lain there in a tail-coat. He has an old, old eye, has Smallweed; and he drinks, and smokes, in a monkeyish way; and his neck is stiff in his collar; and he is never to be taken in; and he knows all about it, whatever it is. In short, in his bringing up, he has been so nursed by Law and Equity that he has become a kind of fossil Imp, to account for whose terrestrial existence it is reported at the public offices that his father was John Doe, and his mother the only female member of the Roe family: also that his first long-clothes were made from a blue bag.

Into the Dining House, unaffected by the seductive show in the window, of artificially whitened cauliflowers and poultry, verdant baskets of peas, coolly blooming cucumbers, and joints ready for the spit, Mr. Smallweed leads the way. They know him there, and defer to him. He has his favorite box, he bespeaks all the papers, he is down upon bald patriarchs, who keep them more than ten minutes afterwards. It is of no use trying him with anything less than a full-sized "bread," or proposing to him any joint in cut, unless it is in the very best cut. In the matter of gravy he is adamant.

Conscious of his elfin power, and submitting to his dread experience, Mr. Guppy consults him in the choice of that day's banquet; turning an appealing look towards him as the waitress repeats the catalogue of viands, and saying "What do *you* take, Chick?" Chick, out of the profundity of his artfulness, preferring "veal and ham and French beans — And don't you forget the stuffing, Polly," (with an unearthly cock of his venerable eye.) Mr. Guppy and Mr. Jobling give the like order. Three pint pots of half-and-half are superadded. Quickly the waitress returns, bearing what is apparently a model of the tower of Babel, but what is really a pile of plates and flat tin dish-covers. Mr. Smallweed, approving of what is set before him, conveys intelligent benignity into his ancient eye, and winks upon her. Then, amid a constant coming in, and going out, and running about, and a clatter of crockery, and a rumbling up and down of the machine which brings the nice cuts from the kitchen, and a shrill crying for more nice cuts down the speaking-pipe, and a shrill reckoning of the cost of nice cuts that have been disposed of, and a general flush and steam of hot joints, cut and uncut, and a considerably heated atmosphere in which the soiled knives and table-cloths seem to break out spontaneously into eruptions of grease and blotches of beer, the legal triumvirate appease their appetites.

Mr. Jobling is buttoned up closer than mere adornment might require. His hat presents at the rims a peculiar appearance of a glistening nature, as if it had been a favorite snail-promenade. The same phenomenon is visible on some parts of his coat, and particularly at the seams. He has the faded appearance of a gentleman in embarrassed circumstances; even his light whiskers droop with something of a shabby air.

His appetite is so vigorous, that it suggests spare living for some little time back. He makes such a speedy end of his plate of veal and ham, bringing it to a close while his companions are yet midway in theirs, that Mr. Guppy proposes another. "Thank you, Guppy," says Mr. Jobling, "I really don't know but what I *will* take another."

Another being brought, he falls to with great good will.

Mr. Guppy takes silent notice of him at intervals, until he is half-way through this second plate and stops to take an enjoying pull at his pint-pot of half-and-half (also renewed), and stretches out his legs and rubs his hands. Beholding him in which glow of contentment, Mr. Guppy says, —

"You are a man again, Tony!"

"Well, not quite, yet," says Mr. Jobling. "Say, just born."

"Will you take any other vegetables? Grass? Peas? Summer cabbage?"

"Thank you, Guppy," says Mr. Jobling. "I really don't know but what I *will* take summer cabbage."

Order given; with the sarcastic addition (from Mr. Smallweed) of "Without slugs, Polly!" And cabbage produced.

"I am growing up, Guppy," says Mr. Jobling, plying his knife and fork with a relishing steadiness.

"Glad to hear it."

"In fact, I have just turned into my teens," says Mr. Jobling.

He says no more until he has performed his task, which he achieves as Messrs. Guppy and Smallweed finish theirs; thus getting over the ground in excellent style, and beating those two gentlemen easily by a veal and ham and a cabbage.

"Now, Small," says Mr. Guppy, "what would you recommend about pastry?"

"Marrow puddings," says Mr. Smallweed, instantly.

"Ay, ay!" cries Mr. Jobling, with an arch look. "You're there, are you? Thank you, Guppy, I don't know but what I *will* take a marrow pudding."

Three marrow puddings being produced, Mr. Jobling adds, in a pleasant humor, that he is coming of age fast. To these succeed, by command of Mr. Smallweed, "three Cheshires;" and to those, "three small rums." This apex of the entertainment happily reached, Mr. Jobling puts up his legs on the carpeted seat (having his own side of the box to himself), leans against the wall, and says, "I am grown up, now, Guppy. I have arrived at maturity."

"What do you think, now," says Mr. Guppy, "about — you don't mind Smallweed?"

"Not the least in the world. I have the pleasure of drinking his good health."

"Sir, to you!" says Mr. Smallweed.

"I was saying, what do you think *now*," pursues Mr. Guppy, "of enlisting?"

"Why, what I may think after dinner," returns Mr.

Jobling, "is one thing, my dear Guppy, and what I may think before dinner is another thing. Still, even after dinner, I ask myself the question, What am I to do? How am I to live? Ill fo manger, you know," says Mr. Jobling, pronouncing that word as if he meant a necessary fixture in an English stable. "Ill fo manger. That's the French saying, and mangering is as necessary to me as it is to a Frenchman. Or more so."

Mr. Smallweed is decidedly of opinion "much more so."

"If any man had told me," pursues Jobling, "even so lately as when you and I had the frisk down in Lincolnshire, Guppy, and drove over to see that house at Castle Wold" —

Mr. Smallweed corrects him — Chesney Wold.

"Chesney Wold. (I thank my honorable friend for that cheer.) If any man had told me, then, that I should be as hard up at the present time as I literally find myself, I should have — well, I should have pitched into him," says Mr. Jobling, taking a little rum-and-water with an air of desperate resignation; "I should have let fly at his head."

"Still, Tony, you were on the wrong side of the post then," remonstrates Mr. Guppy. "You were talking about nothing else in the gig."

"Guppy," says Mr. Jobling, "I will not deny it. I was on the wrong side of the post. But I trusted to things coming round."

That very popular trust in flat things coming round! Not in their being beaten round, or worked round, but in their "coming" round! As though a lunatic should trust in the world's "coming" triangular!

"I had confident expectations that things would come

round and be all square," says Mr. Jobling, with some vagueness of expression, and perhaps of meaning, too. "But I was disappointed. They never did. And when it came to creditors making rows at the office, and to people that the office dealt with making complaints about dirty trifles of borrowed money, why there was an end of that connection. And of any new professional connection, too; for if I was to give a reference to-morrow, it would be mentioned, and would sew me up. Then, what's a fellow to do? I have been keeping out of the way, and living cheap, down about the market-gardens; but what's the use of living cheap when you have got no money? You might as well live dear."

"Better," Mr. Smallweed thinks.

"Certainly. It's the fashionable way; and fashion and whiskers have been my weaknesses, and I don't care who knows it," says Mr. Jobling. "They are great weaknesses — Damme, sir, they are great. Well!" proceeds Mr. Jobling, after a defiant visit to his rum-and-water, "what can a fellow do, I ask you, *but* enlist?"

Mr. Guppy comes more fully into the conversation, to state what, in his opinion, a fellow can do. His manner is the gravely impressive manner of a man who has not committed himself in life, otherwise than as he has become the victim of a tender sorrow of the heart.

"Jobling," says Mr. Guppy, "myself and our mutual friend Smallweed " —

(Mr. Smallweed modestly observes "Gentlemen both!" and drinks.)

"Have had a little conversation on this matter more than once, since you " —

"Say, got the sack!" cries Mr. Jobling, bitterly. "Say it, Guppy. You mean it."

"N-o-o! Left the Inn," Mr. Smallweed delicately suggests.

"Since you left the Inn, Jobling," says Mr. Guppy; "and I have mentioned, to our mutual friend Smallweed, a plan I have lately thought of proposing. You know Snagsby the stationer?"

"I know there is such a stationer," returns Mr. Jobling. "He was not ours, and I am not acquainted with him."

"He *is* ours, Jobling, and I *am* acquainted with him," Mr. Guppy retorts. "Well, sir! I have lately become better acquainted with him, through some accidental circumstances that have made me a visitor of his in private life. Those circumstances it is not necessary to offer in argument. They may — or they may not — have some reference to a subject, which may — or may not — have cast its shadow on my existence."

As it is Mr. Guppy's perplexing way, with boastful misery to tempt his particular friends into this subject, and the moment they touch it, to turn on them with that trenchant severity about the chords in the human mind; both Mr. Jobling and Mr. Smallweed decline the pitfall, by remaining silent.

"Such things may be," repeats Mr. Guppy, "or they may not be. They are no part of the case. It is enough to mention, that both Mr. and Mrs. Snagsby are very willing to oblige me; and that Snagsby has, in busy times, a good deal of copying work to give out. He has all Tulkinghorn's, and an excellent business besides. I believe, if our mutual friend Smallweed were put into the box, he could prove this?"

Mr. Smallweed nods, and appears greedy to be sworn.

"Now, gentlemen of the jury," says Mr. Guppy, "— I

mean, now, Jobling — you may say this is a poor prospect of a living. Granted. But it's better than nothing, and better than enlistment. You want time. There must be time for these late affairs to blow over. You might live through it on much worse terms than by writing for Snagsby."

Mr. Jobling is about to interrupt, when the sagacious Smallweed checks him with a dry cough, and the words, " Hem! Shakspeare!"

" There are two branches to this subject, Jobling," says Mr. Guppy. " That is the first. I come to the second. You know Krook, the Chancellor, across the lane. Come, Jobling," says Mr. Guppy, in his encouraging cross-examination-tone, " I think you know Krook, the Chancellor, across the lane?"

" I know him by sight," says Mr. Jobling.

" You know him by sight. Very well. And you know little Flite?"

" Everybody knows her," says Mr. Jobling.

" Everybody knows her. *Very* well. Now it has been one of my duties of late, to pay Flite a certain weekly allowance, deducting from it the amount of her weekly rent; which I have paid (in consequence of instructions I have received) to Krook himself, regularly, in her presence. This has brought me into communication with Krook, and into a knowledge of his house and his habits. I know he has a room to let. You may live there, at a very low charge, under any name you like, as quietly as if you were a hundred miles off. He'll ask no questions; and would accept you as a tenant, at a word from me — before the clock strikes, if you chose. And I'll tell you another thing, Jobling," says Mr. Guppy, who has suddenly lowered his voice, and become familiar again, " he's an extraordinary old chap — always rummaging among a litter of papers, and grubbing away at teaching himself to read and write; without getting on a bit, as it seems to me. He is a most extraordinary old chap, sir. I don't know but what it might be worth a fellow's while to look him up a bit."

"You don't mean —?" Mr. Jobling begins.

"I mean," returns Mr. Guppy, shrugging his shoulders with becoming modesty, "that *I* can't make him out. I appeal to our mutual friend Smallweed whether he has or has not heard me remark, that I can't make him out."

Mr. Smallweed bears the concise testimony, "A few!"

"I have seen something of the profession, and something of life, Tony," says Mr. Guppy, "and it's seldom I can't make a man out, more or less. But such an old card as this; so deep, so sly, and secret (though I don't believe he is ever sober), I never came across. Now, he must be precious old, you know, and he has not a soul about him, and he is reported to be immensely rich; and whether he is a smuggler, or a receiver, or an unlicensed pawnbroker, or a money-lender — all of which I have thought likely at different times — it might pay you to knock up a sort of knowledge of him. I don't see why you shouldn't go in for it, when everything else suits."

Mr. Jobling, Mr. Guppy, and Mr. Smallweed, all lean their elbows on the table, and their chins upon their hands, and look at the ceiling. After a time, they all drink, slowly lean back, put their hands in their pockets, and look at one another.

"If I had the energy I once possessed, Tony!" says

Mr. Guppy, with a sigh. "But there are chords in the human mind"—

Expressing the remainder of the desolate sentiment in rum-and-water, Mr. Guppy concludes by resigning the adventure to Tony Jobling, and informing him that during the vacation and while things are slack, his purse, "as far as three or four or even five pound goes," will be at his disposal. "For never shall it be said," Mr. Guppy adds with emphasis, "that William Guppy turned his back upon his friend!"

The latter part of the proposal is so directly to the purpose, that Mr. Jobling says with emotion, "Guppy, my trump, your fist!" Mr. Guppy presents it, saying, "Jobling, my boy, there it is!" Mr. Jobling returns, "Guppy we have been pals now for some years!" Mr. Guppy replies, "Jobling, we have." They then shake hands, and Mr. Jobling adds in a feeling manner. "Thank you, Guppy, I don't know but what I *will* take another glass, for old acquaintance sake"

"Krook's last lodger died there," observes Mr. Guppy, in an incidental way.

"Did he, though!" says Mr. Jobling.

"There was a verdict. Accidental death. You don't mind that?"

"No," says Mr. Jobling, "I don't mind it; but he might as well have died somewhere else. It's devilish odd that he need go and die at *my* place!" Mr. Jobling quite resents this liberty; several times returning to it with such remarks as, "There are places enough to die in, I should think!" or, "He wouldn't have liked my dying at *his* place, I dare say!"

However, the compact being virtually made, Mr. Guppy proposes to despatch the trusty Smallweed to ascertain if Mr. Krook is at home, as in that case they may complete the negotiation without delay. Mr. Jobling approving, Smallweed puts himself under the tall hat and conveys it out of the dining-rooms in the Guppy manner. He soon returns with the intelligence that Mr. Krook is at home, and that he has seen him through the shop-door, sitting in his back premises, sleeping, "like one o'clock."

"Then I'll pay," says Mr. Guppy; "and we'll go and see him. Small, what will it be?"

Mr. Smallweed, compelling the attendance of the waitress with one hitch of his eyelash, instantly replies as follows: "Four veals and hams is three, and four potatoes is three and four, and one summer cabbage is three and six, and three marrows is four and six, and six breads is five, and three Cheshires is five and three, and four pints of half-and-half is six and three, and four small rums is eight and three, and three Pollys is eight and six. Eight and six in half a sovereign, Polly, and eighteenpence out!"

Not at all excited by these stupendous calculations, Smallweed dismisses his friends with a cool nod, and remains behind to take a little admiring notice of Polly, as opportunity may serve, and to read the daily papers: which are so very large in proportion to himself, shorn of his hat, that when he holds up The Times to run his eye over the columns, he seems to have retired for the night, and to have disappeared under the bedclothes.

Mr. Guppy and Mr. Jobling repair to the rag and bottle shop, where they find Krook still sleeping like one o'clock; that is to say, breathing stertorously with his chin upon his breast, and quite insensible to any external sounds, or even to gentle shaking. On the table beside him, among the usual lumber, stand an empty gin-bottle and a glass. The unwholesome air is so stained with this liquor, that even the green eyes of the cat upon her shelf, as they open and shut and glimmer on the visitors, look drunk.

"Hold up here!" says Mr. Guppy, giving the relaxed figure of the old man another shake. "Mr. Krook! Halloa, sir!"

But it would seem as easy to wake a bundle of old clothes, with a spirituous heat smouldering in it. "Did you ever see such a stupor as he falls into, between drink and sleep?" says Mr. Guppy.

"If this is his regular sleep," returns Jobling, rather alarmed, "it'll last a long time one of these days, I am thinking."

"It's always more like a fit than a nap," says Mr. Guppy, shaking him again. "Halloa, your lordship! Why he might be robbed, fifty times over! Open your eyes!"

After much ado, he opens them, but without appearing to see his visitors, or any other objects. Though he crosses one leg on another, and folds his hands, and several times closes and opens his parched lips, he seems to all intents and purposes as insensible as before.

"He is alive, at any rate," says Mr. Guppy. "How are you, my Lord Chancellor? I have brought a friend of mine, sir, on a little matter of business."

The old man still sits, often smacking his dry lips, without the least consciousness. After some minutes, he makes an attempt to rise. They help him up, and he staggers against the wall, and stares at them.

"How do you do, Mr. Krook?" says Mr. Guppy, in some discomfiture. "How do you do, sir? You are looking charming, Mr. Krook. I hope you are pretty well?"

The old man, in aiming a purposeless blow at Mr. Guppy, or at nothing, feebly swings himself round, and comes with his face against the wall. So he remains for a minute or two, heaped up against it; and then staggers down the shop to the front-door. The air, the movement in the court, the lapse of time, or the combination of these things, recovers him. He comes back pretty steadily, adjusting his fur-cap on his head, and looking keenly at them.

"Your servant, gentlemen; I've been dozing. Hi! I am hard to wake, odd times."

"Rather so, indeed, sir," responds Mr. Guppy.

"What? You've been a-trying to do it, have you?" says the suspicious Krook.

"Only a little," Mr. Guppy explains.

The old man's eye resting on the empty bottle, he takes it up, examines it, and slowly tilts it upside down.

"I say!" he cries, like the hobgoblin in the story. "Somebody's been making free here!"

"I assure you we found it so," says Mr. Guppy. "Would you allow me to get it filled for you?"

"Yes, certainly I would!" cries Krook, in high glee. "Certainly I would! Don't mention it! Get it filled next door — Sol's Arms — the Lord Chancellor's fourteenpenny. Bless you, they know *me!*"

He so presses the empty bottle upon Mr. Guppy, that that gentleman, with a nod to his friend, accepts the trust, and hurries out and hurries in again with the bottle filled. The old man receives it in his arms like a beloved grandchild, and pats it tenderly.

"But, I say!" he whispers, with his eyes screwed up,

after tasting it, "this a'n't the Lord Chancellor's fourteenpenny. This is eighteenpenny!"

"I thought you might like that better," says Mr. Guppy.

"You're a nobleman, sir," returns Krook, with another taste — and his hot breath seems to come towards them like a flame. "You're a baron of the land."

Taking advantage of this auspicious moment, Mr. Guppy presents his friend under the impromptu name of Mr. Weevle, and states the object of their visit. Krook with his bottle under his arm (he never gets beyond a certain point of either drunkenness or sobriety), takes time to survey his proposed lodger, and seems to approve of him. "You'd like to see the room, young man?" he says. "Ah! It's a good room! Been whitewashed. Been cleaned down with soft soap and soda. Hi! It's worth twice the rent; letting alone my company when you want it, and such a cat to keep the mice away."

Commending the room after this manner, the old man takes them up-stairs, where indeed they do find it cleaner than it used to be, and also containing some old articles of furniture which he has dug up from his inexhaustible stores. The terms are easily concluded — for the Lord Chancellor cannot be hard on Mr. Guppy, associated as he is with Kenge and Carboy, Jarndyce and Jarndyce, and other famous claims on his professional consideration — and it is agreed that Mr. Weevle shall take possession on the morrow. Mr. Weevle and Mr. Guppy then repair to Cook's Court, Cursitor Street, where the personal introduction of the former to Mr. Snagsby is effected, and (more important) the vote and interest of Mrs. Snagsby are secured. They then report progress to the eminent Smallweed, waiting at the office in his tall hat for that purpose, and separate; Mr. Guppy explaining that he would terminate his little entertainment by standing treat at the play, but that there are chords in the human mind which would render it a hollow mockery.

On the morrow, in the dusk of evening, Mr. Weevle modestly appears at Krook's, by no means incommoded with luggage, and establishes himself in his new lodging; where the two eyes in the shutters stare at him in his sleep, as if they were full of wonder. On the following day Mr. Weevle, who is a handy good-for-nothing kind of young fellow, borrows a needle and thread of Miss Flite, and a hammer of his landlord, and goes to work devising apologies for window-curtains, and knocking up apologies for shelves, and hanging up his two teacups, milkpot, and crockery sundries on a pennyworth of little hooks, like a shipwrecked sailor making the best of it.

But what Mr. Weevle prizes most, of all his few possessions (next after his light whiskers, for which he has an attachment that only whiskers can awaken in the breast of man), is a choice collection of copper-plate impressions from that truly national work, the Divinities of Albion, or Galaxy Gallery of British Beauty, representing ladies of title and fashion in every variety of smirk that art, combined with capital, is capable of producing. With these magnificent portraits, unworthily confined in a band-box during his seclusion among the market-gardens, he decorates his apartment; and as the Galaxy Gallery of British Beauty wears every variety of fancy dress, plays every variety of musical instrument, fondles every variety of dog, ogles every variety of prospect, and is backed up by every variety of flower-pot and balustrade, the result is very imposing.

But fashion is Mr. Weevle's, as it was Tony Jobling's weakness. To borrow yesterday's paper from the Sol's Arms of an evening, and read about the brilliant and distinguished meteors that are shooting across the fashionable sky in every direction, is unspeakable consolation to him. To know what member of what brilliant and distinguished circle accomplished the brilliant and distinguished feat of joining it yesterday, or contemplates the no less brilliant and distinguished feat of leaving it to-morrow, gives him a thrill of joy. To be informed what the Galaxy Gallery of British Beauty is about, and means to be about, and what Galaxy marriages are on the tapis, and what Galaxy rumors are in circulation, is to become acquainted with the most glorious destinies of mankind. Mr. Weevle reverts from this intelligence, to the Galaxy portraits implicated; and seems to know the originals, and to be known of them.

For the rest he is a quiet lodger, full of handy shifts and devices as before mentioned, able to cook and clean for himself, as well as to carpenter, and developing social inclinations after the shades of evening have fallen on the court. At those times, when he is not visited by Mr. Guppy, or by a small light in his likeness quenched in a dark hat, he comes out of his dull room — where he has inherited the deal wilderness of desk bespattered with a rain of ink — and talks to Krook, or is "very free," as they call it in the court, commendingly, with any one disposed for conversation. Wherefore, Mrs. Piper, who leads the court, is impelled to offer two remarks to Mrs. Perkins: Firstly, that if her Johnny was to have whiskers, she could wish 'em to be identically like that young man's; and secondly, Mark my words, Mrs. Perkins, ma'am, and don't you be surprised, Lord bless you, if that young man comes in at last for old Krook's money!

CHAPTER XXI.

THE SMALLWEED FAMILY.

In a rather ill-favored and ill-savored neighborhood, though one of its rising grounds bears the name of Mount Pleasant, the Elfin Smallweed, christened Bartholomew, and known on the domestic hearth as Bart, passes that limited portion of his time on which the office and its contingencies have no claim. He dwells in a little narrow street, always solitary, shady, and sad, closely bricked in on all sides like a tomb, but where there yet lingers the stump of an old forest-tree, whose flavor is about as fresh and natural as the Smallweed smack of youth.

There has been only one child in the Smallweed family for several generations. Little old men and women there have been, but no child, until Mr. Smallweed's grandmother, now living, became weak in her intellect, and fell (for the first time) into a childish state. With such infantine graces as a total want of observation, memory, understanding and interest, and an eternal disposition to fall asleep over the fire and into it, Mr. Smallweed's grandmother has undoubtedly brightened the family.

Mr. Smallweed's grandfather is likewise of the party. He is in a helpless condition as to his lower, and nearly so as to his upper limbs; but his mind is unimpaired. It holds, as well as it ever held, the first four rules of arithmetic, and a certain small collection of the hardest facts. In respect of ideality, reverence, wonder, and other such phrenological attributes, it is no worse off than it used to be. Everything that Mr. Smallweed's grandfather ever put away in his mind was a grub at first, and is a grub at last. In all his life he has never bred a single butterfly.

The father of this pleasant grandfather, of the neighborhood of Mount Pleasant, was a horny-skinned, two-legged, money-getting species of spider, who spun webs to catch unwary flies, and retired into holes until they were entrapped. The name of this old pagan's God was Compound Interest. He lived for it, married it, died of it. Meeting with a heavy loss in an honest little enterprise in which all the loss was intended to have been on the other side, he broke something — something necessary to his existence; therefore it couldn't have been his heart — and made an end of his career. As his character was not good, and he had been bred at a Charity School, in a complete course, according to question and answer, of those ancient people the Amorites and Hittites, he was frequently quoted as an example of the failure of education.

His spirit shone through his son, to whom he had always preached of "going out" early in life, and whom he made a clerk in a sharp scrivener's office at twelve years old. There, the young gentleman improved his mind, which was of a lean and anxious character; and, developing the family gifts, gradually elevated himself into the discounting profession. Going out early in life and marrying late, as his father had done before him, he too begat a lean and anxious-minded son; who, in his turn, going out early in life and marrying late, became the father of Bartholomew and Judith Smallweed, twins. During the whole time consumed in the slow growth of this family tree, the house of Smallweed, always early to go out and late to marry, has strengthened itself in its practical character, has discarded all amusements, discountenanced all story-books, fairy-tales, fictions, and fables, and banished all levities whatsoever. Hence the gratifying fact, that it has had no child born to it, and that the complete little men and women whom it has produced, have been observed to bear a likeness to old monkeys with something depressing on their minds.

At the present time, in the dark little parlor certain feet below the level of the street — a grim, hard, uncouth parlor, only ornamented with the coarsest of baize table-covers, and the hardest of sheet-iron tea-trays, and offering in its decorative character no bad allegorical representation of Grandfather Smallweed's mind — seated in two black horsehair porter's chairs, one on each side of the fireplace, the superannuated Mr. and Mrs. Smallweed wile away the rosy hours. On the stove are a couple of trivets for the pots and kettles, which it is Grandfather Smallweed's usual occupation to watch, and projecting from the chimney-piece between them is a sort of brass gallows for roasting, which he also superintends when it is in action. Under the venerable Mr. Smallweed's seat, and guarded by his spindle legs, is a drawer in his chair, reported to contain property to a fabulous amount. Beside him is a spare cushion, with which he is always provided, in order that he may have something to throw at the venerable partner of his respected age whenever she makes an allusion to money — a subject on which he is particularly sensitive.

"And where's Bart?" Grandfather Smallweed inquires of Judy, Bart's twin-sister.

"He a'n't come in yet," says Judy.

"It's his tea-time, isn't it?"

"No."

"How much do you mean to say it wants then?"

"Ten minutes."

"Hey?"

"Ten minutes." — (Loud on the part of Judy.)

"Ho!" says Grandfather Smallweed. "Ten minutes."

Grandmother Smallweed, who has been mumbling and shaking her head at the trivets, hearing figures mentioned, connects them with money, and screeches, like a horrible old parrot without any plumage, "Ten ten-pound notes!"

Grandfather Smallweed immediately throws the cushion at her.

"Drat you, be quiet!" says the good old man.

The effect of this act of jaculation is twofold. It not only doubles up Mrs. Smallweed's head against the side of her porter's chair, and causes her to present, when extricated by her grand-daughter, a highly unbecoming state of cap, but the necessary exertion recoils on Mr. Smallweed himself, whom it throws back into *his* porter's chair, like a broken puppet. The excellent old gentleman being, at these times, a mere clothes-bag with a black skull-cap on the top of it, does not present a very animated appearance, until he has undergone the two operations at the hands of his grand-daughter, of being shaken up like a great bottle, and poked and punched like a great bolster. Some indication of a neck being developed in him by these means, he and the sharer of his life's evening again sit fronting one another in their two porter's chairs, like a couple of sentinels long forgotten on their post by the Black Sergeant, Death.

Judy, the twin, is worthy company for these associates. She is so indubitably sister to Mr. Smallweed the younger, that the two kneaded into one would hardly make a young person of average proportions; while she so happily exemplifies the before-mentioned family likeness to the monkey tribe, that, attired in a spangled robe and cap, she might walk about the table-land on the top of a barrel-organ without exciting much remark as an unusual specimen. Under existing circumstances, however, she is dressed in a plain, spare gown of brown stuff.

Judy never owned a doll, never heard of Cinderella, never played at any game. She once or twice fell into children's company when she was about ten years old, but the children couldn't get on with Judy, and Judy couldn't get on with them. She seemed like an animal of another species, and there was instinctive repugnance on both sides. It is very doubtful whether Judy knows how to laugh. She has so rarely seen the thing done, that the probabilities are strong the other way. Of anything like a youthful laugh, she certainly can have no conception. If she were to try one, she would find her teeth in her way; modelling that action of her face, as she has unconsciously modelled all its other expressions, on her pattern of sordid age. Such is Judy.

And her twin-brother couldn't wind up a top for his life. He knows no more of Jack the Giant Killer, or of Sinbad the Sailor, than he knows of the people in the stars. He could as soon play at leap-frog, or at cricket, as change into a cricket or a frog himself. But, he is so much the better off than his sister, that on his narrow world of fact an opening has dawned, into such broader regions as lie within the ken of Mr. Guppy. Hence, his admiration and his emulation of that shining enchanter.

Judy, with a gong-like clash and clatter, sets one of the sheet-iron tea-trays on the table, and arranges cups and saucers. The bread she puts on in an iron basket; and the butter (and not much of it) in a small pewter plate. Grandfather Smallweed looks hard after the tea as it is served out, and asks Judy where the girl is?

"Charley, do you mean?" says Judy.

"Hey?" from Grandfather Smallweed.

"Charley, do you mean?"

This touches a spring in Grandmother Smallweed, who, chuckling, as usual, at the trivets, cries, — "Over the water! Charley over the water, Charley over the water, over the water to Charley, Charley over the water, over the water to Charley!" and becomes quite energetic about it. Grandfather looks at the cushion, but has not sufficiently recovered his late exertion.

"Ha!" he says, when there is silence, — "if that's her name. She eats a deal. It would be better to allow her for her keep."

Judy, with her brother's wink, shakes her head, and purses up her mouth into No, without saying it.

"No?" returns the old man. "Why not?"

"She'd want sixpence a-day, and we can do it for less," says Judy.

"Sure?"

Judy answers with a nod of deepest meaning, and calls, as she scrapes the butter on the loaf with every precaution against waste, and cuts it into slices, "You Charley, where are you!" Timidly obedient to the summons, a little girl in a rough apron and a large bonnet, with her hands covered with soap and water, and a scrubbing-brush in one of them, appears, and courteseys.

"What work are you about now?" says Judy, making an ancient snap at her, like a very sharp old beldame.

"I'm a-cleaning the up-stairs back-room, miss," replies Charley.

"Mind you do it thoroughly, and don't loiter. Shirking won't do for me. Make haste! Go along!" cries Judy, with a stamp upon the ground. "You girls are more trouble than you're worth, by half."

On this severe matron, as she returns to her task of scraping the butter and cutting the bread, falls the shadow of her brother, looking in at the window. For whom, knife and loaf in hand, she opens the street-door.

"Ay, ay, Bart!" says Grandfather Smallweed. "Here you are, hey?"

"Here I am," says Bart.

"Been along with your friend again, Bart?"

Small nods.

"Dining at his expense, Bart?"

Small nods again.

"That's right. Live at his expense as much as you can, and take warning by his foolish example. That's the use of such a friend. The only use you can put him to," says the venerable sage.

His grandson, without receiving this good counsel as dutifully as he might, honors it with all such acceptance as may lie in a slight wink and a nod, and takes a chair at the tea-table. The four old faces then hover over tea-cups, like a company of ghastly cherubim; Mrs. Smallweed perpetually twitching her head and chattering at the trivets, and Mr. Smallweed requiring to be repeatedly shaken up like a large black draught.

"Yes, yes," says the good old gentleman, reverting to his lesson of wisdom. "That's such advice as your father would have given you, Bart. You never saw your father. More's the pity. He was my true son." Whether it is intended to be conveyed that he was particularly pleasant to look at, on that account, does not appear.

"He was my true son," repeats the old gentleman, folding his bread and butter on his knee; "a good accountant, and died fifteen years ago."

Mrs. Smallweed, following her usual instinct, breaks out with "Fifteen hundred pound. Fifteen hundred pound in a black box, fifteen hundred pound locked up, fifteen hundred pound put away and hid!" Her worthy husband, setting aside his bread and butter, immediately discharges the cushion at her, crushes her against the side of her chair, and falls back in his own, overpowered. His appearance, after visiting Mrs. Smallweed with one of these admonitions, is particularly impressive and not wholly prepossessing: firstly, because the exertion generally twists his black skull-cap over one eye and gives him an air of goblin rakishness; secondly, because he mutters violent imprecations against Mrs. Smallweed; and thirdly, because the contrast between those powerful expressions and his powerless figure is suggestive of a baleful old malignant, who would be very wicked if he could. All this, however, is so common in the Smallweed family circle, that it produces no impression. The old gentleman is merely shaken, and has his internal feathers beaten up; the cushion is restored to its usual place beside him; and the old lady, perhaps with her cap adjusted, and perhaps not, is planted in her chair again, ready to be bowled down like a ninepin.

Some time elapses, in the present instance, before the old gentleman is sufficiently cool to resume his discourse; and even then he mixes it up with several edifying expletives addressed to the unconscious partner of his bosom, who holds communication with nothing on earth but the trivets. As thus:

"If your father, Bart, had lived longer, he might have been worth a deal of money — you brimstone chatterer! — but just as he was beginning to build up the house that he had been making the foundations for, through many a year — you jade of a magpie, jackdaw, and pollparrot, what do you mean! — he took ill and died of a low fever, always being a sparing and a spare man, full of business care — I should like to throw a cat at you instead of a cushion, and I will too if you make such a confounded fool of yourself! — and your mother, who was a prudent woman as dry as a chip, just dwindled away like touchwood after you and Judy were born — You are an old pig. You are a brimstone pig. You're a head of swine!"

Judy, not interested in what she has often heard, begins to collect in a basin various tributary streams of tea, from the bottoms of cups and saucers and from the bottom of the teapot, for the little charwoman's evening meal. In like manner she gets together, in the iron bread-basket, as many outside fragments and worn-down heels of loaves as the rigid economy of the house has left in existence.

"But your father and me were partners, Bart," says the old gentleman; "and when I am gone, you and Judy will have all there is. It's rare for you both, that you went out early in life — Judy to the flower-business, and you to the law. You won't want to spend it. You'll get your living without it, and put more to it. When I am gone, Judy will go back to the flower-business, and you'll still stick to the law."

One might infer, from Judy's appearance, that her business rather lay with the thorns than the flowers; but, she has, in her time, been apprenticed to the art and mystery of artificial flower-making. A close observer might perhaps detect both in her eye and her brother's, when their venerable grandsire anticipates his being gone, some little impatience to know when he may be going, and some resentful opinion that it is time he went.

"Now, if everybody has done," says Judy, completing her preparations, "I'll have that girl in to her tea. She would never leave off, if she took it by herself in the kitchen."

Charley is accordingly introduced, and, under a heavy fire of eyes, sits down to her basin and a Druidical ruin of bread and butter. In the active superintendence of this young person, Judy Smallweed appears to attain a perfectly geological age, and to date from the remotest periods. Her systematic manner of flying at her and pouncing on her, with or without pretence, whether or no, is wonderful; evincing an accomplishment in the art of girl-driving, seldom reached by the oldest practitioners.

"Now, don't stare about you all the afternoon," cries Judy, shaking her head and stamping her foot as she happens to catch the glance which has been previously sounding the basin of tea, "but take your victuals and get back to your work."

"Yes, miss," says Charley.

"Don't say yes," returns Miss Smallweed, "for I know what you girls are. Do it without saying it, and then I may begin to believe you."

Charley swallows a great gulp of tea in token of submission, and so disperses the Druidical ruins that Miss Smallweed charges her not to gormandize, which, "in you girls," she observes, is disgusting. Charley might find some more difficulty in meeting her views on the general subject of girls, but for a knock at the door.

"See who it is, and don't chew when you open it!" cries Judy.

The object of her attentions withdrawing for the purpose, Miss Smallweed takes that opportunity of jumbling the remainder of the bread and butter together, and launching two or three dirty teacups into the ebb-tide of the basin of tea; as a hint that she considers the eating and drinking terminated.

"Now! Who is it, and what's wanted?" says the snappish Judy.

It is one "Mr. George," it appears. Without other announcement or ceremony, Mr. George walks in.

"Whew!" says Mr. George. "You are hot here. Always a fire, eh? Well! Perhaps you do right to get used to one." Mr. George makes the latter remark to himself, as he nods to Grandfather Smallweed.

"Ho! It's you!" cries the old gentleman. "How de do? How de do?"

"Middling," replies Mr. George, taking a chair. "Your grand-daughter I have had the honor of seeing before; my service to you, miss."

"This is my grandson," says Grandfather Smallweed. "You ha'n't seen him before. He is in the law, and not much at home."

"My service to him, too! He is like his sister. He is very like his sister. He is devilish like his sister," says Mr. George, laying a great and not altogether complimentary stress on his last adjective.

"And how does the world use you, Mr. George?" Grandfather Smallweed inquires, slowly rubbing his legs.

"Pretty much as usual. Like a football."

He is a swarthy browned man of fifty; well made, and good-looking; with crisp dark hair, bright eyes, and a broad chest. His sinewy and powerful hands, as sunburnt as his face, have evidently been used to a pretty rough life. What is curious about him is, that he sits forward on his chair as if he were, from long habit, allowing space for some dress or accoutrements that he has altogether laid aside. His step too is measured and heavy, and would go well with a weighty clash and jingle of spurs. He is close-shaved now, but his mouth is set as if his upper lip had been for years familiar with a great moustache; and his manner of occasionally laying the open palm of his broad brown hand upon it, is to the same effect. Altogether, one might guess Mr. George to have been a trooper once upon a time.

A special contrast Mr. George makes to the Smallweed family. Trooper was never yet billeted upon a household more unlike him. It is a broadsword to an oyster-knife. His developed figure, and their stunted forms; his large manner, filling any amount of room, and their little, narrow, pinched ways; his sounding voice, and their sharp, spare tones; are in the strongest and the strangest opposition. As he sits in the middle of the grim parlor, leaning a little forward, with his hands upon his thighs and his elbows squared, he looks as though, if he remained there long, he would absorb into himself the whole family and the whole four-roomed house, extra little back-kitchen and all.

"Do you rub your legs to rub life into 'em?" he asks of Grandfather Smallweed, after looking round the room.

"Why, it's partly a habit, Mr. George, and — yes — it partly helps the circulation," he replies.

"The cir-cu-la-tion!" repeats Mr. George, folding his arms upon his chest, and seeming to become two sizes larger. "Not much of that, I should think."

"Truly, I'm old, Mr. George," says Grandfather Smallweed. "But I can carry my years. I'm older than *her*," nodding at his wife, "and see what she is! — You're a brimstone chatterer!" with a sudden revival of his late hostility.

"Unlucky old soul!" says Mr. George, turning his head in that direction. "Don't scold the old lady. Look at her here, with her poor cap half off her head, and her poor chair all in a muddle. Hold up, ma'am. That's better. There we are! Think of your mother, Mr. Smallweed," says Mr. George, coming back to his seat from assisting her, "if your wife a'n't enough."

"I suppose you were an excellent son, Mr. George," the old man hints, with a leer.

The color of Mr. George's face rather deepens, as he replies, "Why, no. I wasn't."

"I am astonished at it."

"So am I. I ought to have been a good son, and I think I meant to have been one. But I wasn't. I was a thundering bad son, that's the long and the short of it, and never was a credit to anybody."

"Surprising!" cries the old man.

"However," Mr. George resumes, "the less said about it, the better now. Come! You know the agreement.

Always a pipe out of the two months' interest! (Bosh! It's all correct. You needn't be afraid to order the pipe. Here's the new bill, and here's the two months' interest-money, and a devil-and-all of a scrape it is to get it together in my business.)"

Mr. George sits, with his arms folded, consuming the family and the parlor, while Grandfather Smallweed is assisted by Judy to two black leathern cases out of a locked bureau; in one of which he secures the document he has just received, and from the other takes another similar document which he hands to Mr. George, who twists it up for a pipe-light. As the old man inspects, through his glasses, every up-stroke and down-stroke of both documents, before he releases them from their leathern prison,— and as he counts the money three times over, and requires Judy to say every word she utters at least twice, and is as tremulously slow of speech and action as it is possible to be,— this business is a long time in progress. When it is quite concluded, and not before, he disengages his ravenous eyes and fingers from it, and answers Mr. George's last remark by saying, "Afraid to order the pipe? We are not so mercenary as that, sir. Judy, see directly to the pipe and the glass of cold brandy-and-water for Mr. George."

The sportive twins, who have been looking straight before them all this time, except when they have been engrossed by the black leathern cases, retire together, generally disdainful of the visitor, but leaving him to the old man, as two young cubs might leave a traveller to the parental bear.

"And there you sit, I suppose, all the day long, eh?" says Mr. George, with folded arms.

"Just so, just so," the old man nods.

"And don't you occupy yourself at all?"

"I watch the fire — and the boiling and the roasting" —

"When there is any," says Mr. George, with great expression.

"Just so. When there is any."

"Don't you read, or get read to?"

The old man shakes his head with sharp, sly triumph. "No, no. We have never been readers in our family. It don't pay. Stuff. Idleness. Folly. No, no!"

"There's not much to choose between your two states," says the visitor, in a key too low for the old man's dull hearing, as he looks from him to the old woman and back again. "I say!" in a louder voice.

"I hear you."

"You'll sell me up at last, I suppose, when I am a day in arrear."

"My dear friend!" cries Grandfather Smallweed, stretching out both hands to embrace him. "Never! Never, my dear friend! But my friend in the city that I got to lend you the money — *he* might!"

"Oh! you can't answer for him?" says Mr. George; finishing the inquiry, in his lower key, with the words "you lying old rascal!"

"My dear friend, he is not to be depended on. I wouldn't trust him. He will have his bond, my dear friend."

"Devil doubt him," says Mr. George. Charley appearing with a tray, on which are the pipe, a small paper of tobacco, and the brandy-and-water, he asks her, "How do you come here! you haven't got the family face."

"I goes out to work, sir," returns Charley.

The trooper (if trooper he be or have been) takes her

bonnet off, with a light touch for so strong a hand, and pats her on the head. " You give the house almost a wholesome look. It wants a bit of youth as much as it wants fresh air." Then he dismisses her, lights his pipe, and drinks to Mr. Smallweed's friend in the city — the one solitary flight of that esteemed old gentleman's imagination.

" So you think he might be hard upon me, eh ? "

" I think he might, — I am afraid he would. I have known him do it," says Grandfather Smallweed, incautiously, " twenty times."

Incautiously, because his stricken better-half, who has been dozing over the fire for some time, is instantly aroused, and jabbers " Twenty thousand pounds, twenty twenty-pound notes in a money-box, twenty guineas, twenty million twenty per cent., twenty — " and is then cut short by the flying cushion, which the visitor, to whom this singular experiment appears to be a novelty, snatches from her face as it crushes her in the usual manner.

" You're a brimstone idiot. You're a scorpion — a brimstone scorpion ! You're a sweltering toad. You're a chattering, clattering broomstick witch, that ought to be burnt ! " gasps the old man, prostrate in his chair. " My dear friend, will you shake me up a little ? "

Mr. George, who has been looking first at one of them and then at the other, as if he were demented, takes his venerable acquaintance by the throat on receiving this request, and dragging him upright in his chair as easily as if he were a doll, appears in two minds whether or no to shake all future power of cushioning out of him, and shake him into his grave. Resisting the temptation, but agitating him violently enough to make his head roll like a harlequin's, he puts him smartly down in his chair again, and adjusts his skull-cap with such a rub, that the old man winks with both eyes for a minute afterwards.

"O Lord!" gasps Mr. Smallweed. "That'll do. Thank you, my dear friend, that'll do. Oh, dear me, I'm out of breath. O Lord!" And Mr. Smallweed says it, not without evident apprehensions of his dear friend, who still stands over him looming larger than ever.

The alarming presence, however, gradually subsides into its chair, and falls to smoking in long puffs; consoling itself with the philosophical reflection, "The name of your friend in the city begins with a D, comrade, and you're about right respecting the bond."

"Did you speak, Mr. George?" inquires the old man.

The trooper shakes his head; and leaning forward with his right elbow on his right knee and his pipe supported in that hand, while his other hand, resting on his left leg, squares his left elbow in a martial manner, continues to smoke. Meanwhile he looks at Mr. Smallweed with grave attention, and now and then fans the cloud of smoke away, in order that he may see him the more clearly.

"I take it," he says, making just as much and as little change in his position as will enable him to reach the glass to his lips, with a round, full action, "that I am the only man alive (or dead either), that gets the value of a pipe out of *you*?"

"Well!" returns the old man, "it's true that I don't see company, Mr. George, and that I don't treat. I can't afford to it. But as you, in your pleasant way, made your pipe a condition" —

"Why, it's not for the value of it; that's no great

thing. It was a fancy to get it out of you. To have something in for my money."

"Ha! You're prudent, prudent, sir!" cries Grandfather Smallweed, rubbing his legs.

"Very. I always was." Puff. "It's a sure sign of my prudence, that I ever found the way here." Puff. "Also, that I am what I am." Puff. "I am well known to be prudent," says Mr. George, composedly smoking. "I rose in life, that way."

"Don't be down-hearted, sir. You may rise yet."

Mr. George laughs and drinks.

"Ha'n't you no relations, now," asks Grandfather Smallweed, with a twinkle in his eyes, "who would pay off this little principal, or who would lend you a good name or two that I could persuade my friend in the city to make you a further advance upon? Two good names would be sufficient for my friend in the city. Ha'n't you no such relations, Mr. George?"

Mr. George, still composedly smoking, replies, "If I had, I shouldn't trouble them. I have been trouble enough to my belongings in my day. It *may* be a very good sort of penitence in a vagabond, who has wasted the best time of his life, to go back then to decent people that he never was a credit to, and live upon them; but it's not my sort. The best kind of amends then, for having gone away, is to keep away, in my opinion."

"But natural affection, Mr. George," hints Grandfather Smallweed.

"For two good names, hey?" says Mr. George, shaking his head, and still composedly smoking. "No. That's not my sort, either."

Grandfather Smallweed has been gradually sliding down in his chair since his last adjustment, and is now a bundle of clothes, with a voice in it calling for Judy. That Houri appearing, shakes him up in the usual manner, and is charged by the old gentleman to remain near him. For he seems chary of putting his visitor to the trouble of repeating his late attentions.

"Ha!" he observes, when he is in trim again. "If you could have traced out the Captain, Mr. George, it would have been the making of you. If, when you first came here, in consequence of our advertisements in the newspapers — when I say 'our,' I'm alluding to the advertisements of my friend in the city, and one or two others who embark their capital in the same way, and are so friendly towards me as sometimes to give me a lift with my little pittance — if, at that time, you could have helped us, Mr. George, it would have been the making of you."

"I was willing enough to be 'made,' as you call it," says Mr. George, smoking not quite so placidly as before, for since the entrance of Judy he has been in some measure disturbed by a fascination, not of the admiring kind, which obliges him to look at her as she stands by her grandfather's chair; "but, on the whole, I am glad I wasn't now."

"Why, Mr. George? In the name of — of Brimstone, why?" says Grandfather Smallweed, with a plain appearance of exasperation. (Brimstone apparently suggested by his eye lighting on Mrs. Smallweed in her slumber.)

"For two reasons, comrade."

"And what two reasons, Mr. George? In the name of the"—

"Of our friend in the city?" suggests Mr. George, composedly drinking.

"Ay, if you like. What two reasons?"

"In the first place," returns Mr. George; but still looking at Judy, as if, she being so old and so like her grandfather, it is indifferent which of the two he addresses; "you gentlemen took me in. You advertised that Mr. Hawdon (Captain Hawdon, if you hold to the saying 'Once a captain always a captain') was to hear of something to his advantage."

"Well?" returns the old man, shrilly and sharply.

"Well!" says Mr. George, smoking on. "It wouldn't have been much to his advantage to have been clapped into prison by the whole bill and judgment trade of London."

"How do you know that? Some of his rich relations might have paid his debts, or compounded for 'em. Besides, he had taken *us* in. He owed us immense sums, all round. I would sooner have strangled him than had no return. If I sit here thinking of him," snarls the old man, holding up his impotent ten fingers, "I want to strangle him now." And in a sudden access of fury, he throws the cushion at the unoffending Mrs. Smallweed, but it passes harmlessly on one side of her chair.

"I don't need to be told," returns the trooper, taking his pipe from his lips for a moment, and carrying his eyes back from following the progress of the cushion, to the pipe-bowl which is burning low, "that he carried on heavily and went to ruin. I have been at his right hand many a day, when he was charging upon ruin full-gallop. I was with him when he was sick and well, rich and poor. I laid this hand upon him, after he had run through everything and broken down everything beneath him — when he held a pistol to his head."

"I wish he had let it off!" says the benevolent old

man, "and blown his head into as many pieces as he owed pounds!"

"That would have been a smash indeed," returns the trooper, coolly; "any way, he had been young, hopeful, and handsome in the days gone by; and I am glad I never found him, when he was neither, to lead to a result so much to his advantage. That's reason number one."

"I hope number two's as good?" snarls the old man.

"Why, no. It's more of a selfish reason. If I had found him, I must have gone to the other world to look. He was there."

"How do you know he was there?"

"He wasn't here."

"How do you know he wasn't here?"

"Don't lose your temper as well as your money," says Mr. George, calmly knocking the ashes out of his pipe. "He was drowned long before. I am convinced of it. He went over a ship's side. Whether intentionally or accidentally, I don't know. Perhaps your friend in the city does. — Do you know what that tune is, Mr. Smallweed?" he adds, after breaking off to whistle one, accompanied on the table with the empty pipe.

"Tune!" replies the old man. "No. We never have tunes here."

"That's the Dead March in Saul. They bury soldiers to it; so it's the natural end of the subject. Now, if your pretty grand-daughter — excuse me, miss — will condescend to take care of this pipe for two months, we shall save the cost of one next time. Good-evening, Mr. Smallweed!"

"My dear friend!" The old man gives him both his hands.

"So you think your friend in the city will be hard upon me, if I fail in a payment?" says the trooper, looking down upon him like a giant.

"My dear friend, I am afraid he will," returns the old man, looking up at him like a pigmy.

Mr. George laughs; and with a glance at Mr. Smallweed, and a parting salutation to the scornful Judy, strides out of the parlor, clashing imaginary sabres and other metallic appurtenances as he goes.

"You're a damned rogue," says the old gentleman, making a hideous grimace at the door as he shuts it. "But I'll lime you, you dog, I'll lime you!"

After this amiable remark, his spirit soars into those enchanting regions of reflection which its education and pursuits have opened to it; and again he and Mrs. Smallweed wile away the rosy hours, two unrelieved sentinels forgotten as aforesaid by the Black Sergeant.

While the twain are faithful to their post, Mr. George strides through the streets with a massive kind of swagger and a grave-enough face. It is eight o'clock now, and the day is fast drawing in. He stops hard by Waterloo Bridge, and reads a playbill; decides to go to Astley's Theatre. Being there, is much delighted with the horses and the feats of strength; looks at the weapons with a critical eye; disapproves of the combats, as giving evidences of unskilful swordmanship; but is touched home by the sentiments. In the last scene, when the Emperor of Tartary gets up into a cart and condescends to bless the united lovers by hovering over them with the Union-Jack, his eyelashes are moistened with emotion.

The theatre over, Mr. George comes across the water again, and makes his way to that curious region lying about the Haymarket and Leicester Square, which is a centre of attraction to indifferent foreign hotels and indifferent foreigners, racket-courts, fighting-men, swordsmen, footguards, old china, gaming-houses, exhibitions, and a large medley of shabbiness and shrinking out of sight. Penetrating to the heart of this region, he arrives, by a court and a long whitewashed passage, at a great brick building, composed of bare walls, floors, roof-rafters, and skylights; on the front of which, if it can be said to have any front, is painted GEORGE'S SHOOTING GALLERY, &C.

Into George's Shooting Gallery, &c., he goes; and in it there are gaslights (partly turned off now), and two whitened targets for rifle-shooting, and archery accommodation, and fencing appliances, and all necessaries for the British art of boxing. None of these sports or exercises are being pursued in George's Shooting Gallery to-night; which is so devoid of company, that a little grotesque man, with a large head, has it all to himself, and lies asleep upon the floor.

The little man is dressed something like a gunsmith, in a green baize apron and cap; and his face and hands are dirty with gunpowder, and begrimed with the loading of guns. As he lies in the light, before a glaring white target, the black upon him shines again. Not far off, is the strong, rough, primitive table, with a vice upon it, at which he has been working. He is a little man with a face all crushed together, who appears, from a certain blue and speckled appearance that one of his cheeks presents, to have been blown up, in the way of business, at some odd time or times.

"Phil!" says the trooper, in a quiet voice.

"All right!" cries Phil, scrambling to his feet.

"Anything been doing!"

"Flat as ever so much swipes," says Phil. "Five dozen rifle and a dozen pistol. As to aim!" Phil gives a howl at the recollection.

"Shut up shop, Phil!"

As Phil moves about to execute this order, it appears that he is lame, though able to move very quickly. On the speckled side of his face he has no eyebrow, and on the other side he has a bushy black one, which want of uniformity gives him a very singular and rather sinister appearance. Everything seems to have happened to his hands that could possibly take place, consistently with the retention of all the fingers; for they are notched, and seamed, and crumpled all over. He appears to be very strong, and lifts heavy benches about as if he had no idea what weight was. He has a curious way of limping round the gallery with his shoulder against the wall, and tacking off at objects he wants to lay hold of, instead of going straight to them, which has left a smear all round the four walls, conventionally called "Phil's mark."

This custodian of George's Gallery in George's absence concludes his proceedings, when he has locked the great doors, and turned out all the lights but one, which he leaves to glimmer, by dragging out from a wooden cabin in a corner two mattresses and bedding. These being drawn to opposite ends of the gallery, the trooper makes his own bed, and Phil makes his.

"Phil!" says the master, walking towards him without his coat and waistcoat, and looking more soldierly than ever in his braces. "You were found in a doorway, weren't you."

"Gutter," says Phil. "Watchman tumbled over me."

"Then, vagabondizing came natural to *you*, from the beginning."

"As nat'ral as possible," says Phil.

"Good-night!"

"Good-night, guv'ner."

Phil cannot even go straight to bed, but finds it necessary to shoulder round two sides of the gallery, and then tack off at his mattress. The trooper, after taking a turn or two in the rifle-distance, and looking up at the moon now shining through the skylights, strides to his own mattress by a shorter route, and goes to bed too.

CHAPTER XXII.

MR. BUCKET.

ALLEGORY looks pretty cool in Lincoln's Inn Fields, though the evening is hot; for, both Mr. Tulkinghorn's windows are wide open, and the room is lofty, gusty, and gloomy. These may not be desirable characteristics when November comes with fog and sleet, or January with ice and snow; but they have their merits in the sultry long vacation weather. They enable Allegory, though it has cheeks like peaches, and knees like bunches of blossoms, and rosy swellings for calves to its legs and muscles to its arms, to look tolerably cool to-night.

Plenty of dust comes in at Mr. Tulkinghorn's windows, and plenty more has generated among his furniture and papers. It lies thick everywhere. When a breeze from the country that has lost its way, takes fright, and makes a blind hurry to rush out again, it flings as much dust in the eyes of Allegory as the law — or Mr. Tulkinghorn, one of its trustiest representatives — may scatter, on occasion, in the eyes of the laity.

In his lowering magazine of dust, the universal article into which his papers and himself, and all his clients, and all things of earth, animate and inanimate, are resolving, Mr. Tulkinghorn sits at one of the open windows, enjoying a bottle of old port. Though a hard-grained man, close, dry, and silent, he can enjoy old wine with the best.

He has a priceless bin of port in some artful cellar under the Fields, which is one of his many secrets. When he dines alone in chambers, as he has dined to-day, and has his bit of fish and his steak or chicken brought in from the coffee-house, he descends with a candle to the echoing regions below the deserted mansion, and, heralded by a remote reverberation of thundering doors, comes gravely back, encircled by an earthy atmosphere, and carrying a bottle from which he pours a radiant nectar, two score and ten years old, that blushes in the glass to find itself so famous, and fills the whole room with the fragrance of southern grapes.

Mr. Tulkinghorn, sitting in the twilight by the open window, enjoys his wine. As if it whispered to him of its fifty years of silence and seclusion, it shuts him up the closer. More impenetrable than ever, he sits, and drinks, and mellows as it were in secrecy; pondering, at that twilight hour, on all the mysteries he knows, associated with darkening woods in the country, and vast blank shut-up houses in town; and perhaps sparing a thought or two for himself, and his family history, and his money and his will — all a mystery to every one — and that one bachelor friend of his, a man of the same mould and a lawyer too, who lived the same kind of life until he was seventy-five years old, and then, suddenly conceiving (as it is supposed) an impression that it was too monotonous, gave his gold watch to his hair-dresser one summer evening, and walked leisurely home to the Temple, and hanged himself.

But, Mr. Tulkinghorn is not alone to-night, to ponder at his usual length. Seated at the same table, though with his chair modestly and uncomfortably drawn a little way from it, sits a bald, mild, shining man, who coughs respectfully behind his hand when the lawyer bids him fill his glass.

"Now, Snagsby," says Mr. Tulkinghorn, "to go over this odd story again."

"If you please, sir."

"You told me when you were so good as to step round here, last night" —

"For which I must ask you to excuse me if it was a liberty, sir; but I remember that you had taken a sort of an interest in that person, and I thought it possible that you might — just — wish — to" —

Mr. Tulkinghorn is not the man to help him to any conclusion, or to admit anything as to any possibility concerning himself. So Mr. Snagsby trails off into saying, with an awkward cough, "I must ask you to excuse the liberty, sir, I am sure."

"Not at all," says Mr. Tulkinghorn. "You told me, Snagsby, that you put on your hat and came round without mentioning your intention to your wife. That was prudent, I think, because it's not a matter of such importance that it requires to be mentioned."

"Well, sir," returns Mr. Snagsby, "you see my little woman is — not to put too fine a point upon it — inquisitive. She's inquisitive. Poor little thing, she's liable to spasms, and it's good for her to have her mind employed. In consequence of which, she employs it — I should say upon every individual thing she can lay hold of, whether it concerns her or not — especially not. My little woman has a very active mind, sir."

Mr. Snagsby drinks, and murmurs with an admiring cough behind his hand. "Dear me, very fine wine indeed!"

"Therefore you kept your visit to yourself, last night?" says Mr. Tulkinghorn. "And to-night, too?"

"Yes, sir, and to-night, too. My little woman is at present in — not to put too fine a point upon it — in a pious state, or in what she considers such, and attends the Evening Exertions (which is the name they go by) of a reverend party of the name of Chadband. He has a great deal of eloquence at his command undoubtedly, but I am not quite favorable to his style myself. That's neither here nor there. My little woman being engaged in that way, made it easier for me to step round in a quiet manner."

Mr. Tulkinghorn assents. "Fill your glass, Snagsby."

"Thank you, sir, I am sure," returns the stationer with his cough of deference. "This is wonderfully fine wine, sir!"

"It is a rare wine now," says Mr. Tulkinghorn. "It is fifty years old."

"Is it indeed, sir? But I am not surprised to hear it, I am sure. It might be — any age almost." After rendering this general tribute to the port, Mr. Snagsby in his modesty coughs an apology behind his hand for drinking anything so precious.

"Will you run over, once again, what the boy said?" asks Mr. Tulkinghorn, putting his hands into the pockets of his rusty smallclothes and leaning quietly back in his chair.

"With pleasure, sir."

Then, with fidelity, though with some prolixity, the law-stationer repeats Jo's statement made to the assembled guests at his house. On coming to the end of his narrative, he gives a great start, and breaks off with — "Dear me, sir, I wasn't aware there was any other gentleman present!"

Mr. Snagsby is dismayed to see, standing with an attentive face between himself and the lawyer, at a little distance from the table, a person with a hat and stick in his hand who was not there when he himself came in, and has not since entered by the door or by either of the windows. There is a press in the room, but its hinges have not creaked, nor has a step been audible upon the floor. Yet this third person stands there, with his attentive face, and his hat and stick in his hands, and his hands behind him, a composed and quiet listener. He is a stoutly-built, steady-looking, sharp-eyed man in black, of about the middle-age. Except that he looks at Mr. Snagsby as if he were going to take his portrait, there is nothing remarkable about him at first sight but his ghostly manner of appearing.

"Don't mind this gentleman," says Mr. Tulkinghorn, in his quiet way. "This is only Mr. Bucket."

"Oh, indeed, sir?" returns the stationer, expressing by a cough that he is quite in the dark as to who Mr. Bucket may be.

"I wanted him to hear this story," says the lawyer, "because I have half a mind (for a reason) to know more of it, and he is very intelligent in such things. What do you say to this, Bucket?"

"It's very plain, sir. Since our people have moved this boy on, and he's not to be found on his old lay, if Mr. Snagsby don't object to go down with me to Tom-all-Alone's and point him out, we can have him here in less than a couple of hours' time. I can do it without Mr. Snagsby, of course; but this is the shortest way."

"Mr. Bucket is a detective officer, Snagsby," says the lawyer, in explanation.

"Is he indeed, sir?" says Mr. Snagsby, with a strong tendency in his clump of hair to stand on end.

"And if you have no real objection to accompany Mr.

Bucket to the place in question," pursues the lawyer, "I shall feel obliged to you if you will do so."

In a moment's hesitation on the part of Mr. Snagsby, Bucket dips down to the bottom of his mind.

"Don't you be afraid of hurting the boy," he says. "You won't do that. It's all right as far as the boy's concerned. We shall only bring him here to ask him a question or so I want to put to him, and he'll be paid for his trouble, and sent away again. It'll be a good job for him. I promise you, as a man, that you shall see the boy sent away all right. Don't you be afraid of hurting him; you a'n't going to do that."

"Very well, Mr. Tulkinghorn!" cries Mr. Snagsby, cheerfully, and reassured, "since that's the case"—

"Yes! and lookee here, Mr. Snagsby," resumes Bucket, taking him aside by the arm, tapping him familiarly on the breast, and speaking in a confidential tone. "You're a man of the world, you know, and a man of business, and a man of sense. That's what *you* are."

"I am sure I am much obliged to you for your good opinion," returns the stationer, with his cough of modesty, "but"—

"That's what you *are*, you know," says Bucket. "Now, it a'n't necessary to say to a man like you, engaged in your business, which is a business of trust and requires a person to be wide awake and have his senses about him, and his head screwed on tight (I had an uncle in your business once) — it a'n't necessary to say to a man like you, that it's the best and wisest way to keep little matters like this quiet. Don't you see? Quiet!"

"Certainly, certainly," returns the stationer.

"I don't mind telling *you*," says Bucket, with an engaging appearance of frankness, "that, as far as I can understand it, there seems to be a doubt whether this dead person wasn't entitled to a little property, and whether this female hasn't been up to some games respecting that property, don't you see!"

"Oh!" says Mr. Snagsby, but not appearing to see quite distinctly.

"Now, what *you* want," pursues Bucket, again tapping Mr. Snagsby on the breast in a comfortable and soothing manner, "is, that every person should have their rights according to justice. That's what *you* want."

"To be sure," returns Mr. Snagsby, with a nod.

"On account of which, and at the same time to oblige a — do you call it, in your business, customer or client? I forget how my uncle used to call it."

"Why, I generally say customer myself," replies Mr. Snagsby.

"You're right!" returns Mr. Bucket, shaking hands with him quite affectionately, — on account of which, and at the same time to oblige a real good customer, you mean to go down with me, in confidence, to Tom-all-Alone's, and to keep the whole thing quiet ever afterwards and never mention it to any one. That's about your intentions, if I understand you."

"You are right, sir. You are right," says Mr. Snagsby.

"Then here's your hat," returns his new friend, quite as intimate with it as if he had made it; "and if you're ready, I am."

They leave Mr. Tulkinghorn, without a ruffle on the surface of his unfathomable depths, drinking his old wine, and go down into the streets.

"You don't happen to know a very good sort of person of the name of Gridley, do you?" says Bucket, in friendly converse as they descend the stairs.

"No," says Mr. Snagsby, considering, "I don't know anybody of that name. Why?"

"Nothing particular," says Bucket; "only, having allowed his temper to get a little the better of him, and having been threatening some respectable people, he is keeping out of the way of a warrant I have got against him — which it's a pity that a man of sense should do."

As they walk along, Mr. Snagsby observes, as a novelty, that, however quick their pace may be, his companion still seems in some undefinable manner to lurk and lounge; also, that whenever he is going to turn to the right or left, he pretends to have a fixed purpose in his mind of going straight ahead, and wheels off, sharply, at the very last moment. Now and then, when they pass a police constable on his beat, Mr. Snagsby notices that both the constable and his guide fall into a deep abstraction as they come towards each other, and appear entirely to overlook each other, and to gaze into space. In a few instances, Mr. Bucket, coming behind some undersized young man with a shining hat on, and his sleek hair twisted into one flat curl on each side of his head, almost without glancing at him touches him with his stick; upon which the young man, looking round, instantly evaporates. For the most part, Mr. Bucket notices things in general, with a face as unchanging as the great mourning-ring on his little finger, or the brooch, composed of not much diamond and a good deal of setting, which he wears in his shirt.

When they came at last to Tom-all-Alone's, Mr. Bucket stops for a moment at the corner, and takes a lighted bull's-eye from the constable on duty there, who then accompanies him with his own particular bull's-eye at his waist. Between his two conductors, Mr. Snagsby passes along the middle of a villanous street, undrained, unventilated, deep in black mud and corrupt water — though the roads are dry elsewhere — and reeking with such smells and sights that he, who has lived in London all his life, can scarce believe his senses. Branching from this street and its heaps of ruins, are other streets and courts so infamous that Mr. Snagsby sickens in body and mind, and feels as if he were going, every moment deeper down, into the infernal gulf.

"Draw off a bit here, Mr. Snagsby," says Bucket, as a kind of shabby palanquin is borne towards them, surrounded by a noisy crowd. "Here's the fever coming up the street!"

As the unseen wretch goes by, the crowd, leaving that object of attraction, hovers round the three visitors, like a dream of horrible faces, and fades away up alleys and into ruins, and behind walls; and with occasional cries and shrill whistles of warning, thenceforth flits about them until they leave the place.

"Are those the fever-houses, Darby?" Mr. Bucket coolly asks, as he turns his bull's-eye on a line of stinking ruins.

Darby replies that "all them are," and further that in all, for months and months, the people "have been down by dozens," and have been carried out, dead and dying, "like sheep with the rot." Bucket observing to Mr. Snagsby as they go on again, that he looks a little poorly, Mr. Snagsby answers that he feels as if he couldn't breathe the dreadful air.

There is inquiry made, at various houses, for a boy

named Jo. As few people are known in Tom-all-Alone's by any Christian sign, there is much reference to Mr. Snagsby whether he means Carrots, or the Colonel, or Gallows, or Young Chisel, or Terrier Tip, or Lanky, or the Brick. Mr. Snagsby describes over and over again. There are conflicting opinions respecting the original of his picture. Some think it must be Carrots; some say the Brick. The Colonel is produced, but is not at all near the thing. Whenever Mr. Snagsby and his conductors are stationary, the crowd flows round, and from its squalid depths obsequious advice heaves up to Mr. Bucket. Whenever they move, and the angry bull's-eyes glare, it fades away, and flits about them up the alleys, and in the ruins, and behind the walls, as before.

At last there is a lair found out where Toughy, or the Tough Subject, lays him down at night; and it is thought that the Tough Subject may be Jo. Comparison of notes between Mr. Snagsby and the proprietress of the house — a drunken face tied up in a black bundle, and flaring out of a heap of rags on the floor of a dog-hutch which is her private apartment — leads to the establishment of this conclusion. Toughy has gone to the Doctor's to get a bottle of stuff for a sick woman, but will be here anon.

"And who have we got here to-night?" says Mr. Bucket, opening another door and glaring in with his bull's-eye. "Two drunken men, eh? And two women? The men are sound enough," turning back each sleeper's arm from his face to look at him. "Are these your good men, my dears?"

"Yes, sir," returns one of the women. "They are our husbands."

"Brickmakers, eh?"

"Yes, sir."

"What are you doing here? You don't belong to London."

"No, sir. We belong to Hertfordshire."

"Whereabouts in Hertfordshire?"

"Saint Albans."

"Come up on the tramp?"

"We walked up yesterday. There's no work down with us at present, but we have done no good by coming here, and shall do none, I expect."

"That's not the way to do much good," says Mr. Bucket, turning his head in the direction of the unconscious figures on the ground.

"It a'n't, indeed," replies the woman with a sigh. "Jenny and me knows it full well."

The room, though two or three feet higher than the door, is so low that the head of the tallest of the visitors would touch the blackened ceiling if he stood upright. It is offensive to every sense; even the gross candle burns pale and sickly in the polluted air. There are a couple of benches, and a higher bench by way of table. The men lie asleep where they stumbled down, but the women sit by the candle. Lying in the arms of the woman who has spoken, is a very young child.

"Why, what age do you call that little creature?" says Bucket. "It looks as if it was born yesterday." He is not at all rough about it; and as he turns his light gently on the infant, Mr. Snagsby is strangely reminded of another infant, encircled with light, that he has seen in pictures.

"He is not three weeks old yet, sir," says the woman.

"Is he your child?"

"Mine."

The other woman, who was bending over it when they came in, stoops down again, and kisses it as it lies asleep.

"You seem as fond of it as if you were the mother yourself," says Mr. Bucket.

"I was the mother of one like it, master, and it died."

"Ah, Jenny, Jenny!" says the other woman to her; "better so. Much better to think of dead than alive, Jenny! Much better!"

"Why, you a'n't such an unnatural woman, I hope," returns Bucket, sternly, "as to wish your own child dead?"

"God knows you are right, master," she returns. "I am not. I'd stand between it and death, with my own life if I could, as true as any pretty lady."

"Then don't talk in that wrong manner," says Mr. Bucket, mollified again. "Why do you do it?"

"It's brought into my head, master," returns the woman, her eyes filling with tears, "when I look down at the child lying so. If it was never to wake no more, you'd think me mad, I should take on so. I know that very well. I was with Jenny when she lost hers — warn't I, Jenny? — and I know how she grieved. But look around you, at this place. Look at them;" glancing at the sleepers on the ground. "Look at the boy you're waiting for, who's gone out to do me a good turn. Think of the children that your business lays with often and often, and that *you* see grow up!"

"Well, well," says Mr. Bucket, "you train him respectable, and he'll be a comfort to you, and look after you in your old age, you know."

"I mean to try hard," she answers, wiping her eyes. "But I have been a-thinking, being over-tired to-night, and not well with the ague, of all the many things that'll come in his way. My master will be against it, and he'll be beat, and see me beat, and made to fear his home, and perhaps to stray wild. If I work for him ever so much, and ever so hard, there's no one to help me; and if he should be turned bad, 'spite of all I could do, and the time should come when I should sit by him in his sleep, made hard and changed, a'n't it likely I should think of him as he lies in my lap now, and wish he had died as Jenny's child died!"

"There, there!" says Jenny. "Liz, you're tired and ill. Let me take him."

In doing so, she displaces the mother's dress, but quickly readjusts it over the wounded and bruised bosom where the baby has been lying.

"It's my dead child," says Jenny, walking up and down as she nurses, "that makes me love this child so dear, and it's my dead child that makes her love it so dear too, as even to think of its being taken away from her now. While she thinks that, *I* think what fortune would I give to have my darling back. But we mean the same thing, if we knew how to say it, us two mothers does in our poor hearts!"

As Mr. Snagsby blows his nose, and coughs his cough of sympathy, a step is heard without. Mr. Bucket throws his light into the doorway, and says to Mr. Snagsby, "Now, what do you say to Toughy? Will *he* do?"

"That's Jo," says Mr. Snagsby.

Jo stands amazed in the disc of light, like a ragged figure in a magic lantern, trembling to think that he has offended against the law in not having moved on far enough. Mr. Snagsby, however, giving him the consolatory assurance, "It's only a job you will be paid for, Jo," he recovers; and, on being taken outside by Mr. Bucket for a little private confabulation, tells his tale satisfactory, though out of breath.

"I have squared it with the lad," says Mr. Bucket, returning, "and it's all right. Now, Mr. Snagsby, we're ready for you."

First, Jo has to complete his errand of good-nature by handing over the physic he has been to get, which he delivers with the laconic verbal direction that "it's to be took all d'rectly." Secondly, Mr. Snagsby has to lay upon the table half-a-crown, his usual panacea for an immense variety of afflictions. Thirdly, Mr. Bucket has to take Jo by the arm a little above the elbow and walk him on before him: without which observance, neither the Tough Subject nor any other subject could be professionally conducted to Lincoln's Inn Fields. These arrangements completed, they give the women good-night, and come out once more into black and foul Tom-all-Alone's.

By the noisome ways through which they descended into that pit, they gradually emerge from it; the crowd flitting, and whistling, and skulking about them, until they come to the verge, where restoration of the bull's-eyes is made to Darby. Here, the crowd, like a concourse of imprisoned demons, turns back, yelling, and is seen no more. Through the clearer and fresher streets, never so clear and fresh to Mr. Snagsby's mind as now, they walk and ride, until they come to Mr. Tulkinghorn's gate.

As they ascend the dim stairs (Mr. Tulkinghorn's chambers being on the first floor), Mr. Bucket mentions that he has the key of the outer door in his pocket, and that there is no need to ring. For a man so expert in most things of that kind, Bucket takes time to open the door, and makes some noise too. It may be that he sounds a note of preparation.

Howbeit, they come at last into the hall, where a lamp is burning, and so into Mr. Tulkinghorn's usual room — the room where he drank his old wine to-night. He is not there, but his two old-fashioned candlesticks are; and the room is tolerably light.

Mr. Bucket, still having his professional hold of Jo, and appearing to Mr. Snagsby to possess an unlimited number of eyes, makes a little way into this room, when Jo starts and stops.

"What's the matter?" says Bucket in a whisper.

"There she is!" cries Jo.

"Who?"

"The lady!"

(A female figure, closely veiled, stands in the middle of the room, where the light falls upon it. It is quite still, and silent. The front of the figure is towards them, but it takes no notice of their entrance, and remains like a statue.)

"Now, tell me," says Bucket aloud, "how you know that to be the lady."

"I know the wale," replies Jo, staring, "and the bonnet, and the gownd."

"Be quite sure of what you say, Tough," returns Bucket, narrowly observant of him. "Look again."

"I am looking as hard as ever I can look," says Jo, with starting eyes, "and that there's the wale, the bonnet, and the gownd."

"What about those rings you told me of?" asks Bucket.

"A sparkling all over here," says Jo, rubbing the fingers of his left hand on the knuckles of his right, without taking his eyes from the figure.

The figure removes the right-hand glove, and shows the hand.

"Now, what do you say to that?" asks Bucket.

Jo shakes his head. "Not rings a bit like them. Not a hand like that."

"What are you talking of?" says Bucket; evidently pleased though, and well pleased too.

"Hand was a deal whiter, a deal delicater, and a deal smaller," returns Jo.

"Why, you'll tell me I'm my own mother next," says Mr. Bucket. "Do you recollect the lady's voice?"

"I think I does," says Jo.

The figure speaks. "Was it at all like this. I will speak as long as you like if you are not sure. Was it this voice, or at all like this voice?"

Jo looks aghast at Mr. Bucket. "Not a bit!"

"Then, what," retorts that worthy, pointing to the figure, "did you say it was the lady for?"

"Cos," says Jo, with a perplexed stare, but without being at all shaken in his certainty, "Cos that there's the wale, the bonnet, and the gownd. It is her, and it a'n't her. It a'n't her hand, nor yet her rings, nor yet her woice. But that there's the wale, the bonnet, and the gownd, and they're wore the same way wot she wore 'em, and it's her height what she was, and she giv me a sov'ring and hooked it."

"Well!" says Mr. Bucket, slightly, "we haven't got much good out of *you*. But, however, here's five shillings for you. Take care how you spend it, and don't get yourself into trouble." Bucket stealthily tells the coins from one hand into the other like counters — which is a way he has, his principal use of them being in these games of skill — and then puts them, in a little pile, into the boy's hand, and takes him out to the door; leaving Mr. Snagsby, not by any means comfortable under these mysterious circumstances, alone with the veiled figure. But, on Mr. Tulkinghorn's coming into the room, the veil is raised, and a sufficiently good-looking Frenchwoman is revealed, though her expression is something of the intensest.

"Thank you, Mademoiselle Hortense," says Mr. Tulkinghorn, with his usual equanimity. "I will give you no further trouble about this little wager."

"You will do me the kindness to remember, sir, that I am not at present placed?" says Mademoiselle.

"Certainly, certainly!"

"And to confer upon me the favor of your distinguished recommendation?"

"By all means, Mademoiselle Hortense."

"A word from Mr. Tulkinghorn is so powerful." — "It shall not be wanting, Mademoiselle." — "Receive the assurance of my devoted gratitude, dear sir." — "Good-night." Mademoiselle goes out with an air of native gentility; and Mr. Bucket, to whom it is, on an emergency, as natural to be groom of the ceremonies as it is to be anything else, shows her down-stairs, not without gallantry.

"Well, Bucket?" quoth Mr. Tulkinghorn on his return.

"It's all squared, you see, as I squared it myself, sir. There a'n't a doubt that it was the other one with this one's dress on. The boy was exact respecting colors and everything. Mr. Snagsby, I promised you as a man that he should be sent away all right. Don't say it wasn't done!"

"You have kept your word, sir," returns the stationer; "and if I can be of no further use, Mr. Tulkinghorn, I think, as my little woman will be getting anxious" —

"Thank you, Snagsby, no further use," says Mr. Tulkinghorn. "I am quite indebted to you for the trouble you have taken already."

"Not at all, sir. I wish you good-night."

"You see, Mr. Snagsby," says Mr. Bucket, accompanying him to the door, and shaking hands with him over and over again, "what I like in you, is, that you're a man it's of no use pumping; that's what *you* are. When you know you have done a right thing, you put it away, and it's done with and gone, and there's an end of it. That's what *you* do."

"That is certainly what I endeavor to do, sir," returns Mr. Snagsby.

"No, you don't do yourself justice. It a'n't what you endeavor to do," says Mr. Bucket, shaking hands with him and blessing him in the tenderest manner, "it's what you *do*. That's what I estimate in a man in your way of business."

Mr. Snagsby makes a suitable response; and goes homeward so confused by the events of the evening, that he is doubtful of his being awake and out — doubtful of the reality of the streets through which he goes — doubtful of the reality of the moon that shines above him. He is presently reassured on these subjects, by the unchallengeable reality of Mrs. Snagsby, sitting up with her head in a perfect beehive of curl-papers and nightcap: who has dispatched Guster to the police-station with official intelligence of her husband's being made away with, and who, within the last two hours, has passed through every stage of swooning with the greatest decorum. But, as the little woman feelingly says, many thanks she gets for it!

CHAPTER XXIII.

ESTHER'S NARRATIVE.

WE came home from Mr. Boythorn's after six pleasant weeks. We were often in the park, and in the woods, and seldom passed the Lodge where we had taken shelter without looking in to speak to the keeper's wife; but we saw no more of Lady Dedlock, except at church on Sundays. There was company at Chesney Wold; and although several beautiful faces surrounded her, her face retained the same influence on me as at first. I do not quite know, even now, whether it was painful or pleasurable; whether it drew me towards her, or made me shrink from her. I think I admired her with a kind of fear; and I know that in her presence my thoughts always wandered back, as they had done at first, to that old time of my life.

I had a fancy, on more than one of these Sundays, that what this lady so curiously was to me, I was to her — I mean that I disturbed her thoughts as she influenced mine, though in some different way. But when I stole a glance at her, and saw her so composed and distant and unapproachable, I felt this to be a foolish weakness. Indeed, I felt the whole state of my mind in reference to her to be weak and unreasonable; and I remonstrated with myself about it as much as I could.

One incident that occurred before we quitted Mr. Boythorn's house, I had better mention in this place.

I was walking in the garden with Ada, when I was told that some one wished to see me. Going into the breakfast-room where this person was waiting, I found it to be the French maid who had cast off her shoes and walked through the wet grass, on the day when it thundered and lightened.

"Mademoiselle," she began, looking fixedly at me with her too eager eyes, though otherwise presenting an agreeable appearance, and speaking neither with boldness nor servility, "I have taken a great liberty in coming here, but you know how to excuse it, being so amiable, mademoiselle."

"No excuse is necessary," I returned, "if you wish to speak to me."

"That is my desire, mademoiselle. A thousand thanks for the permission. I have your leave to speak. Is it not?" she said, in a quick, natural way.

"Certainly," said I.

"Mademoiselle, you are so amiable! Listen then, if you please. I have left my Lady. We could not agree. My Lady is so high; so very high. Pardon! Mademoiselle, you are right!" Her quickness anticipated what I might have said presently, but as yet had only thought. "It is not for me to come here to complain of my Lady. But I say she is so high, so very high. I will say not a word more. All the world knows that."

"Go on, if you please," said I.

"Assuredly; mademoiselle, I am thankful for your politeness. Mademoiselle, I have an inexpressible desire to find service with a young lady who is good, accomplished, beautiful. You are good, accomplished, and beautiful as an angel. Ah, could I have the honor of being your domestic!"

"I am sorry —" I began.

"Do not dismiss me so soon, mademoiselle!" she said, with an involuntary contraction of her fine black eyebrows. "Let me hope a moment! Mademoiselle, I know this service would be more retired than that which I have quitted. Well! I wish that. I know this service would be less distinguished than that which I have quitted. Well! I wish that. I know that I should win less, as to wages here. Good. I am content."

"I assure you," said I, quite embarrassed by the mere idea of having such an attendant, "that I keep no maid" —

"Ah, mademoiselle, but why not? Why not, when you can have one so devoted to you! Who would be enchanted to serve you; who would be so true, so zealous, and so faithful, every day! Mademoiselle, I wish with all my heart to serve you. Do not speak of money at present. Take me as I am. For nothing!"

She was so singularly earnest that I drew back, almost afraid of her. Without appearing to notice it, in her ardor, she still pressed herself upon me; speaking in a rapid subdued voice, though always with a certain grace and propriety.

"Mademoiselle, I come from the south country, where we are quick, and where we like and dislike very strong. My Lady was too high for me; I was too high for her. It is done — past — finished! Receive me as your domestic, and I will serve you well. I will do more for you, than you figure to yourself now. Chut! mademoiselle, I will — no matter, I will do my utmost possible, in all things. If you accept my service, you will not repent it. Mademoiselle, you will not repent it, and I will serve you well. You don't know how well!"

There was a lowering energy in her face, as she stood

looking at me while I explained the impossibility of my engaging her (without thinking it necessary to say how very little I desired to do so), which seemed to bring visibly before me some woman from the streets of Paris in the reign of terror. She heard me out without interruption; and then said, with her pretty accent, and in her mildest voice, —

"Hey, mademoiselle, I have received my answer! I am sorry of it. But I must go elsewhere, and seek what I have not found here. Will you graciously let me kiss your hand?"

She looked at me more intently as she took it, and seemed to take note, with her momentary touch, of every vein in it. "I fear I surprised you, mademoiselle, on the day of the storm?" she said, with a parting courtesy.

I confessed that she had surprised us all.

"I took an oath, mademoiselle," she said, smiling, "and I wanted to stamp it on my mind, so that I might keep it faithfully. And I will! Adieu, mademoiselle!"

So ended our conference, which I was very glad to bring to a close. I suppose she went away from the village, for I saw her no more; and nothing else occurred to disturb our tranquil summer pleasures, until six weeks were out, and we returned home as I began just now by saying.

At that time, and for a good many weeks after that time, Richard was constant in his visits. Besides coming every Saturday or Sunday, and remaining with us until Monday morning, he sometimes rode out on horseback unexpectedly, and passed the evening with us, and rode back again early next day. He was as vivacious as ever, and told us he was very industrious; but I was not easy in my mind about him. It appeared to me that his industry was all misdirected. I could not find that it led to anything, but the formation of delusive hopes in connection with the suit already the pernicious cause of so much sorrow and ruin. He had got at the core of that mystery now, he told us; and nothing could be plainer than that the will under which he and Ada were to take, I don't know how many thousands of pounds, must be finally established, if there were any sense or justice in the Court of Chancery — but oh, what a great *if* that sounded in my ears — and that this happy conclusion could not be much longer delayed. He proved this to himself by all the weary arguments on that side he had read, and every one of them sunk him deeper in the infatuation. He had even begun to haunt the Court. He told us how he saw Miss Flite there daily; how they talked together, and he did her little kindnesses; and how, while he laughed at her, he pitied her from his heart. But he never thought — never, my poor, dear, sanguine Richard, capable of so much happiness then, and with such better things before him! — what a fatal link was riveting between his fresh youth and her faded age; between his free hopes and her caged birds, and her hungry garret, and her wandering mind.

Ada loved him too well to mistrust him much in anything he said or did; and my Guardian, though he frequently complained of the east wind and read more than usual in the Growlery, preserved a strict silence on the subject. So, I thought, one day when I went to London to meet Caddy Jellyby, at her solicitation, I would ask Richard to be in waiting for me at the coach-office, that we might have a little talk together. I found him there when I arrived, and we walked away arm in arm.

"Well, Richard," said I, as soon as I could begin to be

grave with him, "are you beginning to feel more settled now?"

"Oh, yes, my dear," returned Richard. "I am all right enough."

"But settled?" said I.

"How do you mean, settled?" returned Richard, with his gay laugh.

"Settled in the law," said I.

"Oh, ay," replied Richard, "I'm all right enough."

"You said that before, my dear Richard."

"And you don't think it's an answer, eh? Well! Perhaps it's not. Settled? You mean, do I feel as if I were settling down?"

"Yes."

"Why, no, I can't say I am settling down," said Richard, strongly emphasizing 'down,' as if that expressed the difficulty; "because one can't settle down while this business remains in such an unsettled state. When I say this business, of course I mean the — forbidden subject."

"Do you think it will ever be in a settled state?" said I.

"Not the least doubt of it," answered Richard.

We walked a little way without speaking; and presently Richard addressed me in his frankest and most feeling manner, thus, —

"My dear Esther, I understand you, and I wish to Heaven I were a more constant sort of fellow. I don't mean constant to Ada, for I love her dearly — better and better every day — but constant to myself. (Somehow, I mean something that I can't very well express, but you'll make it out.) If I were a more constant sort of fellow, I should have held on, either to Badger, or to Kenge and Carboy, like grim Death; and should have begun to be steady and systematic by this time, and shouldn't be in debt, and" —

"*Are* you in debt, Richard?"

"Yes," said Richard, "I am a little so, my dear. Also I have taken rather too much to billiards, and that sort of thing. Now the murder's out; you despise me, Esther, don't you?"

"You know I don't," said I.

"You are kinder to me than I often am to myself," he returned. "My dear Esther, I am a very unfortunate dog not to be more settled, but how *can* I be more settled? If you live in an unfinished house, you couldn't settle down in it; if you were condemned to leave everything you undertook, unfinished, you would find it hard to apply yourself to anything; and yet that's my unhappy case. I was born into this unfinished contention with all its chances and changes, and it began to unsettle me before I quite knew the difference between a suit at law and a suit of clothes; and it has gone on unsettling me ever since; and here I am now, conscious sometimes that I am but a worthless fellow to love my confiding cousin Ada."

We were in a solitary place, and he put his hand before his eyes and sobbed as he said the words.

"O Richard!" said I, "do not be so moved. You have a noble nature, and Ada's love may make you worthier every day."

"I know, my dear," he replied, pressing my arm, "I know all that. You mustn't mind my being a little soft now, for I have had all this upon my mind for a long time; and have often meant to speak to you, and have sometimes wanted opportunity and sometimes courage.

I know what the thought of Ada ought to do for me, but it doesn't do it. I am too unsettled even for that. I love her most devotedly; and yet I do her wrong, in doing myself wrong, every day and hour. But it can't last forever. We shall come on for a final hearing, and get judgment in our favor; and then you and Ada shall see what I can really be!"

It had given me a pang to hear him sob, and see the tears start out between his fingers; but that was infinitely less affecting to me, than the hopeful animation with which he said these words.

"I have looked well into the papers, Esther — I have been deep in them for months," he continued, recovering his cheerfulness in a moment, "and you may rely upon it that we shall come out triumphant. As to years of delay, there has been no want of them, Heaven knows! and there is the greater probability of our bringing the matter to a speedy close; in fact, it's on the paper now. It will be all right at last, and then you shall see!"

Recalling how he had just now placed Messrs. Kenge and Carboy in the same category with Mr. Badger, I asked him when he intended to be articled in Lincoln's Inn?

"There again! I think not at all, Esther," he returned, with an effort. "I fancy I have had enough of it. Having worked at Jarndyce and Jarndyce like a galley-slave, I have slaked my thirst for the law, and satisfied myself that I shouldn't like it. Besides, I find it unsettles me more and more to be so constantly upon the scene of action. So what," continued Richard, confident again by this time, "do I naturally turn my thoughts to?"

"I can't imagine," said I.

"Don't look so serious," returned Richard, "because it's the best thing I can do, my dear Esther, I am certain. It's not as if I wanted a profession for life. These proceedings will come to a termination, and then I am provided for. No. I look upon it as a pursuit which is in its nature more or less unsettled, and therefore suited to my temporary condition — I may say, precisely suited. What is it that I naturally turn my thoughts to?"

I looked at him, and shook my head.

"What," said Richard, in a tone of perfect conviction, "but the army!"

"The army?" said I.

"The army, of course. What I have to do, is, to get a commission; and — there I am, you know!" said Richard.

And then he showed me, proved by elaborate calculations in his pocket-book, that supposing he had contracted, say two hundred pounds of debt in six months, out of the army; and that he contracted no debt at all within a corresponding period, in the army — as to which he had quite made up his mind; this step must involve a saving of four hundred pounds in a year, or two thousand pounds in five years — which was a considerable sum. And then he spoke so ingenuously and sincerely, of the sacrifice he made in withdrawing himself for a time from Ada, and of the earnestness with which he aspired — as in thought he always did, I know full well — to repay her love, and to insure her happiness, and to conquer what was amiss in himself, and to acquire the very soul of decision, that he made my heart ache keenly, sorely. For, I thought, how would this end, how could this end, when so soon and so surely all his manly qualities were touched by the fatal blight that ruined everything it rested on!

I spoke to Richard with all the earnestness I felt, and all the hope I could not quite feel then; and implored him, for Ada's sake, not to put any trust in Chancery. To all I said, Richard readily assented; riding over the Court and everything else in his easy way, and drawing the brightest pictures of the character he was to settle into — alas, when the grievous suit should loose its hold upon him! We had a long talk, but it always came back to that, in substance.

At last, we came to Soho Square, where Caddy Jellyby had appointed to wait for me, as a quiet place in the neighborhood of Newman Street. Caddy was in the garden in the centre, and hurried out as soon as I appeared. After a few cheerful words, Richard left us together.

"Prince has a pupil over the way, Esther," said Caddy, "and got the key for us. So, if you will walk round and round here with me, we can lock ourselves in, and I can tell you comfortably what I wanted to see your dear good face about."

"Very well, my dear," said I. "Nothing could be better." So Caddy, after affectionately squeezing the dear good face as she called it, locked the gate, and took my arm, and we began to walk round the garden very cosily.

"You see, Esther," said Caddy, who thoroughly enjoyed a little confidence, "after you spoke to me about its being wrong to marry without Ma's knowledge, or even to keep Ma long in the dark respecting our engagement — though I don't believe Ma cares much for me, I must say — I thought it right to mention your opinions to Prince. In the first place, because I want to profit by everything you tell me ; and in the second place, because I have no secrets from Prince."

"I hope he approved, Caddy?"

"O, my dear! I assure you he would approve of anything you could say. You have no idea what an opinion he has of you!"

"Indeed?"

"Esther, it's enough to make anybody but me jealous," said Caddy, laughing and shaking her head; "but it only makes me joyful, for you are the best friend I ever had, and the best friend I ever can have, and nobody can respect and love you too much to please me."

"Upon my word, Caddy," said I, "you are in the general conspiracy to keep me in a good humor. Well, my dear?"

"Well! I am going to tell you," replied Caddy, crossing her hands confidentially upon my arm. "So we talked a good deal about it, and so I said to Prince, 'Prince, as Miss Summerson'" —

"I hope you didn't say 'Miss Summerson?'"

"No. I didn't!" cried Caddy, greatly pleased, and with the brightest of faces. "I said, 'Esther.' I said to Prince, 'As Esther is decidedly of that opinion, Prince, and has expressed it to me, and always hints it when she writes those kind notes, which you are so fond of hearing me read to you, I am prepared to disclose the truth to Ma whenever you think proper. And I think, Prince,' said I, 'that Esther thinks that I should be in a better, and truer, and more honorable position altogether, if you did the same to your Papa.'"

"Yes, my dear," said I. "Esther certainly does think so."

"So I was right, you see!" exclaimed Caddy. "Well!

this troubled Prince a good deal; not because he had the least doubt about it, but because he is so considerate of the feelings of old Mr. Turveydrop; and he had his apprehensions that old Mr. Turveydrop might break his heart, or faint away, or be very much overcome in some affecting manner or other, if he made such an announcement. He feared old Mr. Turveydrop might consider it undutiful, and might receive too great a shock. For, old Mr. Turveydrop's deportment is very beautiful you know, Esther," added Caddy; "and his feelings are extremely sensitive."

"Are they, my dear?"

"O, extremely sensitive. Prince says so. Now, this has caused my darling child — I didn't mean to use the expression to you, Esther," Caddy apologized, her face suffused with blushes, "but I generally call Prince my darling child."

I laughed; and Caddy laughed and blushed, and went on.

"This has caused him, Esther" —

"Caused whom, my dear?"

"O you tiresome thing!" said Caddy, laughing, with her pretty face on fire. "My darling child, if you insist upon it! — This has caused him weeks of uneasiness, and has made him delay, from day to day, in a very anxious manner. At last he said to me, 'Caddy, if Miss Summerson, who is a great favorite with my father, could be prevailed upon to be present when I broke the subject, I think I could do it.' So I promised I would ask you. And I made up my mind, besides," said Caddy, looking at me hopefully but timidly, "that if you consented, I would ask you afterwards to come with me to Ma. This is what I meant, when I said in my note that I had a great favor and a great assistance to beg of you. And if you thought you could grant it, Esther, we should both be very grateful."

"Let me see, Caddy," said I, pretending to consider. "Really I think I could do a greater thing than that, if the need were pressing. I am at your service and the darling child's, my dear, whenever you like."

Caddy was quite transported by this reply of mine; being, I believe, as susceptible to the least kindness or encouragement as any tender heart that ever beat in this world; and after another turn or two round the garden, during which she put on an entirely new pair of gloves, and made herself as resplendent as possible that she might do no avoidable discredit to the Master of Deportment, we went to Newman Street direct.

Prince was teaching, of course. We found him engaged with a not very hopeful pupil — a stubborn little girl with a sulky forehead, a deep voice, and an inanimate dissatisfied mamma — whose case was certainly not rendered more hopeful by the confusion into which we threw her preceptor. The lesson at last came to an end, after proceeding as discordantly as possible; and when the little girl had changed her shoes, and had had her white muslin extinguished in shawls, she was taken away. After a few words of preparation, we then went in search of Mr. Turveydrop; whom we found, grouped with his hat and gloves, as a model of Deportment, on the sofa in his private apartment — the only comfortable room in the house. He appeared to have dressed at his leisure, in the intervals of a light collation; and his dressing-case, brushes, and so forth, all of quite an elegant kind, lay about.

"Father, Miss Summerson; Miss Jellyby."

"Charmed! Enchanted!" said Mr. Turveydrop, rising with his high-shouldered bow. "Permit me!" handing chairs. "Be seated!" kissing the tips of his left fingers. "Overjoyed!" shutting his eyes and rolling. "My little retreat is made a Paradise." Recomposing himself on the sofa, like the second gentleman in Europe.

"Again you find us, Miss Summerson," said he, "using our little arts to polish, polish! Again the sex stimulates us, and rewards us, by the condescension of its lovely presence. It is much in these times (and we have made an awfully degenerating business of it since the days of His Royal Highness the Prince Regent — my patron, if I may presume to say so) to experience that Deportment is not wholly trodden under foot by mechanics. That it can yet bask in the smile of Beauty, my dear madam."

I said nothing, which I thought a suitable reply; and he took a pinch of snuff.

"My dear son," said Mr. Turveydrop, "you have four schools this afternoon. I would recommend a hasty sandwich."

"Thank you, father," returned Prince; "I will be sure to be punctual. My dear father, may I beg you to prepare your mind for what I am going to say!"

"Good Heaven!" exclaimed the model, pale and aghast, as Prince and Caddy, hand in hand, bent down before him.

"What is this? Is this lunacy! Or what is this?"

"Father," returned Prince, with great submission, "I love this young lady, and we are engaged."

"Engaged!" cried Mr. Turveydrop, reclining on the sofa, and shutting out the sight with his hand. "An arrow launched at my brain, by my own child!"

"We have been engaged for some time, father," faltered Prince; "and Miss Summerson, hearing of it, advised that we should declare the fact to you, and was so very kind as to attend on the present occasion. Miss Jellyby is a young lady who deeply respects you, father."

Mr. Turveydrop uttered a groan.

"No, pray don't! Pray don't, father," urged his son. "Miss Jellyby is a young lady who deeply respects you, and our first desire is to consider your comfort."

Mr. Turveydrop sobbed.

"No, pray don't, father!" cried his son.

"Boy," said Mr. Turveydrop, "it is well that your sainted mother is spared this pang. Strike deep, and spare not. Strike home, sir, strike home!"

"Pray, don't say so, father," implored Prince, in tears. "It goes to my heart. I do assure you, father, that our first wish and intention is to consider your comfort. Caroline and I do not forget our duty — what is my duty is Caroline's, as we have often said together — and, with your approval and consent, father, we will devote ourselves to making your life agreeable."

"Strike home," murmured Mr. Turveydrop. "Strike home!"

But he seemed to listen, I thought, too.

"My dear father," returned Prince, "we well know what little comforts you are accustomed to, and have a right to; and it will always be our study and our pride, to provide those before anything. If you will bless us with your approval and consent, father, we shall not think of being married until it is quite agreeable to you; and when we *are* married, we shall always make you — of course — our first consideration. You must ever be the Head and Master here, father; and we feel how truly unnatural it would be in us, if we failed to know it, or if we failed to exert ourselves in every possible way to please you."

Mr. Turveydrop underwent a severe internal struggle, and came upright on the sofa again, with his cheeks puffing over his stiff cravat: a perfect model of parental deportment.

"My son!" said Mr. Turveydrop. "My children! I cannot resist your prayer. Be happy!"

His benignity, as he raised his future daughter-in-law and stretched out his hand to his son (who kissed it with affectionate respect and gratitude), was the most confusing sight I ever saw.

"My children," said Mr. Turveydrop, paternally encircling Caddy with his left arm as she sat beside him, and putting his right hand gracefully on his hip. "My son and daughter, your happiness shall be my care. I will watch over you. You shall always live with me;" meaning, of course, I will always live with you; "this house is henceforth as much yours as mine; consider it your home. May you long live to share it with me!"

The power of his Deportment was such, that they really were as much overcome with thankfulness as if, instead of quartering himself upon them for the rest of his life, he were making some munificent sacrifice in their favor.

"For myself, my children," said Mr. Turveydrop, "I am falling into the sear and yellow leaf, and it is impossible to say how long the last feeble traces of gentlemanly Deportment may linger in this weaving and spinning age. But, so long, I will do my duty to society, and will show myself, as usual, about town. My wants are few and simple. My little apartment here, my few essentials for the toilet, my frugal morning meal, and my little dinner, will suffice. I charge your dutiful affection with the supply of these requirements, and I charge myself with all the rest."

They were overpowered afresh by his uncommon generosity.

"My son," said Mr. Turveydrop, "for those little points in which you are deficient — points of Deportment which are born with a man — which may be improved by cultivation, but can never be originated — you may still rely on me. I have been faithful to my post, since the days of His Royal Highness the Prince Regent; and I will not desert it now. No, my son. If you ever have contemplated your father's poor position with a feeling of pride, you may rest assured that he will do nothing to tarnish it. For yourself, Prince, whose character is different (we cannot be all alike, nor is it advisable that we should), work, be industrious, earn money, and extend the connection as much as possible."

"That you may depend I will do, dear father, with all my heart," replied Prince.

"I have no doubt of it," said Mr. Turveydrop. "Your qualities are not shining, my dear child, but they are steady and useful. And to both of you, my children, I would merely observe, in the spirit of a sainted Wooman on whose path I had the happiness of casting, I believe, *some* ray of light, — take care of the establishment, take care of my simple wants, and bless you both!"

Old Mr. Turveydrop then became so very gallant, in honor of the occasion, that I told Caddy we must really go to Thavies' Inn at once if we were to go at all that day. So we took our departure, after a very loving farewell between Caddy and her betrothed: and during our walk she was so happy, and so full of old Mr. Turveydrop's praises, that I would not have said a word in his disparagement for any consideration.

The house in Thavies' Inn had bills in the windows announcing that it was to let, and it looked dirtier and gloomier and ghastlier than ever. The name of poor Mr. Jellyby had appeared in the list of Bankrupts, but a day or two before; and he was shut up in the dining-room with two gentlemen, and a heap of blue bags, account-books, and papers, making the most desperate endeavors to understand his affairs. They appeared to me to be quite beyond his comprehension; for when Caddy took me into the dining-room by mistake, and we came upon Mr. Jellyby in his spectacles, forlornly fenced into a corner by the great dining-table and the two gentlemen, he seemed to have given up the whole thing, and to be speechless and insensible.

Going up-stairs to Mrs. Jellyby's room (the children were all screaming in the kitchen, and there was no servant to be seen), we found that lady in the midst of a voluminous correspondence, opening, reading, and sorting letters, with a great accumulation of torn covers on the floor. She was so preoccupied that at first she did not know me, though she sat looking at me with that curious, bright-eyed, far-off look of hers.

"Ah! Miss Summerson?" she said at last. "I was thinking of something so different! I hope you are well. I am happy to see you. Mr. Jarndyce and Miss Clare quite well?"

I hoped in return that Mr. Jellyby was quite well.

"Why, not quite, my dear," said Mrs. Jellyby, in the calmest manner. "He has been unfortunate in his affairs, and is a little out of spirits. Happily for me, I am so much engaged that I have no time to think about it. We have, at the present moment, one hundred and seventy families, Miss Summerson, averaging five persons in each, either gone or going to the left bank of the Niger."

I thought of the one family so near us, who were neither gone nor going to the left bank of the Niger, and wondered how she could be so placid.

"You have brought Caddy back, I see," observed Mrs. Jellyby, with a glance at her daughter. "It has become quite a novelty to see her here. She has almost deserted her old employment, and in fact obliges me to employ a boy."

"I am sure, Ma," — began Caddy.

"Now, you know, Caddy," her mother mildly interposed, "that I *do* employ a boy, who is now at his dinner. What is the use of your contradicting?"

"I was not going to contradict, Ma," returned Caddy. "I was only going to say, that surely you wouldn't have me be a mere drudge all my life."

"I believe, my dear," said Mrs. Jellyby, still opening her letters, casting her bright eyes smilingly over them, and sorting them as she spoke, "that you have a business example before you in your mother. Besides. A mere drudge? If you had any sympathy with the destinies of the human race, it would raise you high above any such idea. But you have none. I have often told you, Caddy, you have no such sympathy."

"Not if it's Africa, Ma, I have not."

"Of course you have not. Now, if I were not happily so much engaged, Miss Summerson," said Mrs. Jellyby, sweetly casting her eyes for a moment on me, and considering where to put the particular letter she had just opened, "this would distress and disappoint me. But I have so much to think of, in connection with Borrioboola Gha, and it is so necessary I should concentrate myself, that there is my remedy, you see."

As Caddy gave me a glance of entreaty, and as Mrs.

Jellyby was looking far away into Africa straight through my bonnet and head, I thought it a good opportunity to come to the subject of my visit, and to attract Mrs. Jellyby's attention.

"Perhaps," I began, "you will wonder what has brought me here to interrupt you."

"I am always delighted to see Miss Summerson," said Mrs. Jellyby, pursuing her employment with a placid smile. "Though I wish," and she shook her head, "she was more interested in the Borrioboolan project."

"I have come with Caddy," said I, "because Caddy justly thinks she ought not to have a secret from her mother; and fancies I shall encourage and aid her (though I am sure I don't know how) in imparting one."

"Caddy," said Mrs. Jellyby, pausing for a moment in her occupation, and then serenely pursuing it after shaking her head, "you are going to tell me some nonsense."

Caddy untied the strings of her bonnet, took her bonnet off, and letting it dangle on the floor by the strings, and crying heartily, said, "Ma, I am engaged."

"Oh, you ridiculous child!" observed Mrs. Jellyby, with an abstracted air, as she looked over the despatch last opened; "what a goose you are!"

"I am engaged, Ma," sobbed Caddy, "to young Mr. Turveydrop, at the Academy; and old Mr. Turveydrop (who is a very gentlemanly man indeed) has given his consent, and I beg and pray you'll give us yours, Ma, because I never could be happy without it. I never, never could!" sobbed Caddy, quite forgetful of her general complainings, and of everything but her natural affection.

"You see again, Miss Summerson," observed Mrs. Jellyby, serenely, "what a happiness it is to be so much occupied as I am, and to have this necessity for self-concentration that I have. Here is Caddy engaged to a dancing-master's son — mixed up with people who have no more sympathy with the destinies of the human race than she has herself! This, too, when Mr. Quale, one of the first philanthropists of our time, has mentioned to me that he was really disposed to be interested in her!"

"Ma, I always hated and detested Mr. Quale!" sobbed Caddy.

"Caddy, Caddy!" returned Mrs. Jellyby, opening another letter with the greatest complacency. "I have no doubt you did. How could you do otherwise, being totally destitute of the sympathies with which he overflows! Now, if my public duties were not a favorite child to me, if I were not occupied with large measures on a vast scale, these petty details might grieve me very much, Miss Summerson. But can I permit the film of a silly proceeding on the part of Caddy (from whom I expect nothing else), to interpose between me and the great African continent? No. No," repeated Mrs. Jellyby, in a calm clear voice, and with an agreeable smile as she opened more letters and sorted them. "No, indeed."

I was so unprepared for the perfect coolness of this reception, though I might have expected it, that I did not know what to say. Caddy seemed equally at a loss. Mrs. Jellyby continued to open and sort letters; and to repeat occasionally, in quite a charming tone of voice, and with a smile of perfect composure, "No, indeed."

"I hope, Ma," sobbed poor Caddy at last, "you are not angry?"

"Oh, Caddy, you really are an absurd girl," returned Mrs. Jellyby, "to ask such questions, after what I have said of the preoccupation of my mind."

"And I hope, Ma, you give us your consent, and wish us well?" said Caddy.

"You are a nonsensical child to have done anything of this kind," said Mrs. Jellyby; "and a degenerate child, when you might have devoted yourself to the great public measure. But the step is taken, and I have engaged a boy, and there is no more to be said. Now, pray, Caddy," said Mrs. Jellyby — for Caddy was kissing her, "don't delay me in my work, but let me clear off this heavy batch of papers before the afternoon post comes in!"

I thought I could not do better than take my leave; I was detained for a moment by Caddy's saying —

"You won't object to my bringing him to see you, Ma?"

"Oh, dear me, Caddy," cried Mrs. Jellyby, who had relapsed into that distant contemplation, "have you begun again? Bring whom?"

"Him, Ma."

"Caddy, Caddy!" said Mrs. Jellyby, quite weary of such little matters. "Then you must bring him some evening which is not a Parent Society night, or a Branch night, or a Ramification night. You must accommodate the visit to the demands upon my time. My dear Miss Summerson, it was very kind of you to come here to help out this silly chit. Good-by! When I tell you that I have fifty-eight new letters from manufacturing families anxious to understand the details of the Native and Coffee Cultivation question, this morning, I need not apologize for having very little leisure."

I was not surprised by Caddy's being in low spirits, when we went down-stairs; or by her sobbing afresh on my neck, or by her saying she would far rather have been scolded than treated with such indifference, or by her confiding to me that she was so poor in clothes, that how she was ever to be married creditably she didn't know. I gradually cheered her up, by dwelling on the many things she would do for her unfortunate father, and for Peepy, when she had a home of her own; and finally we went down-stairs into the damp dark kitchen, where Peepy and his little brothers and sisters were grovelling on the stone floor, and where we had such a game of play with them, that to prevent myself from being quite torn to pieces I was obliged to fall back on my fairy tales. From time to time, I heard loud voices in the parlor overhead, and occasionally a violent tumbling about of the furniture. The last effect I am afraid was caused by poor Mr. Jellyby's breaking away from the dining-table, and making rushes at the window with the intention of throwing himself into the area, whenever he made any new attempt to understand his affairs.

As I rode quietly home at night after the day's bustle, I thought a good deal of Caddy's engagement, and felt confirmed in my hopes (in spite of the elder Mr. Turveydrop), that she would be the happier and better for it. And if there seemed to be but a slender chance of her and her husband ever finding out what the model of Deportment really was, why that was all for the best too, and who would wish them to be wiser? I did not wish them to be any wiser, and indeed was half ashamed of not entirely believing in him myself. And I looked up at the stars, and thought about travellers in distant countries and the stars *they* saw, and hoped I might always be so blest and happy as to be useful to some one in my small way.

They were so glad to see me when I got home, as

they always were, that I could have sat down and cried for joy, if that had not been a method of making myself disagreeable. Everybody in the house, from the lowest to the highest, showed me such a bright face of welcome, and spoke so cheerily, and was so happy to do anything for me, that I suppose there never was such a fortunate little creature in the world.

We got into such a chatty state that night, through Ada and my Guardian drawing me out to tell them all about Caddy, that I went on prose, prose, prosing, for a length of time. At last I got up to my own room, quite red to think how I had been holding forth; and then I heard a soft tap at my door. So I said, "Come in!" and there came in a pretty little girl, neatly dressed in mourning, who dropped a courtesy.

"If you please, miss," said the little girl, in a soft voice, " I am Charley."

"Why, so you are," said I, stooping down in astonishment, and giving her a kiss. " How glad I am to see you, Charley!"

" If you please, miss," pursued Charley, in the same soft voice, " I'm your maid."

" Charley?"

" If you please, miss, I'm a present to you, with Mr. Jarndyce's love."

I sat down with my hand on Charley's neck, and looked at Charley.

"And oh, miss," says Charley, clapping her hands, with the tears starting down her dimpled cheeks, " Tom's at school, if you please, and learning so good! And little Emma, she's with Mrs. Blinder, miss, a being took such care of! And Tom, he would have been at school — and Emma, she would have been left with Mrs.

Blinder — and me, I should have been here — all a deal sooner, miss; only Mr. Jarndyce thought that Tom and Emma and me had better get a little used to parting first, we was so small. Don't cry, if you please, miss!"

"I can't help it, Charley."

"No, miss, nor I can't help it," says Charley. "And if you please, miss, Mr. Jarndyce's love, and he thinks you'll like to teach me now and then. And if you please, Tom and Emma and me is to see each other once a month. And I'm so happy and so thankful, miss," cried Charley, with a heaving heart, "and I'll try to be such a good maid!"

"O Charley, dear, never forget who did all this!"

"No, miss, I never will. Nor Tom won't. Nor yet Emma. It was all you, miss."

"I have known nothing of it. It was Mr. Jarndyce, Charley."

"Yes, miss, but it was all done for the love of you, and that you might be my mistress. If you please, miss, I am a little present with his love, and it was all done for the love of you. Me and Tom was to be sure to remember it."

Charley dried her eyes, and entered on her functions: going in her matronly little way about and about the room, and folding up everything she could lay her hands upon. Presently, Charley came creeping back to my side, and said, —

"O, don't cry, if you please, miss."

And I said again, "I can't help it, Charley."

And Charley said again, "No, miss, nor I can't help it." And so, after all, I did cry for joy indeed, and so did she.

CHAPTER XXIV.

AN APPEAL CASE.

As soon as Richard and I had held the conversation of which I have given an account, Richard communicated the state of his mind to Mr. Jarndyce. I doubt if my Guardian were altogether taken by surprise, when he received the representation; though it caused him much uneasiness and disappointment. He and Richard were often closeted together, late at night and early in the morning, and passed whole days in London, and had innumerable appointments with Mr. Kenge, and labored through a quantity of disagreeable business. While they were thus employed, my Guardian, though he underwent considerable inconvenience from the state of the wind, and rubbed his head so constantly that not a single hair upon it ever rested in its right place, was as genial with Ada and me as at any other time, but maintained a steady reserve on these matters. And as our utmost endeavors could only elicit from Richard himself sweeping assurances that everything was going on capitally, and that it really was all right at last, our anxiety was not much relieved by him.

We learnt, however, as the time went on, that a new application was made to the Lord Chancellor on Richard's behalf, as an Infant and a Ward, and I don't know what; and that there was a quantity of talking; and that the Lord Chancellor described him, in open court, as a vexatious and capricious infant; and that the matter was adjourned and readjourned, and referred, and reported on, and petitioned about, until Richard began to doubt (as he told us) whether, if he entered the army at all, it would not be as a veteran of seventy or eighty years of age. At last an appointment was made for him to see the Lord Chancellor again in his private room, and there the Lord Chancellor very seriously reproved him for trifling with time, and not knowing his mind — "a pretty good joke, I think," said Richard, "from that quarter!" — and at last it was settled that his application should be granted. His name was entered at the Horse Guards, as an applicant for an Ensign's commission; the purchase-money was deposited at an Agent's; and Richard, in his usual characteristic way, plunged into a violent course of military study, and got up at five o'clock every morning to practise the broadsword exercise.

Thus, vacation succeeded term, and term succeeded vacation. We sometimes heard of Jarndyce and Jarndyce, as being in the paper or out of the paper, or as being to be mentioned, or as being to be spoken to; and it came on, and it went off. Richard, who was now in a Professor's house in London, was able to be with us less frequently than before; my Guardian still maintained the same reserve; and so time passed until the commission was obtained, and Richard received directions with it to join a regiment in Ireland.

He arrived post-haste with the intelligence one evening, and had a long conference with my Guardian. Upwards of an hour elapsed before my Guardian put his head into the room where Ada and I were sitting, and said, "Come in, my dears!" We went in, and found Richard, whom we had last seen in high spirits, leaning on the chimney-piece, looking mortified and angry.

"Rick and I, Ada," said Mr. Jarndyce, "are not quite of one mind. Come, come, Rick, put a brighter face upon it!"

"You are very hard with me, sir," said Richard. "The harder, because you have been so considerate to me in all other respects, and have done me kindnesses that I can never acknowledge. I never could have been set right without you, sir."

"Well, well!" said Mr. Jarndyce, "I want to set you more right yet. I want to set you more right with yourself."

"I hope you will excuse my saying, sir," returned Richard in a fiery way, but yet respectfully, "that I think I am the best judge about myself."

"I hope you will excuse my saying, my dear Rick," observed Mr. Jarndyce with the sweetest cheerfulness and good humor, "that it's quite natural in you to think so, but I don't think so. I must do my duty, Rick, or you could never care for me in cool blood; and I hope you will always care for me, cool and hot."

Ada had turned so pale, that he made her sit down in his reading-chair, and sat beside her.

"It's nothing, my dear," he said; "it's nothing. Rick and I have only had a friendly difference, which we must state to you, for you are the theme. Now you are afraid of what's coming."

"I am not, indeed, cousin John," replied Ada, with a smile, "if it is to come from you."

"Thank you, my dear. Do you give me a minute's calm attention, without looking at Rick. And, little woman, do you likewise. My dear girl," putting his hand on hers, as it lay on the side of the easy-chair, "you recollect the talk we had, we four, when the little woman told me of a little love-affair?"

"It is not likely that either Richard or I can ever forget your kindness, that day, cousin John."

"I can never forget it," said Richard.

"And I can never forget it," said Ada.

"So much the easier what I have to say, and so much the easier for us to agree," returned my Guardian, his face irradiated by the gentleness and honor of his heart. "Ada, my bird, you should know that Rick has now chosen his profession for the last time. All that he has of certainty will be expended when he is fully equipped. He has exhausted his resources, and is bound henceforward to the tree he has planted."

"Quite true that I have exhausted my present resources, and I am quite content to know it. But what I have of certainty, sir," said Richard, "is not all I have."

"Rick, Rick!" cried my Guardian, with a sudden terror in his manner, and in an altered voice, and putting up his hands as if he would have stopped his ears, "for the love of God, don't found a hope or expectation on the family curse! Whatever you do on this side the grave, never give one lingering glance towards the horrible phantom that has haunted us so many years. Better to borrow, better to beg, better to die!"

We were all startled by the fervor of this warning. Richard bit his lip and held his breath, and glanced at me, as if he felt, and knew that I felt too, how much he needed it.

"Ada, my dear," said Mr. Jarndyce, recovering his cheerfulness, "these are strong words of advice; but I live in Bleak House, and have seen a sight here. Enough of that. All Richard had, to start him in the race of life, is ventured. I recommend to him and you, for his sake and your own, that he should depart from us with the understanding that there is no sort of contract between you. I must go further. I will be plain with you both. You were to confide freely in me, and I will confide freely in you. I ask you wholly to relinquish, for the present, any tie but your relationship."

"Better to say at once, sir," returned Richard, "that you renounce all confidence in me, and that you advise Ada to do the same."

"Better to say nothing of the sort, Rick, because I don't mean it."

"You think I have begun ill, sir," retorted Richard. "I *have*, I know."

"How I hoped you would begin, and how go on, I told you when we spoke of these things last," said Mr. Jarndyce, in a cordial and encouraging manner. "You have not made that beginning yet; but there is a time for all things, and yours is not gone by — rather, it is just now fully come. Make a clear beginning altogether. You two (very young, my dears) are cousins. As yet, you are nothing more. What more may come, must come of being worked out, Rick; and no sooner."

"You are very hard with me, sir," said Richard. "Harder than I could have supposed you would be."

"My dear boy," said Mr. Jarndyce, "I am harder with myself when I do anything that gives you pain. You have your remedy in your own hands. Ada, it is better for him that he should be free, and that there should be no youthful engagement between you. Rick, it is better for her, much better; you owe it to her. Come! Each of you will do what is best for the other, if not what is best for yourselves."

"Why is it best, sir?" returned Richard, hastily. "It was not, when we opened our hearts to you. You did not say so, then."

"I have had experience since. I don't blame you, Rick, — but I have had experience since."

"You mean of me, sir."

"Well! Yes, both of you," said Mr. Jarndyce, kindly. "The time is not come for your standing pledged to one another. It is not right, and I must not recognize it. Come, come, my young cousins, begin afresh! Bygones shall be bygones, and a new page turned for you to write your lives in."

Richard gave an anxious glance at Ada, but said nothing.

"I have avoided saying one word to either of you, or to Esther," said Mr. Jarndyce, "until now, in order that we might be open as the day, and all on equal terms. I now affectionately advise, I now most earnestly entreat, you two, to part as you came here. Leave all else to time, truth, and steadfastness. If you do otherwise, you will do wrong; and you will have made me do wrong, in ever bringing you together."

A long silence succeeded.

"Cousin Richard," said Ada, then, raising her blue eyes tenderly to his face, "after what our cousin John has said, I think no choice is left us. Your mind may be quite at ease about me; for you will leave me here under his care, and will be sure that I can have nothing to wish for; quite sure, if I guide myself by his advice. I — I don't doubt, cousin Richard," said Ada, a little confused, "that you are very fond of me, and I — I don't think you will fall in love with anybody else. But I should like you to consider well about it, too; as I should like you to be in all things very happy. You may trust in me, cousin Richard. I am not at all changeable; but I am not unreasonable, and should never blame you. Even cousins may be sorry to part; and in truth I am very, very sorry, Richard, though I know it's for your welfare. I shall always think of you affectionately, and often talk of you with Esther, and — and perhaps you will sometimes think a little of me, cousin Richard. So now," said Ada, going up to him and giving him her trembling hand, "we are only cousins again, Richard — for the time perhaps — and I pray for a blessing on my dear cousin, wherever he goes!"

It was strange to me that Richard should not be able to forgive my Guardian, for entertaining the very same opinion of him which he himself had expressed of himself in much stronger terms to me. But, it was certainly the case. I observed, with great regret, that from this hour he never was as free and open with Mr. Jarndyce as he had been before. He had every reason given him to be so, but he was not; and, solely on his side, an estrangement began to arise between them.

In the business of preparation and equipment he soon lost himself, and even his grief at parting from Ada, who remained in Hertfordshire, while he, Mr. Jarndyce, and I went up to London for a week. He remembered her by fits and starts, even with bursts of tears; and at such times would confide to me the heaviest self-reproaches. But, in a few minutes he would recklessly conjure up some undefinable means by which they were both to be made rich and happy forever, and would become as gay as possible.

It was a busy time, and I trotted about with him all day long, buying a variety of things, of which he stood in need. Of the things he would have bought, if he had been left to his own ways, I say nothing. He was perfectly confidential with me, and often talked so sensibly and feelingly about his faults and his vigorous resolutions, and dwelt so much upon the encouragement he derived from these conversations, that I could never have been tired if I had tried.

There used, in that week, to come backward and forward to our lodging, to fence with Richard, a person who had formerly been a cavalry soldier; he was a fine bluff-looking man, of a frank free bearing, with whom Richard had practised for some months. I heard so much about him, not only from Richard, but from my Guardian too, that I was purposely in the room, with my work, one morning after breakfast when he came.

"Good-morning, Mr. George," said my Guardian, who happened to be alone with me. "Mr. Carstone will be here directly. Meanwhile, Miss Summerson is very happy to see you, I know. Sit down."

He sat down, a little disconcerted by my presence, I thought; and, without looking at me, drew his heavy sunburnt hand across and across his upper lip.

"You are as punctual as the sun," said Mr. Jarndyce.

"Military time, sir," he replied. "Force of habit. A mere habit in me, sir. I am not at all business-like."

"Yet you have a large establishment, too, I am told?" said Mr. Jarndyce.

"Not much of a one, sir. I keep a shooting-gallery, but not much of a one."

"And what kind of a shot, and what kind of a swordsman, do you make of Mr. Carstone?" said my Guardian.

"Pretty good, sir," he replied, folding his arms upon his broad chest, and looking very large. "If Mr. Carstone was to give his full mind to it, he would come out very good."

"But he don't, I suppose?" said my Guardian.

"He did at first, sir, but not afterwards. Not his full mind. Perhaps he has something else upon it — some young lady, perhaps." His bright dark eyes glanced at me for the first time.

"He has not me upon his mind, I assure you, Mr. George," said I, laughing, "though you seem to suspect me."

He reddened a little through his brown, and made me a trooper's bow. "No offence, I hope, miss. I am one of the Roughs."

"Not at all," said I. "I take it as a compliment."

If he had not looked at me before, he looked at me now, in three or four quick successive glances. "I beg your pardon, sir," he said to my Guardian, with a manly kind of diffidence, "but you did me the honor to mention the young lady's name" —

"Miss Summerson."

"Miss Summerson," he repeated, and looked at me again.

"Do you know the name?" I asked.

"No, miss. To my knowledge, I never heard it. I thought I had seen you somewhere."

"I think not," I returned, raising my head from my work to look at him; and there was something so genuine in his speech and manner, that I was glad of the opportunity. "I remember faces very well."

"So do I, miss!" he returned, meeting my look with the fulness of his dark eyes and broad forehead. "Humph! What set me off, now, upon that!"

His once more reddening through his brown, and being disconcerted by his efforts to remember the association, brought my Guardian to his relief.

"Have you many pupils, Mr. George?"

"They vary in their number, sir. Mostly, they're but a small lot to live by."

"And what classes of chance people come to practise at your gallery?"

"All sorts, sir. Natives and foreigners. From gentlemen to 'prentices. I have had French women come, before now, and show themselves dabs at pistol-shooting. Mad people out of number, of course, — but *they* go everywhere, where the doors stand open."

"People don't come with grudges and schemes of finishing their practice with live targets, I hope?" said my Guardian, smiling.

"Not much of that, sir, though that *has* happened. Mostly they come for skill — or idleness. Six of one, and half a dozen of the other. I beg your pardon," said Mr. George, sitting stiffly upright, and squaring an elbow on each knee, "but I believe you're a Chancery suitor, if I have heard correct?"

"I am sorry to say I am."

"I have had one of *your* compatriots in my time, sir."

"A Chancery suitor?" returned my Guardian. "How was that?"

"Why, the man was so badgered, and worried, and tortured, by being knocked about from post to pillar, and from pillar to post," said Mr. George, "that he got out of sorts. I don't believe he had any idea of taking aim at anybody; but he was in that condition of resentment and violence, that he would come and pay for fifty shots, and fire away till he was red-hot. One day I said to him when there was nobody by, and he had been talking to me angrily about his wrongs, 'If this practice is a safety-valve, comrade, well and good; but I don't altogether like your being so bent upon it, in your present state of mind; I'd rather you took to something else.' I was on my guard for a blow, he was that passionate; but he received it in very good part, and left off directly. We shook hands, and struck up a sort of friendship."

"What was that man?" asked my Guardian, in a new tone of interest.

"Why, he began by being a small Shropshire farmer, before they made a baited bull of him," said Mr. George.

"Was his name Gridley?"

"It was, sir."

Mr. George directed another succession of quick bright glances at me, as my Guardian and I exchanged a word or two of surprise at the coincidence; and I therefore explained to him how we knew the name. He made me another of his soldierly bows, in acknowledgment of what he called my condescension.

"I don't know," he said, as he looked at me, "what it is that sets me off again — but — bosh, what's my head running against!" He passed one of his heavy hands over his crisp dark hair, as if to sweep the broken thoughts out of his mind; and sat a little forward, with one arm akimbo and the other resting on his leg, looking in a brown study at the ground.

"I am sorry to learn that the same state of mind has

got this Gridley into new troubles, and that he is in hiding," said my Guardian.

"So I am told, sir," returned Mr. George, still musing and looking on the ground. "So I am told."

"You don't know where?"

"No, sir," returned the trooper, lifting up his eyes and coming out of his revery. "I can't say anything about him. He will be worn out soon, I expect. You may file a strong man's heart away for a good many years, but it will tell all of a sudden at last."

Richard's entrance stopped the conversation. Mr. George rose, made me another of his soldierly bows, wished my Guardian a good day, and strode heavily out of the room.

This was the morning of the day appointed for Richard's departure. We had no more purchases to make now; I had completed all his packing early in the afternoon; and our time was disengaged until night, when he was to go to Liverpool for Holyhead. Jarndyce and Jarndyce being again expected to come on that day, Richard proposed to me that we should go down to the Court and hear what passed. As it was his last day, and he was eager to go, and I had never been there, I gave my consent, and we walked down to Westminster, where the Court was then sitting. We beguiled the way with arrangements concerning the letters that Richard was to write to me, and the letters that I was to write to him; and with a great many hopeful projects. My Guardian knew where we were going, and therefore was not with us.

When we came to the Court, there was the Lord Chancellor — the same whom I had seen in his private room in Lincoln's Inn — sitting, in great state and gravity, on the bench; with the mace and seals on a red table below him, and an immense flat nosegay, like a little garden, which scented the whole Court. Below the table, again, was a long row of solicitors, with bundles of papers on the matting at their feet; and then there were the gentlemen of the bar in wigs and gowns — some awake and some asleep, and one talking, and nobody paying much attention to what he said. The Lord Chancellor leaned back in his very easy-chair, with his elbow on the cushioned arm, and his forehead resting on his hand; some of those who were present, dozed; some read the newspapers; some walked about, or whispered in groups: all seemed perfectly at their ease, by no means in a hurry, very unconcerned, and extremely comfortable.

To see everything going on so smoothly, and to think of the roughness of the suitors' lives and deaths; to see all that full dress and ceremony, and to think of the waste, and want, and beggared misery it represented; to consider that, while the sickness of hope deferred was raging in so many hearts, this polite show went calmly on from day to day, and year to year, in such good order and composure; to behold the Lord Chancellor, and the whole array of practitioners under him, looking at one another and at the spectators, as if nobody had ever heard that all over England the name in which they were assembled was a bitter jest: was held in universal horror, contempt, and indignation; was known for something so flagrant and bad, that little short of a miracle could bring any good out of it to any one: this was so curious and self-contradictory to me, who had no experience of it, that it was at first incredible, and I could not comprehend it. I sat where Richard put me, and tried to listen, and looked about me; but there seemed to be no reality in the whole scene, except poor little Miss Flite, the madwoman, standing on a bench, and nodding at it.

Miss Flite soon espied us, and came to where we sat. She gave me a gracious welcome to her domain, and indicated, with much gratification and pride, its principal attractions. Mr. Kenge also came to speak to us, and did the honors of the place in much the same way; with the bland modesty of a proprietor. It was not a very good day for a visit, he said; he would have preferred the first day of term; but it was imposing, it was imposing.

When we had been there half an hour or so, the case in progress — if I may use a phrase so ridiculous in such a connection — seemed to die out of its own vapidity, without coming, or being by anybody expected to come, to any result. The Lord Chancellor then threw down a bundle of papers from his desk to the gentlemen below him, and somebody said "JARNDYCE AND JARNDYCE." Upon this there was a buzz, and a laugh, and a general withdrawal of the bystanders, and a bringing in of great heaps, and piles, and bags and bagsful of papers.

I think it came on "for further directions," — about some bill of costs, to the best of my understanding, which was confused enough. But I counted twenty-three gentlemen in wigs, who said they were "in it"; and none of them appeared to understand it much better than I. They chatted about it with the Lord Chancellor, and contradicted and explained among themselves, and some of them said it was this way, and some of them said it was that way, and some of them jocosely proposed to read huge volumes of affidavits, and there was more buzzing and laughing, and everybody concerned was in a state of idle entertainment, and nothing could be made of it by anybody. After an hour or so of this, and a good many speeches being begun and cut short, it was "referred back for the present," as Mr. Kenge said, and the papers were bundled up again. before the clerks had finished bringing them in.

I glanced at Richard, on the termination of these hopeless proceedings, and was shocked to see the worn look of his handsome young face. "It can't last forever, Dame Durden. Better luck next time!" was all he said.

I had seen Mr. Guppy bringing in papers, and arranging them for Mr. Kenge; and he had seen me and made me a forlorn bow, which rendered me desirous to get out of the Court. Richard had given me his arm and was taking me away, when Mr. Guppy came up.

"I beg your pardon, Mr. Carstone," said he, in a whisper, "and Miss Summerson's also; but there's a lady here, a friend of mine, who knows her, and wishes to have the pleasure of shaking hands." As he spoke, I saw before me, as if she had started into bodily shape from my remembrance, Mrs. Rachael of my godmother's house.

"How do you do, Esther?" said she. "Do you recollect me?"

I gave her my hand, and told her yes, and that she was very little altered.

"I wonder you remember those times, Esther," she returned with her old asperity. "They are changed now. Well! I am glad to see you, and glad you are not too proud to know me." But, indeed she seemed disappointed that I was not.

"Proud, Mrs. Rachael!" I remonstrated.

"I am married, Esther," she returned, coldly correcting me, "and am Mrs. Chadband. Well! I wish you good-day, and I hope you'll do well."

Mr. Guppy, who had been attentive to this short dialogue, heaved a sigh in my ear, and elbowed his own and Mrs. Rachael's way through the confused little crowd of people coming in and going out, which we were in the midst of, and which the change in the business had brought together. Richard and I were making our way through it, and I was yet in the first chill of the late unexpected recognition, when I saw, coming towards us, but not seeing us, no less a person than Mr. George. He made nothing of the people about him as he tramped on, staring over their heads into the body of the Court.

"George!" said Richard, as I called his attention to him.

"You are well met, sir," he returned. "And you, miss. Could you point a person out for me, I want? I don't understand these places."

Turning as he spoke, and making an easy way for us, he stopped when we were out of the press, in a corner behind a great red curtain.

"There's a little cracked old woman," he began, "that"—

I put up my finger, for Miss Flite was close by me; having kept beside me all the time, and having called the attention of several of her legal acquaintance to me (as I had overheard to my confusion), by whispering in their ears, "Hush! Fitz-Jarndyce on my left!"

"Hem!" said Mr. George. "You remember, miss, that we passed some conversation on a certain man this morning?—Gridley," in a low whisper behind his hand.

"Yes," said I.

"He is hiding at my place. I couldn't mention it. Hadn't his authority. He is on his last march, miss, and has a whim to see her. He says they can feel for one another, and she has been almost as good as a friend to him here. I came down to look for her; for when I sat by Gridley this afternoon, I seemed to hear the roll of the muffled drums."

"Shall I tell her?" said I.

"Would you be so good?" he returned, with a glance of something like apprehension at Miss Flite. "It's a Providence I met you, miss; I doubt if I should have known how to get on with that lady." And he put one hand in his breast, and stood upright in a martial attitude, as I informed little Miss Flite, in her ear, of the purport of his kind errand.

"My angry friend from Shropshire! Almost as celebrated as myself!" she exclaimed. Now really! My dear, I will wait upon him with the greatest pleasure."

"He is living concealed at Mr. George's," said I.

"Hush! This is Mr. George."

"In—deed!" returned Miss Flite. "Very proud to have the honor! A military man, my dear. You know, a perfect General!" she whispered to me.

Poor Miss Flite deemed it necessary to be so courtly and polite, as a mark of her respect for the army, and to courtesy so very often, that it was no easy matter to get her out of the Court. When this was at last done, and addressing Mr. George as "General," she gave him her arm, to the great entertainment of some idlers who were looking on, he was so discomposed, and begged me so respectfully "not to desert him," that I could not make up my mind to do it; especially as Miss Flite was always tractable with me, and as she too said, "Fitz-

Jarndyce, my dear, you will accompany us, of course." As Richard seemed quite willing, and even anxious, that we should see them safely to their destination, we agreed to do so. And as Mr. George informed us that Gridley's mind had run on Mr. Jarndyce all the afternoon, after hearing of their interview in the morning, I wrote a hasty note in pencil to my Guardian to say where we were gone, and why. Mr. George sealed it at a coffee-house, that it might lead to no discovery, and we sent it off by a ticket-porter.

We then took a hackney-coach, and drove away to the neighborhood of Leicester Square. We walked through some narrow courts, for which Mr. George apologized, and soon came to the Shooting Gallery, the door of which was closed. As he pulled a bell-handle which hung by a chain to the door-post, a very respectable old gentleman, with gray hair, wearing spectacles, and dressed in a black spencer and gaiters and a broad-brimmed hat, and carrying a large gold-headed cane, addressed him.

"I ask your pardon, my good friend," said he; "but is this George's Shooting Gallery?"

"It is, sir," returned Mr. George, glancing up at the great letters in which that inscription was printed on the whitewashed wall.

"Oh! To be sure!" said the old gentleman, following his eyes. "Thank you. Have you rung the bell?"

"My name is George, sir, and I have rung the bell."

"Oh, indeed?" said the old gentleman. "Your name is George? Then I am here as soon as you, you see. You came for me, no doubt?"

"No, sir. You have the advantage of me."

"Oh, indeed?" said the old gentleman. "Then it was your young man who came for me. I am a physician, and was requested — five minutes ago — to come and visit a sick man, at George's Shooting Gallery."

"The muffled drums," said Mr. George, turning to Richard and me, and gravely shaking his head. "It's quite correct, sir. Will you please to walk in."

The door being at that moment opened, by a very singular-looking little man in a green baize cap and apron, whose face, and hands, and dress were blackened all over, we passed along a dreary passage into a large building with bare brick walls; where there were targets, and guns, and swords, and other things of that kind. When we had all arrived here, the physician stopped, and, taking off his hat, appeared to vanish by magic, and to leave another and quite a different man in his place.

"Now look'ee here, George," said the man, turning quickly round upon him, and tapping him on the breast with a large forefinger. "You know me, and I know you. You're a man of the world, and I'm a man of the world. My name's Bucket, as you are aware, and I have got a peace-warrant against Gridley. You have kept him out of the way a long time, and you have been artful in it, and it does you credit."

Mr. George, looking hard at him, bit his lip and shook his head.

"Now, George," said the other, keeping close to him, "you're a sensible man, and a well-conducted man; that's what *you* are, beyond a doubt. And mind you, I don't talk to you as a common character, because you have served your country, and you know that when duty calls we must obey. Consequently, you're very far from wanting to give trouble. If I required assistance, you'd assist me; that's what *you*'d do. Phil Squod, don't you go a-sidling round the gallery like that;" the dirty little man was shuffling about with his shoulder against the wall, and his eyes on the intruder, in a manner that looked threatening; "because I know you, and I won't have it."

"Phil!" said Mr. George.

"Yes, Guv'ner."

"Be quiet."

The little man, with a low growl, stood still.

"Ladies and gentlemen," said Mr. Bucket, "you'll excuse anything that may appear to be disagreeable in this, for my name's Inspector Bucket of the Detective, and I have a duty to perform. George, I know where my man is, because I was on the roof last night, and saw him through the skylight, and you along with him. He is in there, you know," pointing; "that's where *he* is — on a sofy. Now I must see my man, and I must tell my man to consider himself in custody; but, you know me, and you know I don't want to take any uncomfortable measures. You give me your word, as from one man to another (and an old soldier, mind you, likewise!), that it's honorable between us two, and I'll accommodate you to the utmost of my power."

"I give it," was the reply. "But it wasn't handsome in you, Mr. Bucket."

"Gammon, George! Not handsome?" said Mr. Bucket, tapping him on his broad breast again, and shaking hands with him. "I don't say it wasn't handsome in you to keep my man so close, do I? Be equally good-tempered to me, old boy! Old William Tell! Old Shaw, the Life Guardsman! Why, he's a model of the whole British army in himself, ladies and gentlemen. I'd give a fifty-pun' note to be such a figure of a man!"

The affair being brought to this head, Mr. George, after a little consideration, proposed to go in first to his comrade (as he called him), taking Miss Flite with him. Mr. Bucket agreeing, they went away to the further end of the gallery, leaving us sitting and standing by a table covered with guns. Mr. Bucket took this opportunity of entering into a little light conversation: asking me if I were afraid of fire-arms, as most young ladies were; asking Richard if he were a good shot; asking Phil Squod which he considered the best of those rifles, and what it might be worth, first-hand; telling him, in return, that it was a pity he ever gave way to his temper, for he was naturally so amiable that he might have been a young woman; and making himself generally agreeable.

After a time he followed us to the further end of the gallery, and Richard and I were going quietly away, when Mr. George came after us. He said that if we had no objection to see his comrade, he would take a visit from us very kindly. The words had hardly passed his lips, when the bell was rung, and my Guardian appeared; "on the chance," he slightly observed, "of being able to do any little thing for a poor fellow involved in the same misfortune as himself." We all four went back together, and went into the place where Gridley was.

It was a bare room, partitioned off from the gallery with unpainted wood. As the screening was not more than eight or ten feet high, and only enclosed the sides, not the top, the rafters of the high gallery roof were overhead, and the skylight, through which Mr. Bucket had looked down. The sun was low — near setting — and its light came redly in above, without descending to the ground. Upon a plain canvas-covered sofa lay the man from Shropshire — dressed much as we had seen him last, but so changed, that at first I recognized no likeness in his colorless face to what I recollected.

He had been still writing in his hiding-place, and still dwelling on his grievances, hour after hour. A table and some shelves were covered with manuscript papers, and with worn pens, and a medley of such tokens. Touchingly and awfully drawn together, he and the little mad woman were side by side, and, as it were, alone. She sat on a chair holding his hand, and none of us went close to them.

His voice had faded, with the old expression of his face, with his strength, with his anger, with his resistance to the wrongs that had at last subdued him. The faintest shadow of an object full of form and color, is such a picture of it, as he was of the man from Shropshire whom we had spoken with before.

He inclined his head to Richard and me, and spoke to my Guardian.

"Mr. Jarndyce, it is very kind of you to come to see me. I am not long to be seen, I think. I am very glad to take your hand, sir. You are a good man, superior to injustice, and God knows I honor you."

They shook hands earnestly, and my Guardian said some words of comfort to him.

"It may seem strange to you, sir," returned Gridley; "I should not have liked to see you, if this had been the first time of our meeting. But, you know, I made a fight for it; you know I stood up with my single hand against them all; you know I told them the truth to the last, and told them what they were, and what they had done to me; so I don't mind your seeing me, this wreck."

"You have been courageous with them, many and many a time," returned my Guardian.

"Sir, I have been;" with a faint smile. "I told you what would come of it, when I ceased to be so; and, see here! Look at us — look at us!" He drew the hand Miss Flite held through her arm, and brought her something nearer to him.

"This ends it. Of all my old associations, of all my old pursuits and hopes, of all the living and the dead world, this one poor soul alone comes natural to me, and I am fit for. There is a tie of many suffering years between us two, and it is the only tie I ever had on earth that Chancery has not broken."

"Accept my blessing, Gridley," said Miss Flite, in tears. "Accept my blessing!"

"I thought, boastfully, that they never could break my heart, Mr. Jarndyce. I was resolved that they should not. I did believe that I could, and would, charge them with being the mockery they were, until I died of some bodily disorder. But I am worn out. How long I have been wearing out, I don't know; I seemed to break down in an hour. I hope they may never come to hear of it. I hope everybody here will lead them to believe that I died defying them, consistently and perseveringly, as I did through so many years."

Here Mr. Bucket, who was sitting in a corner, by the door, good-naturedly offered such consolation as he could administer.

"Come, come!" he said, from his corner. "Don't go on in that way, Mr. Gridley. You are only a little low. We are all of us a little low, sometimes. *I* am. Hold up, hold up! You'll lose your temper with the whole round of 'em, again and again; and I shall take you on a score of warrants yet, if I have luck."

He only shook his head.

"Don't shake your head," said Mr. Bucket. "Nod it; that's what I want to see you do. Why, Lord bless your soul, what times we have had together! Haven't I seen you in the Fleet over and over again, for contempt? Haven't I come into Court, twen-ty afternoons, for no other purpose than to see you pin the Chancellor like a bulldog? Don't you remember, when you first began to threaten the lawyers, and the peace was sworn against you two or three times a-week? Ask the little old lady there; she has been always present. Hold up, Mr. Gridley; hold up, sir!"

"What are you going to do about him?" asked George, in a low voice.

"I don't know yet," said Bucket, in the same tone. Then resuming his encouragement, he pursued aloud:

"Worn out, Mr. Gridley? After dodging me for all these weeks, and forcing me to climb the roof here like a Tom Cat, and to come to see you as a Doctor? That a'n't like being worn out. *I* should think not! Now, I tell you what you want. You want excitement, you know, to keep *you* up; that's what *you* want. You're used to it, and you can't do without it. I couldn't myself. Very well, then; here's this warrant got by Mr. Tulkinghorn of Lincoln's Inn Fields, and backed into half-a-dozen counties since. What do you say to coming along with me, upon this warrant, and having a good angry argument before the magistrates? It'll do you good; it'll freshen you up, and get you into training for another turn at the Chancellor. Give in? Why I am surprised to hear a man of your energy talk of giving in. You mustn't do that. You're half the fun of the fair, in the Court of Chancery. George, you lend Mr. Gridley a hand, and let's see now whether he won't be better up than down."

"He is very weak," said the trooper, in a low voice.

"Is he?" returned Bucket, anxiously. "I only want to rouse him. I don't like to see an old acquaintance giving in like this. It would cheer him up more than anything if I could make him a little waxy with me. He's welcome to drop into me, right and left, if he likes. *I* shall never take advantage of it."

The roof rang with a scream from Miss Flite, which still rings in my ears.

"Oh, no, Gridley!" she cried, as he fell heavily and calmly back from before her. "Not without my blessing. After so many years!"

The sun was down, the light had gradually stolen from the roof, and the shadow had crept upward. But, to me, the shadow of that pair, one living and one dead, fell heavier on Richard's departure than the darkness of the darkest night. And through Richard's farewell words I heard it echoed:

"Of all my old associations, of all my old pursuits and hopes, of all the living and the dead world, this one poor soul alone comes natural to me, and I am fit for. There is a tie of many suffering years between us two, and it is the only tie I ever had on earth that Chancery has not broken!"

CHAPTER XXV.

MRS. SNAGSBY SEES IT ALL.

There is disquietude in Cook's Court, Cursitor Street. Black suspicion hides in that peaceful region. The mass of Cook's Courtiers are in their usual state of mind, no better and no worse; but, Mr. Snagsby is changed, and his little woman knows it.

For, Tom-all-Alone's and Lincoln's Inn Fields persist in harnessing themselves, a pair of ungovernable coursers, to the chariot of Mr. Snagsby's imagination; and Mr. Bucket drives; and the passengers are Jo and Mr. Tulkinghorn; and the complete equipage whirls through the Law Stationery business at wild speed, all round the clock. Even in the little front kitchen where the family meals are taken, it rattles away at a smoking pace from the dinner-table, when Mr. Snagsby pauses in carving the first slice of the leg of mutton baked with potatoes, and stares at the kitchen wall.

Mr. Snagsby cannot make out what it is that he has had to do with. Something is wrong, somewhere; but what something, what may come of it, to whom, when, and from which unthought-of and unheard-of quarter, is the puzzle of his life. His remote impressions of the robes and coronets, the stars and garters, that sparkle through the surface-dust of Mr. Tulkinghorn's chambers; his veneration for the mysteries presided over by that best and closest of his customers, whom all the Inns of Court, all Chancery Lane, and all the legal neighborhood agree to hold in awe; his remembrance of Detective Mr. Bucket with his forefinger, and his confidential manner impossible to be evaded or declined; persuade him that he is a party to some dangerous secret, without knowing what it is. And it is the fearful peculiarity of this condition, that, at any hour of his daily life, at any opening of the shop-door, at any pull of the bell, at any entrance of a messenger, or any delivery of a letter, the secret may take air and fire, explode, and blow up — Mr. Bucket only knows whom.

For which reason, whenever a man unknown comes into the shop (as many men unknown do), and says, "Is Mr. Snagsby in?" or words to that innocent effect, Mr. Snagsby's heart knocks hard at his guilty breast. He undergoes so much from such injuries, that when they are made by boys he revenges himself by flipping at their ears over the counter, and asking the young dogs what they mean by it, and why they can't speak out at once? More impracticable men and boys persist in walking into Mr. Snagsby's sleep, and terrifying him with unaccountable questions; so that often, when the cock at the little dairy in Cursitor Street breaks out in his usual absurd way about the morning, Mr. Snagsby finds himself in a crisis of nightmare, with his little woman shaking him, and saying "What's the matter with the man!"

The little woman herself is not the least item in his difficulty. To know that he is always keeping a secret from her; that he has, under all circumstances, to conceal and hold fast a tender double tooth, which her sharpness is ever ready to twist out of his head; gives Mr. Snagsby, in her dentistical presence, much of the air of a dog who has a reservation from his master, and will look anywhere rather than meet his eye.

These various signs and tokens, marked by the little woman, are not lost upon her. They impel her to say, "Snagsby has something on his mind!" And thus suspicion get's into Cook's Court, Cursitor Street. From suspicion to jealousy, Mrs. Snagsby finds the road as natural and short as from Cook's Court to Chancery Lane. And thus jealousy gets into Cook's Court, Cursitor Street. Once there (and it was always lurking thereabout), it is very active and nimble in Mrs. Snagsby's breast, — prompting her to nocturnal examinations of Mr. Snagsby's pockets; to secret perusals of Mr. Snagsby's letters; to private researches in the Day Book and Ledger, till, cash-box, and iron safe; to watchings at windows, listenings behind doors, and a general putting of this and that together by the wrong end.

Mrs. Snagsby is so perpetually on the alert, that the house becomes ghostly with creaking boards and rustling garments. The 'prentices think somebody may have been murdered there, in bygone times. Guster holds certain loose atoms of an idea (picked up at Tooting, where they were found floating among the orphans), that there is buried money underneath the cellar, guarded by an old man with a white beard, who cannot get out for seven thousand years, because he said the Lord's Prayer backwards.

"Who was Nimrod?" Mrs. Snagsby repeatedly inquires of herself. "Who was that lady — that creature? And who is that boy?" Now, Nimrod being as dead as the mighty hunter whose name Mrs. Snagsby has appropriated, and the lady being unproducible, she directs her mental eye, for the present, with redoubled vigilance, to the boy. "And who," quoth Mrs. Snagsby, for the thousand and first time, "is that boy? Who is that——!" And there Mrs. Snagsby is seized with an inspiration.

He has no respect for Mr. Chadband. No, to be sure, and he wouldn't have, of course. Naturally he wouldn't, under those contagious circumstances. He was invited and appointed by Mr. Chadband — why, Mrs. Snagsby heard it herself with her own ears! — to come back, and be told where he was to go, to be addressed by Mr. Chadband; and he never came! Why did he never come? Because he was told not to come. Who told him not to come? Who? Ha, ha! Mrs. Snagsby sees it all.

But happily (and Mrs. Snagsby tightly shakes her head and tightly smiles), that boy was met by Mr. Chadband yesterday in the streets; and that boy, as affording a subject which Mr. Chadband desires to improve for the spiritual delight of a select congregation, was seized by Mr. Chadband and threatened with being delivered over to the police, unless he showed the reverend gentleman where he lived, and unless he entered into, and fulfilled, an undertaking to appear in Cook's Court to-morrow night — "to — mor — row — night," Mrs. Snagsby repeats for mere emphasis, with another tight smile, and another tight shake of her head; and to-morrow night that boy will be here, and to-morrow night Mrs. Snagsby will have her eye upon him and upon some one else; and oh, you may walk a long while in your secret ways (says Mrs. Snagsby, with haughtiness and scorn), but you can't blind ME!

Mrs. Snagsby sounds no timbrel in anybody's ears, but holds her purpose quietly, and keeps her counsel. Tomorrow comes, the savory preparations for the Oil Trade come, the evening comes. Comes, Mr. Snagsby in his black coat; come, the Chadbands; come (when the gorging vessel is replete), the 'prentices and Guster, to be edified; comes, at last, with his slouching hat, and his shuffle backward, and his shuffle forward, and his shuffle to the right, and his shuffle to the left, and his bit of fur-cap in his muddy hand, which he picks as if it were some mangy bird he had caught, and was plucking before eating raw, Jo, the very, very tough subject Mr. Chadband is to improve.

Mrs. Snagsby screws a watchful glance on Jo, as he is brought into the little drawing-room by Guster. He looks at Mr. Snagsby the moment he comes in. Aha! Why does he look at Mr. Snagsby? Mr. Snagsby looks at him. Why should he do that, but that Mrs. Snagsby sees it all? Why else should that look pass between them, why else should Mr. Snagsby be confused, and cough a signal cough behind his hand? It is as clear as crystal that Mr. Snagsby is that boy's father.

"Peace, my friends," says Chadband, rising and wiping the oily exudations from his reverend visage. "Peace be with us! My friends, why with us? Because," with his fat smile, "it cannot be against us, because it must be for us; because it is not hardening, because it is softening; because it does not make war like the hawk, but comes home untoe us like the dove. Therefore, my friends, peace be with us! My human boy, come forward!"

Stretching forth his flabby paw, Mr. Chadband lays the same on Jo's arm, and considers where to station him. Jo, very doubtful of his reverend friend's intentions, and not at all clear but that something practical and painful is going to be done to him, mutters, "You let me alone. I never said nothink to you. You let me alone."

"No, my young friend," says Chadband, smoothly, "I will not let you alone. And why? Because I am a harvest-laborer, because I am a toiler and a moiler, because you are delivered over untoe me, and are become as a precious instrument in my hands. My friends, may I so employ this instrument as to use it toe your advantage, toe your profit, toe your gain, toe your welfare, toe your enrichment! My young friend, sit upon this stool."

Jo, apparently possessed by an impression that the reverend gentleman wants to cut his hair, shields his head with both arms, and is got into the required position with great difficulty, and every possible manifestation of reluctance.

When he is at last adjusted like a lay-figure, Mr. Chadband, retiring behind the table, holds up his bear's-paw, and says, " My friends!" This is the signal for a general settlement of the audience. The 'prentices giggle internally, and nudge each other. Guster falls into a staring and vacant state, compounded of a stunned admiration of Mr. Chadband and pity for the friendless outcast whose condition touches her nearly. Mrs. Snagsby silently lays trains of gunpowder. Mrs. Chadband composes herself grimly by the fire, and warms her knees: finding that sensation favorable to the reception of eloquence.

It happens that Mr. Chadband has a pulpit habit of fixing some member of his congregation with his eye, and fatly arguing his points with that particular person; who is understood to be expected to be moved to an occasional grunt, groan, gasp, or other audible expression of inward working; which expression of inward working, being echoed by some elderly lady in the next pew, and so communicated, like a game of forfeits, through a circle of the more fermentable sinners present, serves the purpose of parliamentary cheering, and gets Mr. Chadband's steam up. From mere force of habit, Mr. Chadband in saying "My friends!" has rested his eye on Mr. Snagsby; and proceeds to make that ill-starred stationer, already sufficiently confused, the immediate recipient of his discourse.

"We have here among us, my friends," says Chadband, "a Gentile and a Heathen, a dweller in the tents of Tom-all-Alone's, and a mover-on upon the surface of the earth. We have here among us, my friends," and Mr. Chadband, untwisting the point with his dirty thumbnail, bestows an oily smile on Mr. Snagsby, signifying that he will throw him an argumentative back-fall presently if he be not already down, "a brother and a boy. Devoid of parents, devoid of relations, devoid of flocks and herds, devoid of gold and silver, and of precious stones. Now, my friends, why do I say he is devoid of these possessions? Why? Why is he?" Mr. Chadband states the question as if he were propounding an entirely new riddle, of much ingenuity and merit, to Mr. Snagsby, and entreating him not to give it up.

Mr. Snagsby, greatly perplexed by the mysterious look he received just now from his little woman — at about the period when Mr. Chadband mentioned the word parents — is tempted into modestly remarking, "I don't know, I'm sure, sir." On which interruption Mrs. Chadband glares, and Mrs. Snagsby says, "For shame!"

"I hear a voice," says Chadband; "is it a still, small voice, my friends? I fear not, though I fain would hope so" —

("Ah—h!" from Mrs. Snagsby.)

"Which says, 'I don't know.' Then I will tell you why. I say this brother, present here among us, is devoid of parents, devoid of relations, devoid of flocks and herds, devoid of gold, of silver, and of precious stones, because he is devoid of the light that shines in upon some of us. What is that light? What is it? I ask you, what is that light?"

Mr. Chadband draws back his head and pauses, but Mr. Snagsby is not to be lured on to his destruction again. Mr. Chadband, leaning forward over the table, pierces what he has got to follow, directly into Mr. Snagsby, with the thumb-nail already mentioned.

"It is," says Chadband, "the ray of rays, the sun of suns, the moon of moons, the star of stars. It is the light of Terewth."

Mr. Chadband draws himself up again, and looks triumphantly at Mr. Snagsby, as if he would be glad to know how he feels after that.

"Of Terewth," says Mr. Chadband, hitting him again. "Say not to me that it is *not* the lamp of lamps. I say to you, it is. I say to you, a million of times over, it is. It is! I say to you that I will proclaim it to you, whether you like it or not; nay, that the less you like it, the more I will proclaim it to you. With a speaking-trumpet! I say to you that if you rear yourself against it, you shall fall, you shall be bruised, you shall be battered, you shall be flawed, you shall be smashed."

The present effect of this flight of oratory — much admired for its general power by Mr. Chadband's followers — being not only to make Mr. Chadband unpleasantly warm, but to represent the innocent Mr. Snagsby in the light of a determined enemy to virtue, with a forehead of brass and a heart of adamant, that unfortunate tradesman becomes yet more disconcerted; and is in a very advanced state of low spirits and false position, when Mr. Chadband accidentally finishes him.

"My friends," he resumes, after dabbing his fat head for some time, — and it smokes to such an extent that he seems to light his pocket-handkerchief at it, which smokes, too, after every dab, — "to pursue the subject we are endeavoring with our lowly gifts to improve, let us in a spirit of love inquire what is that Terewth to which I have alluded. For, my young friends," suddenly addressing the 'prentices and Guster, to their consternation, "if I am told by the doctor that calomel or castor-oil is good for me, I may naturally ask what is calomel, and what is castor-oil. I may wish to be informed of that, before I dose myself with either or with both. Now, my young friends, what is this Terewth, then? Firstly (in a spirit of love), what is the common sort of Terewth — the working-clothes — the every-day wear, my young friends? Is it deception?"

("Ah—h!" from Mrs. Snagsby.)

"Is it suppression?"

(A shiver in the negative from Mrs. Snagsby.)

"Is is reservation?"

(A shake of the head from Mrs. Snagsby — very long and very tight.)

"No, my friends, it is neither of these. Neither of these names belongs to it. When this young Heathen now among us, — who is now, my friends, asleep, the seal of indifference and perdition being set upon his eyelids; but do not wake him, for it is right that I should have to wrestle, and to combat, and to struggle, and to conquer, for his sake, — when this young, hardened Heathen told us a story of a Cock, and of a Bull, and of a lady, and of a sovereign, was *that* the Terewth? No. Or, if it was partly, was it wholly, and entirely? No, my friends, no!"

If Mr. Snagsby could withstand his little woman's look, as it enters at his eyes, the windows of his soul, and searches the whole tenement, he were other than the man he is. He cowers and droops.

"Or, my juvenile friends," says Chadband, descending to the level of their comprehension, with a very obtrusive demonstration, in his greasily meek smile, of coming a long way down-stairs for the purpose, "if the master of this house was to go forth into the city and there see an eel, and was to come back, and was to call untoe him the mistress of this house, and was to say, 'Sarah, rejoice with me, for I have seen an elephant!' would *that* be Terewth?"

Mrs. Snagsby in tears.

"Or put it, my juvenile friends, that he saw an elephant, and returning said, 'Lo, the city is barren, I have seen but an eel!' would *that* be Terewth?"

Mrs. Snagsby sobbing loudly.

"Or put it, my juvenile friends," says Chadband, stimulated by the sound, "that the unnatural parents of this slumbering Heathen — for parents he had, my juvenile friends, beyond a doubt — after casting him forth to the wolves and the vultures, and the wild dogs and the young gazelles, and the serpents, went back to their dwellings and had their pipes, and their pots, and their flutings, and their dancings, and their malt liquors, and their butcher's meat and poultry, would *that* be Terewth?"

Mrs. Snagsby replies by delivering herself a prey to spasms; not an unresisting prey, but a crying and a tearing one, so that Cook's Court reëchoes with her shrieks. Finally, becoming cataleptic, she has to be carried up the narrow staircase like a grand piano. After unspeakable suffering, productive of the utmost consternation, she is pronounced, by expresses from the bedroom, free from pain, though much exhausted; in which state of affairs Mr. Snagsby, trampled and crushed in the pianoforte removal, and extremely timid and feeble, ventured to come out from behind the door in the drawing-room.

All this time, Jo has been standing on the spot where he woke up, ever picking his cap, and putting bits of fur in his mouth. He spits them out with a remorseful air, for he feels that it is in his nature to be an unimprovable reprobate, and that it's no good *his* trying to keep awake, for *he* won't never know nothink. Though it may be, Jo, that there is a history so interesting and affecting even to minds as near the brutes as thine, recording deeds done on this earth for common men, that if the Chadbands, removing their own persons from the light, would but show it thee in simple reverence, would but leave it unimproved, would but regard it as being eloquent enough without their modest aid — it might hold thee awake, and thou might learn from it yet!

Jo never heard of any such book. Its compilers, and the Reverend Chadband, are all one to him — except that he knows the Reverend Chadband, and would rather run away from him for an hour than hear him talk for five minutes. "It a'n't no good my waiting here no longer," thinks Jo. "Mr. Snagsby a'n't a-going to say nothink to me to-night." And down-stairs he shuffles.

But down-stairs is the charitable Guster, holding by the handrail of the kitchen-stairs, and warding off a fit, as yet doubtfully, the same having been induced by Mrs.

Snagsby's screaming. She has her own supper of bread and cheese to hand to Jo; with whom she ventures to interchange a word or so, for the first time.

"Here's something to eat, poor boy," says Guster.

"Thank'ee, mum," says Jo.

"Are you hungry?"

"Jist!" says Jo.

"What's gone of your father and your mother, eh?"

Jo stops in the middle of a bite, and looks petrified. For this orphan charge of the Christian Saint whose shrine was at Tooting, has patted him on the shoulder; and it is the first time in his life that any decent hand has been so laid upon him.

"I never know'd nothink about 'em," says Jo.

"No more didn't I of mine," cries Guster. She is repressing symptoms favorable to the fit, when she seems to take alarm at something, and vanishes down the stairs.

"Jo," whispers the law-stationer softly, as the boy lingers on the step.

"Here I am, Mr. Snagsby."

"I didn't know you were gone — there's another half-crown, Jo. It was quite right of you to say nothing about the lady the other night when we were out together. It would breed trouble. You can't be too quiet, Jo."

"I am fly, master!"

And so, good-night.

A ghostly shade, frilled and night-capped, follows the law-stationer to the room he came from, and glides higher up. And henceforth he begins, go where he will, to be attended by another shadow than his own, hardly less constant than his own, hardly less quiet than his own.

And into whatsoever atmosphere of secrecy his own shadow may pass, let all concerned in the secrecy beware! For the watchful Mrs. Snagsby is there too — bone of his bone, flesh of his flesh, shadow of his shadow.

CHAPTER XXVI.

SHARPSHOOTERS.

WINTRY morning, looking with dull eyes and sallow face upon the neighborhood of Leicester Square, finds its inhabitants unwilling to get out of bed. Many of them are not early risers at the brightest of times, being birds of night who roost when the sun is high, and are wide-awake and keen for prey when the stars shine out. Behind dingy blind and curtain, in upper story and garret, skulking more or less under false names, false hair, false titles, false jewelry, and false histories, a colony of brigands lie in their first sleep. Gentlemen of the green baize road who could discourse, from personal experience, of foreign galleys and home treadmills; spies of strong governments that eternally quake with weakness and miserable fear, broken traitors, cowards, bullies, gamesters, shufflers, swindlers, and false witnesses; some not unmarked by the branding-iron, beneath their dirty braid; all with more cruelty in them than was in Nero, and more crime than is in Newgate. For, howsoever bad the devil can be in fustian or smock-frock (and he can be very bad in both), he is a more designing, callous, and intolerable devil when he sticks a pin in his shirt-front, calls himself a gentleman, backs a card or color, plays a game or so of billiards, and knows a little about bills and promissory notes, than in any other form he wears. And in such form Mr. Bucket shall find him, when he will, pervading the tributary channels of Leicester Square.

But the wintry morning wants him not and wakes him not. It wakes Mr. George of the Shooting Gallery, and his Familiar. They arise, roll up and stow away their mattresses. Mr. George, having shaved himself before a looking-glass of minute proportions, then marches out, bareheaded and bare-chested, to the Pump, in the little yard, and anon comes back shining with yellow soap, friction, drifting rain, and exceedingly cold water. As he rubs himself upon a large jack-towel, blowing like a military sort of diver just come up, — his crisp hair curling tighter and tighter on his sunburnt temples, the more he rubs it, so that it looks as if it never could be loosened by any less coercive instrument than an iron rake or a currycomb, — as he rubs, and puffs, and polishes, and blows, turning his head from side to side, the more conveniently to excoriate his throat, and standing with his body well bent forward, to keep the wet from his martial legs, — Phil, on his knees lighting a fire, looks round as if it were enough washing for him to see all that done, and sufficient renovation, for one day, to take in the superfluous health his master throws off.

When Mr. George is dry, he goes to work to brush his head with two hard brushes at once, to that unmerciful degree that Phil, shouldering his way round the gallery in the act of sweeping it, winks with sympathy. This chafing over, the ornamental part of Mr. George's toilet is soon performed. He fills his pipe, lights it, and marches up and down smoking, as his custom is, while Phil, raising a powerful odor of hot rolls and coffee, prepares breakfast. He smokes gravely, and marches in slow time.

Perhaps this morning's pipe is devoted to the memory of Gridley in his grave.

"And so, Phil," says George of the Shooting Gallery, after several turns in silence; "you were dreaming of the country last night?"

Phil, by the by, said as much, in a tone of surprise, as he scrambled out of bed.

"Yes, guv'ner."

"What was it like?"

"I hardly know what it was like, guv'ner," says Phil, considering.

"How did you know it was the country?"

"On accounts of the grass, I think. And the swans upon it," says Phil, after further consideration.

"What were the swans doing on the grass?"

"They was a-eating of it, I expect," says Phil.

The master resumes his march, and the man resumes his preparation of breakfast. It is not necessarily a lengthened preparation, being limited to the setting forth of very simple breakfast-requisites for two, and the broiling of a rasher of bacon at the fire in the rusty grate; but as Phil has to sidle round a considerable part of the gallery for every object he wants, and never brings two objects at once, it takes time under the circumstances. At length the breakfast is ready. Phil announcing it, Mr. George knocks the ashes out of his pipe on the hob, stands his pipe itself in the chimney-corner, and sits down to the meal. When he has helped himself, Phil follows suit; sitting at the extreme end of the little oblong table, and taking his plate on his knees, — either in humility, or to hide his blackened hands, or because it is his natural manner of eating.

"The country," says Mr. George, plying his knife and

fork; "why, I suppose you never clapped your eyes on the country, Phil?"

"I see the marshes once," says Phil, contentedly eating his breakfast.

"What marshes?"

"*The* marshes, commander," returns Phil.

"Where are they?"

"I don't know where they are," says Phil; "but I see 'em, guv'ner. They was flat. And miste."

Governor and Commander are interchangeable terms with Phil, expressive of the same respect and deference, and applicable to nobody but Mr. George.

"I was born in the country, Phil."

"Was you indeed, commander?"

"Yes. And bred there."

Phil elevates his one eyebrow, and, after respectfully staring at his master to express interest, swallows a great gulp of coffee, still staring at him.

"There's not a bird's note that I don't know," says Mr. George. "Not many an English leaf or berry that I couldn't name. Not many a tree that I couldn't climb yet, if I was put to it. I was a real country boy once. My good mother lived in the country."

"She must have been a fine old lady, guv'ner," Phil observes.

"Ay! and not so old either, five-and-thirty years ago," says Mr. George. "But I'll wager that at ninety she would be near as upright as me, and near as broad across the shoulders."

"Did she die at ninety, guv'ner?" inquires Phil.

"No. Bosh! Let her rest in peace, God bless her!" says the trooper. "What set me on about country boys, and runaways and good-for-nothings? You, to be sure!

So you never clapped your eyes upon the country — marshes and dreams excepted. Eh?"

Phil shakes his head.

" Do you want to see it ? "

" N-no, I don't know as I do, particular," says Phil.

" The town's enough for you, eh ? "

" Why you see, commander," says Phil, " I a'n't acquainted with anythink else, and I doubt if I a'n't a-getting too old to take to novelties."

" How old *are* you, Phil ? " asks the trooper, pausing as he conveys his smoking saucer to his lips.

" I'm something with a eight in it," says Phil. " It can't be eighty. Nor yet eighteen. It's betwixt 'em somewheres."

Mr. George, slowly putting down his saucer without tasting the contents, is laughingly beginning, " Why, what the deuce, Phil " — when he stops, seeing that Phil is counting on his dirty fingers.

" I was just eight," says Phil, " agreeable to the parish calculation, when I went with the tinker. I was sent on an errand, and I see him a-sittin under a old buildin with a fire all to himself wery comfortable, and he says, ' Would you like to come along a me, my man ? ' I says ' Yes,' and him and me and the fire goes home to Clerkenwell together. That was April Fool Day. I was able to count up to ten; and when April Fool Day come round again, I says to myself, ' Now, old chap, you're one and a eight in it.' April Fool Day after that, I says, ' Now, old chap, you're two and a eight in it.' In course of time, I come to ten and a eight in it; two tens and a eight in it. When it got so high, it got the upper hand of me; but this is how I always know there's a eight in it."

"Ah," says Mr. George, resuming his breakfast. "And where's the tinker?"

"Drink put him in the hospital, guv'ner, and the hospital put him — in a glass case, I *have* heerd," Phil replies mysteriously.

"By that means you got promotion? Took the business, Phil?"

"Yes, commander, I took the business. Such as it was. It wasn't much of a beat — round Saffron Hill, Hatton Garden, Clerkenwell, Smiffeld, and there — poor neighborhood, where they uses up the kettles till they're past mending. Most of the tramping tinkers used to come and lodge at our place; that was the best part of my master's earnings. But they didn't come to me. I warn't like him. He could sing 'em a good song. *I* couldn't! He could play 'em a tune on any sort of pot you please, so as it was iron or block tin. *I* never could do nothing with a pot, but mend it or bile it — never had a note of music in me. Besides, I was too ill-looking, and their wives complained of me."

"They were mighty particular. You would pass muster in a crowd, Phil!" says the trooper, with a pleasant smile.

"No, guv'ner," returns Phil, shaking his head. "No, I shouldn't. I was passable enough when I went with the tinker, though nothing to boast of then: but what with blowing the fire with my mouth when I was young, and spileing my complexion, and singeing my hair off, and swallering the smoke; and what with being nat'rally unfort'nate in the way of running against hot metal, and marking myself by sich means; and what with having turn-ups with the tinker as I got older, almost whenever he was too far gone in drink — which was almost always —

my beauty was queer, wery queer, even at that time. As to since; what with a dozen years in a dark forge, where the men was given to larking; and what with being scorched in a accident at a gasworks; and what with being blowed out of winder, case-filling at the firework business; I am ugly enough to be made a show on!"

Resigning himself to which condition with a perfectly satisfied manner, Phil begs the favor of another cup of coffee. While drinking it, he says, —

"It was after the case-filling blow-up, when I first see you, commander. You remember?"

"I remember, Phil. You were walking along in the sun."

"Crawling, guv'ner, again a wall"—

"True, Phil — shouldering your way on"—

"In a nightcap!" exclaims Phil, excited.

"In a nightcap"—

"And hobbling with a couple of sticks!" cries Phil, still more excited.

"With a couple of sticks. When"—

"When you stops, you know," cries Phil, putting down his cup and saucer, and hastily removing his plate from his knees, "and says to me, 'What, comrade! You have been in the wars!' I didn't say much to you, commander, then, for I was took by surprise, that a person so strong and healthy and bold as you was, should stop to speak to such a limping bag of bones as I was. But you says to me, says you, delivering it out of your chest as hearty as possible, so that it was like a glass of something hot, 'What accident have you met with? You have been badly hurt. What's amiss, old boy? Cheer up, and tell us about it!' Cheer up! I was cheered already! I says as much to you, you says more to me,

I says more to you, you says more to me, and here I am, commander! Here I am, commander!" cries Phil, who has started from his chair and unaccountably begun to sidle away. "If a mark's wanted, or if it will improve the business, let the customers take aim at me. They can't spoil *my* beauty. *I*'m all right. Come on! If they want a man to box at, let 'em box at me. Let 'em knock me well about the head. *I* don't mind! If they want a light-weight, to be throwed for practice, Cornwall, Devonshire, or Lancashire, let 'em throw me. They won't hurt *me*. I have been throwed, all sorts of styles, all my life!"

With this unexpected speech, energetically delivered, and accompanied by action illustrative of the various exercises referred to, Phil Squod shoulders his way round three sides of the gallery, and abruptly tacking off at his commander, makes a butt at him with his head, intended to express devotion to his service. He then begins to clear away the breakfast.

Mr. George, after laughing cheerfully, and clapping him on the shoulder, assists in these arrangements, and helps to get the gallery into business order. That done, he takes a turn at the dumb-bells; and afterwards weighing himself, and opining that he is getting "too fleshy," engages with great gravity in solitary broadsword practice. Meanwhile, Phil has fallen to work at his usual table, where he screws and unscrews, and cleans, and files, and whistles into small apertures, and blackens himself more and more, and seems to do and undo everything that can be done and undone about a gun.

Master and man are at length disturbed by footsteps in the passage, where they make an unusual sound, denoting the arrival of unusual company. These steps, advancing nearer and nearer to the gallery, bring into it a group, at first sight scarcely reconcilable with any day in the year but the fifth of November.

It consists of a limp and ugly figure carried in a chair by two bearers, and attended by a lean female with a face like a pinched mask, who might be expected immediately to recite the popular verses, commemorative of the time when they did contrive to blow Old England up alive, but for her keeping her lips tightly and defiantly closed as the chair is put down. At which point, the figure in it gasping, "O Lord! Oh, dear me! I am shaken!" adds, "How de do, my dear friend, how de do?" Mr. George then descries, in the procession, the venerable Mr. Smallweed out for an airing, attended by his grand-daughter Judy as body-guard.

"Mr. George, my dear friend," says Grandfather Smallweed, removing his right arm from the neck of one of his bearers, whom he has nearly throttled coming along, "how de do? You're surprised to see me, my dear friend."

"I should hardly have been more surprised to have seen your friend in the city," returns Mr. George.

"I am very seldom out," pants Mr. Smallweed. "I haven't been out for many months. It's inconvenient — and it comes expensive. But I longed so much to see you, my dear Mr. George. How de do, sir?"

"I am well enough," says Mr. George. "I hope you are the same."

"You can't be too well, my dear friend." Mr. Smallweed takes him by both hands. "I have brought my grand-daughter Judy. I couldn't keep her away. She longed so much to see you."

"Hum! She bears it calmly!" mutters Mr. George.

"So we got a hackney-cab, and put a chair in it, and just round the corner they lifted me out of the cab and into the chair, and carried me here, that I might see my dear friend in his own establishment! This," says Grandfather Smallweed, alluding to the bearer, who has been in danger of strangulation, and who withdraws adjusting his windpipe, " is the driver of the cab. He has nothing extra. It is by agreement included in his fare. This person," the other bearer, " we engaged in the street outside for a pint of beer. Which is twopence. Judy, give the person twopence. I was not sure you had a workman of your own here, my dear friend, or we needn't have employed this person."

Grandfather Smallweed refers to Phil, with a glance of considerable terror, and a half-subdued " O Lord! Oh, dear me!" Nor is his apprehension, on the surface of things, without some reason ; for Phil, who has never beheld the apparition in the black-velvet cap before, has stopped short with a gun in his hand, with much of the air of a dead shot, intent on picking Mr. Smallweed off as an ugly old bird of the crow species.

" Judy, my child," says Grandfather Smallweed, " give the person his twopence. It's a great deal for what he has done."

The person, who is one of those extraordinary specimens of human fungus that spring up spontaneously in the western streets of London, ready dressed in an old red jacket, with a " Mission " for holding horses and calling coaches, receives his twopence with anything but transport, tosses the money into the air, catches it overhanded, and retires.

" My dear Mr. George," says Grandfather Smallweed, " would you be so kind as help to carry me to the fire?

I am accustomed to a fire, and I am an old man, and I soon chill. Oh, dear me!"

His closing exclamation is jerked out of the venerable gentleman by the suddenness with which Mr. Squod, like a genie, catches him up, chair and all, and deposits him on the hearthstone.

"O Lord!" says Mr. Smallweed, panting. "Oh, dear me! Oh, my stars! My dear friend, your workman is very strong — and very prompt. O Lord, he is very prompt! Judy, draw me back a little. I'm being scorched in the legs;" which indeed is testified to the noses of all present by the smell of his worsted stockings.

The gentle Judy, having backed her grandfather a little way from the fire, and having shaken him up as usual, and having released his overshadowed eye from its black-velvet extinguisher, Mr. Smallweed again says, "Oh, dear me! O Lord!" and looking about, and meeting Mr. George's glance, again stretches out both hands.

"My dear friend! So happy in this meeting! And this is your establishment? It's a delightful place. It's a picture! You never find that anything goes off here, accidentally; do you, my dear friend?" adds Grandfather Smallweed, very ill at ease.

"No, no. No fear of that."

"And your workman. He — Oh, dear me! —he never lets anything off without meaning it; does he, my dear friend?"

"He has never hurt anybody but himself," says Mr. George, smiling.

"But he might, you know. He seems to have hurt himself a good deal, and he might hurt somebody else," the old gentleman returns. " He mightn't mean it — or he even might. Mr. George, will you order him to leave his infernal fire-arms alone, and go away?"

Obedient to a nod from the trooper, Phil retires, empty-handed, to the other end of the gallery. Mr. Smallweed, reassured, falls to rubbing his legs.

" And you're doing well, Mr. George?" he says to the trooper, squarely standing faced about towards him with his broadsword in his hand. " You are prospering, please the Powers?"

Mr. George answers with a cool nod, adding, " Go on. You have not come to say that, I know."

" You are so sprightly, Mr. George," returns the venerable grandfather. " You are such good company."

" Ha ha! Go on!" says Mr. George.

" My dear friend!—But that sword looks awful gleaming and sharp. It might cut somebody, by accident. It makes me shiver, Mr. George — Curse him!" says the excellent old gentleman apart to Judy, as the trooper takes a step or two away to lay it aside. " He owes me money, and might think of paying off all scores in this murdering place. I wish your brimstone grandmother was here, and he'd shave her head off."

Mr. George, returning, folds his arms, and looking down at the old man, sliding every moment lower and lower in his chair, says quietly, " Now for it!"

" Ho!" cries Mr. Smallweed, rubbing his hands with an artful chuckle. " Yes. Now for it. Now for what, my dear friend?"

" For a pipe," says Mr. George; who with great composure sets his chair in the chimney-corner, takes his pipe from the grate, fills it and lights it, and falls to smoking peacefully.

This tends to the discomfiture of Mr. Smallweed, who finds it so difficult to resume his object, whatever it may be, that he becomes exasperated, and secretly claws the air with an impotent vindictiveness expressive of an intense desire to tear and rend the visage of Mr. George. As the excellent old gentleman's nails are long and leaden, and his hands lean and veinous, and his eyes green and watery; and, over and above this, as he continues, while he claws, to slide down in his chair and to collapse into a shapeless bundle; he becomes such a ghastly spectacle, even in the accustomed eyes of Judy, that that young virgin pounces at him with something more than the ardor of affection, and so shakes him up, and pats and pokes him in divers parts of his body, but particularly in that part which the science of self-defence would call his wind, that in his grievous distress he utters enforced sounds like a pavior's rammer.

When Judy has by these means set him up again in his chair, with a white face and a frosty nose (but still clawing), she stretches out her weazen forefinger, and gives Mr. George one poke in the back. The trooper raising his head, she makes another poke at her esteemed grandfather; and, having thus brought them together, stares rigidly at the fire.

"Ay, ay! Ho, ho! U—u—u—ugh!" chatters Grandfather Smallweed, swallowing his rage. "My dear friend!" (still clawing.)

"I tell you what," says Mr. George. "If you want to converse with me, you must speak out. I am one of the Roughs, and I can't go about and about. I haven't the art to do it. I am not clever enough. It don't suit me. When you go winding round and round me," says the trooper, putting his pipe between his lips again, "damme, if I don't feel as if I was being smothered!"

And he inflates his broad chest to its utmost extent, as if to assure himself that he is not smothered yet.

"If you have come to give me a friendly call," continues Mr. George, "I am obliged to you; how are you? If you have come to see whether there's any property on the premises, look about you; you are welcome. If you want to out with something, out with it!"

The blooming Judy, without removing her gaze from the fire, gives her grandfather one ghostly poke.

"You see! It's her opinion, too. And why the devil that young woman won't sit down like a Christian," says Mr. George, with his eyes musingly fixed on Judy, "I can't comprehend."

"She keeps at my side to attend to me, sir," says Grandfather Smallweed. "I am an old man, my dear Mr. George, and I need some attention. I can carry my years; I am not a Brimstone poll-parrot;" (snarling and looking unconsciously for the cushion;) "but I need attention, my dear friend."

"Well!" returns the trooper, wheeling his chair to face the old man. "Now then?"

"My friend in the city, Mr. George, has done a little business with a pupil of yours."

"Has he?" says Mr. George. "I am sorry to hear it."

"Yes, sir." Grandfather Smallweed rubs his legs. "He is a fine young soldier now, Mr. George, by the name of Carstone. Friends came forward, and paid it all up, honorable."

"Did they?" returns Mr. George. "Do you think your friend in the city would like a piece of advice?"

"I think he would, my dear friend. From you."

"I advise him, then, to do no more business in that quarter. There's no more to be got by it. The young gentleman, to my knowledge, is brought to a dead halt."

"No, no, my dear friend. No, no, Mr. George. No, no, no, sir," remonstrates Grandfather Smallweed, cunningly rubbing his spare legs. "Not quite a dead halt, I think. He has good friends, and he is good for his pay, and he is good for the selling price of his commission, and he is good for his chance in a lawsuit, and he is good for his chance in a wife, and — oh, do you know, Mr. George, I think my friend would consider the young gentleman good for something yet?" says Grandfather Smallweed, turning up his velvet cap, and scratching his ear like a monkey.

Mr. George, who has put aside his pipe and sits with an arm on his chair-back, beats a tattoo on the ground with his right foot, as if he were not particularly pleased with the turn the conversation has taken.

"But to pass from one subject to another," resumes Mr. Smallweed. "To promote the conversation, as a joker might say. To pass, Mr. George, from the ensign to the captain."

"What are you up to, now?" asks Mr. George, pausing with a frown in stroking the recollection of his moustache. "What captain?"

"Our captain. The captain we know of. Captain Hawdon."

O! that's it, is it?" says Mr. George, with a low whistle, as he sees both grandfather and grand-daughter looking hard at him; "you are there! Well? what about it? Come, I won't be smothered any more. Speak!"

"My dear friend," returns the old man, "I was applied — Judy, shake me up a little! — I was applied to, yesterday, about the captain; and my opinion still is, that the captain is not dead."

"Bosh!" observes Mr. George.

"What was your remark, my dear friend?" inquires the old man with his hand to his ear.

"Bosh!"

"Ho!" says Grandfather Smallweed. "Mr. George, of my opinion you can judge for yourself, according to the questions asked of me, and the reasons given for asking 'em. Now, what do you think the lawyer making the inquiries wants?"

"A job," says Mr. George.

"Nothing of the kind!"

"Can't be a lawyer, then," says Mr. George, folding his arms with an air of confirmed resolution.

"My dear friend, he is a lawyer, and a famous one. He wants to see some fragment in Captain Hawdon's writing. He don't want to keep it. He only wants to see it, and compare it with a writing in his possession."

"Well?"

"Well, Mr. George. Happening to remember the advertisement concerning Captain Hawdon, and any information that could be given respecting him, he looked it up and came to me — just as you did, my dear friend. *Will* you shake hands? So glad you came, that day! I should have missed forming such a friendship, if you hadn't come!"

"Well, Mr. Smallweed?" says Mr. George again, after going through the ceremony with some stiffness.

"I had no such thing. I have nothing but his signature. Plague, pestilence and famine, battle, murder and sudden death upon him," says the old man, making a curse out of one of his few remembrances of a prayer, and squeezing up his velvet cap between his angry hands, "I have half a million of his signatures, I think! But you," breathlessly recovering his mildness of speech, as Judy readjusts the cap on his skittle-ball of a head; "you, my dear Mr. George, are likely to have some letter or paper that would suit the purpose. Anything would suit the purpose, written in the hand."

"Some writing in that hand," says the trooper, pondering, "maybe, I have."

"My dearest friend!"

"Maybe, I have not."

"Ho!" says Grandfather Smallweed, crestfallen.

"But if I had bushels of it, I would not show as much as would make a cartridge, without knowing why."

"Sir, I have told you why. My dear Mr. George, I have told you why."

"Not enough," says the trooper, shaking his head. "I must know more, and approve it."

"Then, will you come to the lawyer? My dear friend, will you come and see the gentleman?" urges Grandfather Smallweed, pulling out a lean old silver watch, with hands like the legs of a skeleton. "I told him it was probable I might call upon him between ten and eleven this forenoon; and it's now half-after ten. Will you come and see the gentleman, Mr. George?"

"Hum!" says he, gravely. "I don't mind that. Though why this should concern you so much, I don't know."

"Everything concerns me, that has a chance in it of bringing anything to light about him. Didn't he take us all in? Didn't he owe us immense sums, all round?

Concern me? Who can anything about him concern, more than me? Not, my dear friend," says Grandfather Smallweed, lowering his tone, " that I want *you* to betray anything. Far from it. Are you ready to come, my dear friend?"

"Ay! I'll come in a moment. I promise nothing, you know."

" No, my dear Mr. George ; no."

" And you mean to say you're going to give me a lift to this place, wherever it is, without charging for it?" Mr. George inquires, getting his hat and thick washleather gloves.

This pleasantry so tickles Mr. Smallweed that he laughs, long and low, before the fire. But ever while he laughs, he glances over his paralytic shoulder at Mr. George, and eagerly watches him as he unlocks the padlock of a homely cupboard at the distant end of the gallery, looks here and there upon the higher shelves, and ultimately takes something out with a rustling of paper, folds it, and puts it in his breast. Then Judy pokes Mr. Smallweed once, and Mr. Smallweed pokes Judy once.

"I am ready," says the trooper, coming back. " Phil, you can carry this old gentleman to his coach, and make nothing of him."

" Oh, dear me! O Lord! Stop a moment!" says Mr. Smallweed. " He's so very prompt! Are you sure you can do it carefully, my worthy man?"

Phil makes no reply ; but, seizing the chair and its load, sidles away, tightly hugged by the now speechless Mr. Smallweed, and bolts along the passage as if he had an acceptable commission to carry the old gentleman to the nearest volcano. His shorter trust, however, terminating at the cab, he deposits him there; and the fair Judy takes her place beside him, and the chair embellishes the roof, and Mr. George takes the vacant place upon the box.

Mr. George is quite confounded by the spectacle he beholds from time to time as he peeps into the cab, through the window behind him; where the grim Judy is always motionless, and the old gentleman with his cap over one eye is always sliding off the seat into the straw, and looking upward at him, out of his other eye, with a helpless expression of being jolted in the back.

CHAPTER XXVII.

MORE OLD SOLDIERS THAN ONE.

Mr. George has not far to ride with folded arms upon the box, for their destination is Lincoln's Inn Fields. When the driver stops his horses, Mr. George alights, and looking in at the window, says, —

"What, Mr. Tulkinghorn's your man, is he?"

"Yes, my dear friend. Do you know him, Mr. George?"

"Why, I have heard of him — seen him too, I think. But I don't know him, and he don't know me."

There ensues the carrying of Mr. Smallweed up-stairs; which is done to perfection with the trooper's help. He is borne into Mr. Tulkinghorn's great room, and deposited on the Turkey rug before the fire. Mr. Tulkinghorn is not within at the present moment, but will be back directly. The occupant of the pew in the hall, having said thus much, stirs the fire, and leaves the triumvirate to warm themselves.

Mr. George is mightily curious in respect of the room. He looks up at the painted ceiling, looks round at the old law-books, contemplates the portraits of the great clients, reads aloud the names on the boxes.

"'Sir Leicester Dedlock, Baronet,'" Mr. George reads thoughtfully. "Ha! 'Manor of Chesney Wold.' Humph!" Mr. George stands looking at these boxes a

long while — as if they were pictures — and comes back
to the fire repeating, " Sir Leicester Dedlock, Baronet,
and Manor of Chesney Wold, hey ? "

" Worth a mint of money, Mr. George ! " whispers
Grandfather Smallweed, rubbing his legs. " Powerfully
rich ! "

" Who do you mean ? This old gentleman, or the
Baronet ? "

" This gentleman, this gentleman."

" So I have heard ; and knows a thing or two, I'll hold
a wager. Not bad quarters either," says Mr. George,
looking round again. " See the strong box, yonder ! "

This reply is cut short by Mr. Tulkinghorn's arrival.
There is no change in him, of course. Rustily dressed,
with his spectacles in his hand, and their very case worn
threadbare. In manner, close and dry. In voice, husky
and low. In face, watchful behind a blind ; habitually
not uncensorious and contemptuous perhaps. The peerage may have warmer worshippers and faithfuller believers than Mr. Tulkinghorn, after all, if everything
were known.

" Good morning, Mr. Smallweed, good morning ! " he
says as he comes in. " You have brought the sergeant, I
see. Sit down, sergeant."

As Mr. Tulkinghorn takes off his gloves and puts them
in his hat, he looks with half-closed eyes across the room
to where the trooper stands, and says within himself perchance, " You'll do, my friend ! "

" Sit down, sergeant," he repeats, as he comes to his
table, which is set on one side of the fire, and takes his
easy-chair. " Cold and raw this morning, cold and raw ! "
Mr. Tulkinghorn warms before the bars, alternately, the
palms and knuckles of his hands, and looks (from behind

that blind which is always down) at the trio sitting in a little semicircle before him.

"Now, I can feel what I am about!" (as perhaps he can in two senses) "Mr. Smallweed." The old gentleman is newly shaken up by Judy, to bear his part in the conversation. "You have brought our good friend the sergeant, I see."

"Yes, sir," returns Mr. Smallweed, very servile to the lawyer's wealth and influence.

"And what does the sergeant say about this business?"

"Mr. George," says Grandfather Smallweed, with a tremulous wave of his shrivelled hand, "this is the gentleman, sir."

Mr. George salutes the gentleman; but otherwise sits bolt upright and profoundly silent — very forward in his chair, as if the full complement of regulation appendages for a field-day hung about him.

Mr. Tulkinghorn proceeds: "Well, George? — I believe your name is George?"

"It is so, sir."

"What do you say, George?"

"I ask your pardon, sir," returns the trooper, "but I should wish to know what *you* say?"

"Do you mean in point of reward?"

"I mean in point of everything, sir."

This is so very trying to Mr. Smallweed's temper, that he suddenly breaks out with "You're a brimstone beast!" and as suddenly asks pardon of Mr. Tulkinghorn; excusing himself for this slip of the tongue, by saying to Judy, "I was thinking of your grandmother, my dear."

"I supposed, sergeant," Mr. Tulkinghorn resumes, as

he leans on one side of his chair and crosses his legs, "that Mr. Smallweed might have sufficiently explained the matter. It lies in the smallest compass, however. You served under Captain Hawdon at one time, and were his attendant in illness, and rendered him many little services, and were rather in his confidence, I am told. That is so, is it not?"

"Yes, sir, that is so," says Mr. George, with military brevity.

"Therefore you may happen to have in your possession something — anything, no matter what — accounts, instructions, orders, a letter, anything — in Captain Hawdon's writing. I wish to compare his writing with some that I have. If you can give me the opportunity, you shall be rewarded for your trouble. Three, four, five guineas, you would consider handsome, I dare say."

"Noble, my dear friend!" cries Grandfather Smallweed, screwing up his eyes.

"If not, say how much more, in your conscience as a soldier, you can demand. There is no need for you to part with the writing against your inclination — though I should prefer to have it."

Mr. George sits squared in exactly the same attitude, looks at the ground, looks at the painted ceiling, and says never a word. The irascible Mr. Smallweed scratches the air.

"The question is," says Mr. Tulkinghorn in his methodical, subdued, uninterested way, "first, whether you have any of Captain Hawdon's writing?"

"First, whether I have any of Captain Hawdon's writing, sir," repeats Mr. George.

"Secondly, what will satisfy you for the trouble of producing it."

"Secondly, what will satisfy me for the trouble of producing it, sir," repeats Mr. George.

"Thirdly, you can judge for yourself whether it is at all like that," says Mr. Tulkinghorn, suddenly handing him some sheets of written paper tied together.

"Whether it is at all like that, sir. Just so," repeats Mr. George.

All three repetitions Mr. George pronounces in a mechanical manner, looking straight at Mr. Tulkinghorn; nor does he so much as glance at the affidavit in Jarndyce and Jarndyce, that has been given to him for his inspection (though he still holds it in his hand), but continues to look at the lawyer with an air of troubled meditation.

"Well?" says Mr. Tulkinghorn. "What do you say?"

"Well, sir," replies Mr. George, rising erect and looking immense, "I would rather, if you'll excuse me, have nothing to do with this."

Mr. Tulkinghorn, outwardly quite undisturbed, demands "Why not?"

"Why, sir," returns the trooper. "Except on military compulsion, I am not a man of business. Among civilians I am what they call in Scotland a ne'er-do-weel. I have no head for papers, sir. I can stand any fire better than a fire of cross-questions. I mentioned to Mr. Smallweed, only an hour or so ago, that when I come into things of this kind I feel as if I was being smothered. And that is my sensation," says Mr. George, looking round upon the company, "at the present moment."

With that, he takes three strides forward, to replace the papers on the lawyer's table, and three strides backward to resume his former station: where he stands perfectly upright, now looking at the ground, and now at the painted ceiling, with his hands behind him as if to prevent himself from accepting any other document whatever.

Under this provocation, Mr. Smallweed's favorite adjective of disparagement is so close to his tongue, that he begins the words " my dear friend " with the monosyllable " Brim "; thus converting the possessive pronoun into Brimmy, and appearing to have an impediment in his speech. Once past this difficulty, however, he exhorts his dear friend in the tenderest manner not to be rash, but to do what so eminent a gentleman requires, and to do it with a good grace: confident that it must be unobjectionable as well as profitable. Mr. Tulkinghorn merely utters an occasional sentence, as "You are the best judge of your own interest, sergeant." "Take care you do no harm by this." "Please yourself, please yourself." "If you know what you mean, that's quite enough." These he utters with an appearance of perfect indifference, as he looks over the papers on his table, and prepares to write a letter.

Mr. George looks distrustfully from the painted ceiling to the ground, from the ground to Mr. Smallweed, from Mr. Smallweed to Mr. Tulkinghorn, and from Mr. Tulkinghorn to the painted ceiling again; often in his perplexity changing the leg on which he rests.

"I do assure you, sir," says Mr. George, "not to say it offensively, that between you and Mr. Smallweed here, I really am being smothered fifty times over. I really am, sir. I am not a match for you gentlemen. Will you allow me to ask, why you want to see the captain's hand, in the case that I could find any specimen of it?"

Mr. Tulkinghorn quietly shakes his head. "No. If

you were a man of business, sergeant, you would not need to be informed, that there are confidential reasons, very harmless in themselves, for many such wants, in the profession to which I belong. But if you are afraid of doing any injury to Captain Hawdon, you may set your mind at rest about that."

"Ay! he is dead, sir."

"*Is* he?" Mr. Tulkinghorn quietly sits down to write.

"Well, sir," says the trooper, looking into his hat after another disconcerted pause; "I am sorry not to have given you more satisfaction. If it would be any satisfaction to any one, that I should be confirmed in my judgment that I would rather have nothing to do with this, by a friend of mine, who has a better head for business than I have, and who is an old soldier, I am willing to consult with him. I — I really am so completely smothered myself at present," says Mr. George, passing his hand hopelessly across his brow, "that I don't know but what it might be a satisfaction to me."

Mr. Smallweed, hearing that this authority is an old soldier, so strongly inculcates the expediency of the trooper's taking counsel with him, and particularly informing him of its being a question of five guineas or more, that Mr. George engages to go and see him. Mr. Tulkinghorn says nothing either way.

"I'll consult my friend, then, by your leave, sir," says the trooper, "and I'll take the liberty of looking in again with a final answer in the course of the day. Mr. Smallweed, if you wish to be carried down-stairs"—

"In a moment, my dear friend, in a moment. Will you first let me speak half a word with this gentleman, in private?"

"Certainly, sir. Don't hurry yourself on my account." The trooper retires to a distant part of the room, and resumes his curious inspection of the boxes; strong and otherwise.

"If I wasn't as weak as a Brimstone Baby, sir," whispers Grandfather Smallweed, drawing the lawyer down to his level by the lappel of his coat, and flashing some half-quenched green fire out of his angry eyes, "I'd tear the writing away from him. He's got it buttoned in his breast. I saw him put it there. Judy saw him put it there. Speak up, you crabbed image for the sign of a walking-stick shop, and say you saw him put it there!"

This vehement conjuration the old gentleman accompanies with such a thrust at his grand-daughter, that it is too much for his strength, and he slips away out of his chair, drawing Mr. Tulkinghorn with him, until he is arrested by Judy, and well shaken.

"Violence will not do for me, my friend," Mr. Tulkinghorn then remarks coolly.

"No, no, I know; I know, sir. But it's chafing and galling — it's — it's worse than your smattering chattering Magpie of a grandmother," to the imperturbable Judy, who only looks at the fire, "to know he has got what's wanted, and won't give it up. He, not to give it up! *He!* A vagabond! But never mind, sir, never mind. At the most, he has only his own way for a little while. I have him periodically in a vice. I'll twist him, sir. I'll screw him, sir. If he won't do it with a good grace, I'll make him do it with a bad one, sir! — Now, my dear Mr. George," says Grandfather Smallweed, winking at the lawyer hideously, as he releases him, "I am ready for your kind assistance, my excellent friend!"

Mr. Tulkinghorn, with some shadowy sign of amusement manifesting itself through his self-possession, stands on the hearth-rug with his back to the fire, watching the disappearance of Mr. Smallweed, and acknowledging the trooper's parting salute with one slight nod.

It is more difficult to get rid of the old gentleman, Mr. George finds, than to bear a hand in carrying him downstairs; for, when he is replaced in his conveyance, he is so loquacious on the subject of the guineas, and retains such an affectionate hold of his button — having, in truth, a secret longing to rip his coat open, and rob him — that some degree of force is necessary on the trooper's part to effect a separation. It is accomplished at last, and he proceeds alone in quest of his adviser.

By the cloisterly Temple, and by Whitefriars (there, not without a glance at Hanging-Sword Alley, which would seem to be something in his way), and by Blackfriars Bridge, and Blackfriars Road, Mr. George sedately marches to a street of little shops lying somewhere in that ganglion of roads from Kent and Surrey, and of streets from the bridges of London, centering in the far-famed Elephant who has lost his castle formed of a thousand four-horse coaches, to a stronger iron monster than he, ready to chop him into mince-meat any day he dares. To one of the little shops in this street, which is a musician's shop, having a few fiddles in the window, and some Pan's pipes and a tambourine, and a triangle, and certain elongated scraps of music, Mr. George directs his massive tread. And halting at a few paces from it, as he sees a soldierly-looking woman, with her outer skirts tucked up, come forth with a small wooden tub, and in that tub commence a whisking and a splashing on the margin of the pavement, Mr. George says to himself,

"She's, as usual, washing greens. I never saw her, except upon a baggage-wagon, when she wasn't washing greens!"

The subject of this reflection is at all events so occupied in washing greens at present, that she remains unsuspicious of Mr. George's approach; until, lifting up herself and her tub together, when she has poured the water off into the gutter, she finds him standing near her. Her reception of him is not flattering.

"George, I never see you, but I wish you was a hundred mile away!"

The trooper, without remarking on this welcome, follows into the musical-instrument shop, where the lady places her tub of greens upon the counter, and having shaken hands with him, rests her arms upon it.

"I never," she says, "George, consider Matthew Bagnet safe a minute when you're near him. You are that restless and that roving"—

"Yes! I know I am, Mrs. Bagnet. I know I am."

"You know you are!" says Mrs. Bagnet. "What's the use of that? *Why* are you?"

"The nature of the animal, I suppose," returns the trooper good-humoredly.

"Ah!" cries Mrs. Bagnet, something shrilly, "but what satisfaction will the nature of the animal be to me, when the animal shall have tempted my Mat away from the musical business to New Zealand or Australey?"

Mrs. Bagnet is not at all an ill-looking woman. Rather large-boned, a little coarse in the grain, and freckled by the sun and wind which have tanned her hair upon the forehead; but healthy, wholesome, and bright-eyed. A strong, busy, active, honest-faced woman, of from forty-five to fifty. Clean, hardy, and so economically dressed (though substantially), that the only article of ornament of which she stands possessed appears to be her wedding-ring; around which her finger has grown to be so large since it was put on, that it will never come off again until it shall mingle with Mrs. Bagnet's dust.

"Mrs. Bagnet," says the trooper, "I am on my parole with you. Mat will get no harm from me. You may trust me so far."

"Well, I think I may. But the very looks of you are unsettling," Mrs. Bagnet rejoins. "Ah, George, George! If you had only settled down, and married Joe Pouch's widow when he died in North America, *she*'d have combed your hair for you."

"It was a chance for me, certainly," returns the trooper, half laughingly, half seriously, "but I shall never settle down into a respectable man now. Joe Pouch's widow might have done me good — there was something in her — and something of her — but I couldn't make up my mind to it. If I had had the luck to meet with such a wife as Mat found!"

Mrs. Bagnet, who seems in a virtuous way to be under little reserve with a good sort of fellow, but to be another good sort of fellow herself for that matter, receives this compliment by flicking Mr. George in the face with a head of greens, and taking her tub into the little room behind the shop.

"Why, Quebec, my poppet," says George, following, on invitation, into that apartment. "And little Malta, too! Come and kiss your Bluffy!"

These young ladies — not supposed to have been actually christened by the names applied to them, though always so called in the family, from the places of their birth in barracks — are respectively employed on three-legged stools: the younger (some five or six years old), in learning her letters out of a penny-primer: the elder (eight or nine perhaps), in teaching her, and sewing with great assiduity. Both hail Mr. George with acclamations as an old friend, and after some kissing and romping plant their stools beside him.

"And how's young Woolwich?" says Mr. George.

"Ah! There now!" cries Mrs. Bagnet, turning about from her saucepans (for she is cooking dinner), with a bright flush on her face. "Would you believe it? Got an engagement at the Theayter, with his father, to play the fife in a military piece."

"Well done, my godson!" cries Mr. George, slapping his thigh.

"I believe you!" says Mrs. Bagnet. "He's a Briton. That's what Woolwich is. A Briton."

"And Mat blows away at his bassoon, and you're respectable civilians one and all," says Mr. George. "Family people. Children growing up. Mat's old mother in Scotland, and your old father somewhere else, corresponded with; and helped a little; and — well, well! To be sure, I don't know why I shouldn't be wished a hundred mile away, for I have not much to do with all this!"

Mr. George is becoming thoughtful; sitting before the fire in the whitewashed room, which has a sanded floor, and a barrack smell, and contains nothing superfluous, and has not a visible speck of dirt or dust in it, from the faces of Quebec and Malta to the bright tin pots and pannikins upon the dresser-shelves;— Mr. George is becoming thoughtful, sitting here while Mrs. Bagnet is busy, when Mr. Bagnet and young Woolwich opportunely come home. Mr. Bagnet is an ex-artilleryman, tall and upright, with shaggy eyebrows, and whiskers like the fibres of a cocoa-nut, not a hair upon his head, and a torrid complexion. His voice, short, deep, and resonant, is not at all unlike the tones of the instrument to which he is devoted. Indeed there may be generally observed in him an unbending, unyielding, brass-bound air, as if he were himself the bassoon of the human orchestra. Young Woolwich is the type and model of a young drummer.

Both father and son salute the trooper heartily. He saying, in due season, that he has come to advise with Mr. Bagnet, Mr. Bagnet hospitably declares that he will hear of no business until after dinner; and that his friend shall not partake of his counsel, without first partaking of boiled pork and greens. The trooper yielding to this invitation, he and Mr. Bagnet, not to embarrass the domestic preparations, go forth to take a turn up and down the little street, which they promenade with measured tread and folded arms, as if it were a rampart.

"George," says Mr. Bagnet. "You know me. It's my old girl that advises. She has the head. But I never own to it before her. Discipline must be maintained. Wait till the greens is off her mind. Then, we'll consult. Whatever the old girl says, do — do it!"

"I intend to, Mat," replies the other. "I would sooner take her opinion than that of a college."

"College," returns Mr. Bagnet, in short sentences, bassoon-like. "What college could you leave — in another quarter of the world — with nothing but a gray cloak and an umbrella — to make its way home to Europe? The old girl would do it to-morrow. Did it once!"

"You are right," says Mr. George.

"What college," pursues Bagnet, "could you set up in life — with two penn'orth of white lime — a penn'orth of fuller's earth — a ha'porth of sand — and the rest of the change out of sixpence, in money? That's what the old girl started on. In the present business."

"I am rejoiced to hear it's thriving, Mat."

"The old girl," says Mr. Bagnet, acquiescing, "saves. Has a stocking somewhere. With money in it. I never saw it. But I know she's got it. Wait till the greens is off her mind. Then she'll set you up."

"She is a treasure!" exclaims Mr. George.

"She's more. But I never own to it before her. Discipline must be maintained. It was the old girl that brought out my musical abilities. I should have been in the artillery now, but for the old girl. Six years I hammered at the fiddle. Ten at the flute. The old girl said it wouldn't do; intention good, but want of flexibility; try the bassoon. The old girl borrowed a bassoon from the bandmaster of the Rifle Regiment. I practised in the trenches. Got on, got another, get a living by it!"

George remarks that she looks as fresh as a rose, and as sound as an apple.

"The old girl," says Mr. Bagnet in reply, "is a thoroughly fine woman. Consequently, she is like a thoroughly fine day. Gets finer as she gets on. I never saw the old girl's equal. But I never own to it before her. Discipline must be maintained!"

Proceeding to converse on different matters, they walk up and down the little street, keeping step and time, until summoned by Quebec and Malta to do justice to the pork and greens; over which Mrs. Bagnet, like a military chaplain, says a short grace. In the distribution of these comestibles, as in every other household duty, Mrs. Bagnet develops an exact system; sitting with every dish before her; allotting to every portion of pork its own portion of pot-liquor, greens, potatoes, and even mustard; and serving it out complete. Having likewise served out the beer from a can, and thus supplied the mess with all things necessary, Mrs. Bagnet proceeds to satisfy her own hunger, which is in a healthy state. The kit of the mess, if the table furniture may be so denominated, is chiefly composed of utensils of horn and tin, that have done duty in several parts of the world. Young Woolwich's knife, in particular, which is of the oyster kind, with the additional feature of a strong shutting-up movement which frequently balks the appetite of that young musician, is mentioned as having gone in various hands the complete round of foreign service.

The dinner done, Mrs. Bagnet, assisted by the younger branches (who polish their own cups and platters, knives and forks), makes all the dinner garniture shine as brightly as before, and puts it all away; first sweeping the hearth to the end that Mr. Bagnet and the visitor may not be retarded in the smoking of their pipes. These household cares involve much pattening and counter-pattening in the back yard, and considerable use of a pail, which is finally so happy as to assist in the ablutions of Mrs. Bagnet herself. That old girl reappearing by and by, quite fresh, and sitting down to her needlework, then and only then — the greens being only then to be considered as entirely off her mind — Mr. Bagnet requests the trooper to state his case.

This Mr. George does with great discretion; appearing to address himself to Mr. Bagnet, but having an eye solely on the old girl all the time, as Bagnet has himself.

She, equally discreet, busies herself with her needlework. The case fully stated, Mr. Bagnet resorts to his standard artifice for the maintenance of discipline.

"That's the whole of it, is it, George?" says he.

"That's the whole of it."

"You act according to my opinion?"

"I shall be guided," replies George, "entirely by it."

"Old girl," says Mr. Bagnet, "give him my opinion. You know it. Tell him what it is."

It is, that he cannot have too little to do with people who are too deep for him, and cannot be too careful of interference with matters he does not understand; that the plain rule is to do nothing in the dark, to be a party to nothing underhanded or mysterious, and never to put his foot where he cannot see the ground. This, in effect, is Mr. Bagnet's opinion, as delivered through the old girl; and it so relieves Mr. George's mind, by confirming his own opinion and banishing his doubts, that he composes himself to smoke another pipe on that exceptional occasion, and to have a talk over old times with the whole Bagnet family, according to their various ranges of experience.

Through these means it comes to pass that Mr. George does not again rise to his full height in that parlor until the time is drawing on when the bassoon and fife are expected by a British public at the theatre; and as it takes time even then for Mr. George, in his domestic character of Bluffy, to take leave of Quebec and Malta, and insinuate a sponsorial shilling into the pocket of his godson, with felicitations on his success in life, it is dark when Mr. George again turns his face towards Lincoln's Inn Fields.

"A family home," he ruminates, as he marches along,

"however small it is, makes a man like me look lonely. But it's well I never made that evolution of matrimony. I shouldn't have been fit for it. I am such a vagabond still, even at my present time of life, that I couldn't hold to the gallery a month together, if it was a regular pursuit, or if I didn't camp there, gypsy fashion. Come! I disgrace nobody and cumber nobody: that's something. I have not done that, for many a long year!"

So he whistles it off, and marches on.

Arrived in Lincoln's Inn Fields, and mounting Mr. Tulkinghorn's stair, he finds the outer door closed, and the chambers shut; but the trooper not knowing much about outer doors, and the staircase being dark besides, he is yet fumbling and groping about, hoping to discover a bell-handle or to open the door for himself, when Mr. Tulkinghorn comes up the stairs (quietly, of course), and angrily asks, —

"Who is that? What are you doing there?"

"I ask your pardon, sir. It's George. The sergeant."

"And couldn't George, the sergeant, see that my door was locked?"

"Why, no, sir, I couldn't. At any rate, I didn't," says the trooper; rather nettled.

"Have you changed your mind? or are you in the same mind?" Mr. Tulkinghorn demands. But he knows well enough at a glance.

"In the same mind, sir."

"I thought so. That's sufficient. You can go. So, you are the man," says Mr. Tulkinghorn, opening his door with the key, "in whose hiding-place Mr. Gridley was found?"

"Yes, I *am* the man," says the trooper, stopping two or three stairs down. "What then, sir?"

"What then? I don't like your associates. You should not have seen the inside of my door this morning, if I had thought of your being that man. Gridley? A threatening, murderous, dangerous fellow."

With these words, spoken in an unusually high tone for him, the lawyer goes into his rooms, and shuts the door with a thundering noise.

Mr. George takes this dismissal in great dudgeon; the greater, because a clerk coming up the stairs has heard the last words of all, and evidently applies them to him. "A pretty character to bear," the trooper growls with a hasty oath, as he strides down-stairs. "A threatening, murderous, dangerous fellow!" and looking up, he sees the clerk looking down at him, and marking him as he passes a lamp. This so intensifies his dudgeon, that for five minutes he is in an ill-humor. But he whistles that off, like the rest of it; and marches home to the Shooting Gallery.

CHAPTER XXVIII.

THE IRONMASTER.

Sir Leicester Dedlock has got the better, for the time being, of the family gout; and is once more, in a literal no less than in a figurative point of view, upon his legs. He is at his place in Lincolnshire; but the waters are out again on the low-lying grounds, and the cold and damp steal into Chesney Wold, though well defended, and eke into Sir Leicester's bones. The blazing fires of fagot and coal — Dedlock timber and antediluvian forest — that blaze upon the broad wide hearths, and wink in the twilight on the frowning woods, sullen to see how trees are sacrificed, do not exclude the enemy. The hot-water pipes that trail themselves all over the house, the cushioned doors and windows, and the screens and curtains, fail to supply the fires' deficiencies, and to satisfy Sir Leicester's need. Hence the fashionable intelligence proclaims one morning to the listening earth, that Lady Dedlock is expected shortly to return to town for a few weeks.

It is a melancholy truth, that even great men have their poor relations. Indeed, great men have often more than their fair share of poor relations; inasmuch as very red blood of the superior quality, like inferior blood unlawfully shed, *will* cry aloud, and *will* be heard. Sir Leicester's cousins, in the remotest degree, are so many

Murders, in the respect that they "will out." Among whom there are cousins who are so poor, that one might almost dare to think it would have been the happier for them never to have been plated links upon the Dedlock chain of gold, but to have been made of common iron at first, and done base service.

Service, however (with a few limited reservations: genteel but not profitable), they may not do, being of the Dedlock dignity. So they visit their richer cousins, and get into debt when they can, and live but shabbily when they can't, and find — the women no husbands, and the men no wives — and ride in borrowed carriages, and sit at feasts that are never of their own making, and so go through high life. The rich family sum has been divided by so many figures, and they are the something over that nobody knows what to do with.

Everybody on Sir Leicester Dedlock's side of the question, and of his way of thinking, would appear to be his cousin more or less. From my Lord Boodle, through the Duke of Foodle, down to Noodle, Sir Leicester, like a glorious spider, stretches his threads of relationship. But while he is stately in the cousinship of the Everybodys, he is a kind and generous man, according to his dignified way, in the cousinship of the Nobodys; and at the present time, in despite of the damp, he stays out the visit of several such cousins at Chesney Wold, with the constancy of a martyr.

Of these, foremost in the first rank stands Volumnia Dedlock, a young lady (of sixty), who is doubly highly related; having the honor to be a poor relation, by the mother's side, to another great family. Miss Volumnia, displaying in early life a pretty talent for cutting ornaments out of colored paper, and also for singing to the guitar in the Spanish tongue, and propounding French conundrums in country houses, passed the twenty years of her existence between twenty and forty in a sufficiently agreeable manner. Lapsing then out of date, and being considered to bore mankind by her vocal performances in the Spanish language, she retired to Bath; where she lives slenderly on an annual present from Sir Leicester, and whence she makes occasional resurrections in the country houses of her cousins. She has an extensive acquaintance at Bath among appalling old gentlemen with thin legs and nankeen trousers, and is of high standing in that dreary city. But she is a little dreaded elsewhere, in consequence of an indiscreet profusion in the article of rouge, and persistency in an obsolete pearl necklace like a rosary of little bird's-eggs.

In any country in a wholesome state, Volumnia would be a clear case for the pension list. Efforts have been made to get her on it; and when William Buffy came in, it was fully expected that her name would be put down for a couple of hundred a-year. But William Buffy somehow discovered, contrary to all expectation, that these were not times when it could be done; and this was the first clear indication Sir Leicester Dedlock had conveyed to him, that the country was going to pieces.

There is likewise the Honorable Bob Stables, who can make warm mashes with the skill of a veterinary surgeon, and is a better shot than most gamekeepers. He has been for some time particularly desirous to serve his country in a post of good emoluments, unaccompanied by any trouble or responsibility. In a well-regulated body politic, this natural desire on the part of a spirited young gentleman so highly connected, would be speedily recognized; but somehow William Buffy found when he came in, that these were not times in which he could manage that little matter, either; and this was the second indication Sir Leicester Dedlock had conveyed to him, that the country was going to pieces.

The rest of the cousins are ladies and gentlemen of various ages and capacities; the major part, amiable and sensible, and likely to have done well enough in life if they could have overcome their cousinship; as it is, they are almost all a little worsted by it, and lounge in purposeless and listless paths, and seem to be quite as much at a loss how to dispose of themselves, as anybody else can be how to dispose of them.

In this society, and where not, my Lady Dedlock reigns supreme. Beautiful, elegant, accomplished, and powerful in her little world (for the world of fashion does not stretch *all* the way from pole to pole), her influence in Sir Leicester's house, however haughty and indifferent her manner, is greatly to improve it and refine it. The cousins, even those older cousins who were paralyzed when Sir Leicester married her, do her feudal homage; and the Honorable Bob Stables daily repeats to some chosen person, between breakfast and lunch, his favorite original remark that she is the best-groomed woman in the whole stud.

Such the guests in the long drawing-room at Chesney Wold this dismal night, when the step on the Ghost's Walk (inaudible here, however), might be the step of a deceased cousin shut out in the cold. It is near bedtime. Bedroom fires blaze brightly all over the house, raising ghosts of grim furniture on wall and ceiling. Bedroom candlesticks bristle on the distant table by the door, and cousins yawn on ottomans. Cousins at the piano, cousins at the soda-water tray, cousins rising from the card-table, cousins gathered round the fire. Standing on one side of his own peculiar fire (for there are two), Sir Leicester. On the opposite side of the broad hearth, my Lady at her table. Volumnia, as one of the more privileged cousins, in a luxurious chair between them. Sir Leicester glancing, with magnificent displeasure, at the rouge and the pearl necklace.

"I occasionally meet on my staircase here," drawls Volumnia, whose thoughts perhaps are already hopping up it to bed, after a long evening of very desultory talk, "one of the prettiest girls, I think, that I ever saw in my life."

"A *protégée* of my Lady's," observes Sir Leicester.

"I thought so. I felt sure that some uncommon eye must have picked that girl out. She really is a marvel. A dolly sort of beauty perhaps," says Miss Volumnia, reserving her own sort, "but in its way, perfect; such bloom I never saw!"

Sir Leicester, with his magnificent glance of displeasure at the rouge, appears to say so too.

"Indeed," remarks my Lady, languidly, "if there is any uncommon eye in the case, it is Mrs. Rouncewell's, and not mine. Rosa is her discovery."

"Your maid, I suppose?"

"No. My anything; pet — secretary — messenger — I don't know what."

"You like to have her about you, as you would like to have a flower, or a bird, or a picture, or a poodle — no, not a poodle, though — or anything else that was equally pretty?" says Volumnia, sympathizing. "Yes, how charming now! and how well that delightful old soul Mrs. Rouncewell is looking. She must be an immense age, and yet she is as active and handsome! — She is the dearest friend I have, positively!"

Sir Leicester feels it to be right and fitting that the housekeeper of Chesney Wold should be a remarkable person. Apart from that, he has a real regard for Mrs. Rouncewell, and likes to hear her praised. So he says, "You are right, Volumnia;" which Volumnia is extremely glad to hear.

"She has no daughter of her own, has she?"

"Mrs. Rouncewell? No, Volumnia. She has a son. Indeed, she had two."

My Lady, whose chronic malady of boredom has been sadly aggravated by Volumnia this evening, glances wearily towards the candlesticks and heaves a noiseless sigh.

"And it is a remarkable example of the confusion into which the present age has fallen; of the obliteration of landmarks, the opening of floodgates, and the uprooting of distinctions," says Sir Leicester with stately gloom; "that I have been informed, by Mr. Tulkinghorn, that Mrs. Rouncewell's son has been invited to go into Parliament."

Miss Volumnia utters a little sharp scream.

"Yes, indeed," repeats Sir Leicester. "Into Parliament."

"I never heard of such a thing! Good gracious, what is the man?" exclaims Volumnia.

"He is called, I believe — an — Ironmaster." Sir Leicester says it slowly, and with gravity and doubt, as not being sure but that he is called a Leadmistress; or that the right word may be some other word expressive of some other relationship to some other metal.

Volumnia utters another little scream.

"He has declined the proposal, if my information from Mr. Tulkinghorn be correct, as I have no doubt it is, Mr. Tulkinghorn being always correct and exact; still, that does not," says Sir Leicester, " that does not lessen the anomaly ; which is fraught with strange considerations — startling considerations, as it appears to me."

Miss Volumnia rising with a look candlestick-wards, Sir Leicester politely performs the grand tour of the drawing-room, brings one, and lights it at my Lady's shaded lamp.

"I must beg you, my Lady," he says while doing so, "to remain a few moments ; for this individual of whom I speak arrived this evening shortly before dinner, and requested — in a very becoming note ;" Sir Leicester, with his habitual regard to truth, dwells upon it; "I am bound to say, in a very becoming and well-expressed note — the favor of a short interview with yourself and *my*self, on the subject of this young girl. As it appeared that he wished to depart to-night, I replied that we would see him before retiring."

Miss Volumnia with a third little scream takes flight, wishing her hosts — O Lud! — well rid of the — what is it ? — Ironmaster!

The other cousins soon disperse, to the last cousin there. Sir Leicester rings the bell. "Make my compliments to Mr. Rouncewell, in the housekeeper's apartments, and say I can receive him now."

My Lady, who has heard all this with slight attention outwardly, looks towards Mr. Rouncewell as he comes in. He is a little over fifty perhaps, of a good figure, like his mother ; and has a clear voice, a broad forehead from which his dark hair has retired, and a shrewd, though open face. He is a responsible-looking gentleman dressed in black, portly enough, but strong and active. Has a perfectly natural and easy air, and is not in the least embarrassed by the great presence into which he comes.

"Sir Leicester and Lady Dedlock, as I have already apologized for intruding on you, I cannot do better than be very brief. I thank you, Sir Leicester."

The head of the Dedlocks has motioned towards a sofa between himself and my Lady. Mr. Rouncewell quietly takes his seat there.

"In these busy times, when so many great undertakings are in progress, people like myself have so many workmen in so many places, that we are always on the flight."

Sir Leicester is content enough that the ironmaster should feel that there is no hurry there; there, in that ancient house, rooted in that quiet park, where the ivy and the moss have had time to mature, and the gnarled and warted elms, and the umbrageous oaks, stand deep in the fern and leaves of a hundred years; and where the sun-dial on the terrace has dumbly recorded for centuries that time, which was as much the property of every Dedlock — while he lasted — as the house and lands. Sir Leicester sits down in an easy-chair, opposing his repose and that of Chesney Wold to the restless flights of ironmasters.

"Lady Dedlock has been so kind," proceeds Mr. Rouncewell, with a respectful glance and a bow that way, "as to place near her a young beauty of the name of Rosa. Now, my son has fallen in love with Rosa; and has asked my consent to his proposing marriage to her, and to their becoming engaged if she will take him — which I suppose she will. I have never seen Rosa until to-day, but I have some confidence in my son's good sense — even in love. I find her what he represents her, to the best of my judgment; and my mother speaks of her with great commendation."

"She in all respects deserves it," says my Lady.

"I am happy, Lady Dedlock, that you say so; and I need not comment on the value to me of your kind opinion of her."

"That," observes Sir Leicester, with unspeakable grandeur, for he thinks the ironmaster a little too glib, "must be quite unnecessary."

"Quite unnecessary, Sir Leicester. Now, my son is a very young man, and Rosa is a very young woman. As I made my way, so my son must make his; and his being married at present is out of the question. But supposing I gave my consent to his engaging himself to this pretty girl, if this pretty girl will engage herself to him, I think it a piece of candor to say at once — I am sure, Sir Leicester and Lady Dedlock, you will understand and excuse me — I should make it a condition that she did not remain at Chesney Wold. Therefore, before communicating further with my son, I take the liberty of saying, that if her removal would be in any way inconvenient or objectionable, I will hold the matter over with him for any reasonable time, and leave it precisely where it is."

Not remain at Chesney Wold! Make it a condition! All Sir Leicester's old misgivings relative to Wat Tyler, and the people in the iron districts who do nothing but turn out by torchlight, come in a shower upon his head: the fine gray hair of which, as well as of his whiskers, actually stirs with indignation.

"Am I to understand, sir," says Sir Leicester, "and is my Lady to understand;" he brings her in thus specially, first, as a point of gallantry, and next as a point of prudence, having great reliance on her sense; "am I to understand, Mr. Rouncewell, and is my Lady to understand, sir, that you consider this young woman too good for Chesney Wold, or likely to be injured by remaining here?"

"Certainly not, Sir Leicester."

"I am glad to hear it." Sir Leicester very lofty indeed.

"Pray, Mr. Rouncewell," says my Lady, warning Sir Leicester off with the slightest gesture of her pretty hand, as if he were a fly, "explain to me what you mean."

"Willingly, Lady Dedlock. There is nothing I could desire more."

Addressing her composed face, whose intelligence, however, is too quick and active to be concealed by any studied impassiveness, however habitual, to the strong Saxon face of the visitor, a picture of resolution and perseverance, my Lady listens with attention, occasionally slightly bending her head.

"I am the son of your housekeeper, Lady Dedlock, and passed my childhood about this house. My mother has lived here half a century, and will die here I have no doubt. She is one of those examples — perhaps as good a one as there is — of love, and attachment, and fidelity in such a station, which England may well be proud of; but of which no order can appropriate the whole pride or the whole merit, because such an instance bespeaks high worth on two sides; on the great side assuredly; on the small one, no less assuredly."

Sir Leicester snorts a little to hear the law laid down in this way; but in his honor and his love of truth, he freely, though silently, admits the justice of the iron-master's proposition.

"Pardon me for saying what is so obvious, but I

wouldn't have it hastily supposed," with the least turn of his eyes towards Sir Leicester, "that I am ashamed of my mother's position here, or wanting in all just respect for Chesney Wold and the family. I certainly may have desired — I certainly have desired, Lady Dedlock — that my mother should retire after so many years, and end her days with me. But, as I have found that to sever this strong bond would be to break her heart, I have long abandoned that idea."

Sir Leicester very magnificent again, at the notion of Mrs. Rouncewell being spirited off from her natural home, to end her days with an ironmaster.

"I have been," proceeds the visitor, in a modest, clear way, "an apprentice, and a workman. I have lived on workman's wages, years and years, and beyond a certain point have had to educate myself. My wife was a foreman's daughter, and plainly brought up. We have three daughters, besides this son of whom I have spoken; and being fortunately able to give them greater advantages than we had ourselves, we have educated them well; very well. It has been one of our great cares and pleasures to make them worthy of any station."

A little boastfulness in his fatherly tone here, as if he added in his heart, "even of the Chesney Wold station." Not a little more magnificence, therefore, on the part of Sir Leicester.

"All this is so frequent, Lady Dedlock, where I live, and among the class to which I belong, that what would be generally called unequal marriages are not of such rare occurrence with us as elsewhere. A son will sometimes make it known to his father that he has fallen in love, say with a young woman in the factory. The father, who once worked in a factory himself, will be a little disappointed at first, very possibly. It may be that he had other views for his son. However, the chances are, that having ascertained the young woman to be of unblemished character, he will say to his son, 'I must be quite sure that you are in earnest here. This is a serious matter for both of you. Therefore I shall have this girl educated for two years' — or, it may be — ' I shall place this girl at the same school with your sisters for such a time, during which you will give me your word and honor to see her only so often. If, at the expiration of that time, when she has so far profited by her advantages as that you may be upon a fair equality, you are both in the same mind, I will do my part to make you happy.' I know of several cases such as I describe, my Lady, and I think they indicate to me my own course now."

Sir Leicester's magnificence explodes. Calmly, but terribly.

"Mr. Rouncewell," says Sir Leicester, with his right hand in the breast of his blue coat — the attitude of state in which he is painted in the gallery: " do you draw a parallel between Chesney Wold and a ———" here he resists a disposition to choke — " a factory ? "

" I need not reply, Sir Leicester, that the two places are very different; but, for the purposes of this case, I think a parallel may be justly drawn between them."

Sir Leicester directs his majestic glance down one side of the long drawing-room, and up the other, before he can believe that he is awake.

" Are you aware, sir, that this young woman whom my Lady — my Lady — has placed near her person, was brought up at the village school outside the gates ? "

" Sir Leicester, I am quite aware of it. A very good

school it is, and handsomely supported by this family."

"Then, Mr. Rouncewell," returns Sir Leicester, "the application of what you have said, is, to me, incomprehensible."

"Will it be more comprehensible, Sir Leicester, if I say," the ironmaster is reddening a little, "that I do not regard the village school as teaching everything desirable to be known by my son's wife?"

From the village school of Chesney Wold, intact as it is this minute, to the whole framework of society; from the whole framework of society, to the aforesaid framework receiving tremendous cracks in consequence of people (ironmasters, leadmistresses, and what not) not minding their catechism, and getting out of the station unto which they are called — necessarily and forever, according to Sir Leicester's rapid logic, the first station in which they happen to find themselves; and from that, to their educating other people out of *their* stations, and so obliterating the landmarks, and opening the floodgates, and all the rest of it; this is the swift progress of the Dedlock mind.

"My Lady, I beg your pardon. Permit me, for one moment!" She has given a faint indication of intending to speak. "Mr. Rouncewell, our views of duty, and our views of station, and our views of education, and our views of — in short, *all* our views — are so diametrically opposed, that to prolong this discussion must be repellent to your feelings, and repellent to my own. This young woman is honored with my Lady's notice and favor. If she wishes to withdraw herself from that notice and favor, or if she chooses to place herself under the influence of any one who may, in his peculiar opinions —

you will allow me to say, in his peculiar opinions, though I readily admit that he is not accountable for them to me — who may, in his peculiar opinions, withdraw her from that notice and favor, she is at any time at liberty to do so. We are obliged to you for the plainness with which you have spoken. It will have no effect of itself, one way or other, on the young woman's position here. Beyond this, we can make no terms; and here we beg — if you will be so good — to leave the subject."

The visitor pauses a moment to give my Lady an opportunity, but she says nothing. He then rises and replies, —

"Sir Leicester and Lady Dedlock, allow me to thank you for your attention, and only to observe that I shall very seriously recommend my son to conquer his present inclinations. Good-night!"

"Mr. Rouncewell," says Sir Leicester, with all the nature of a gentleman shining in him, "it is late, and the roads are dark. I hope your time is not so precious but that you will allow my Lady and myself to offer you the hospitality of Chesney Wold, for to-night at least."

"I hope so," adds my Lady.

"I am much obliged to you, but I have to travel all night, in order to reach a distant part of the country, punctually at an appointed time in the morning."

Therewith the ironmaster takes his departure; Sir Leicester ringing the bell, and my Lady rising as he leaves the room.

When my Lady goes to her boudoir, she sits down thoughtfully by the fire; and, inattentive to the Ghost's Walk, looks at Rosa, writing in an inner room. Presently my Lady calls her.

"Come to me, child. Tell me the truth. Are you in love?"

"Oh! My Lady!"

My Lady, looking at the downcast and blushing face, says, smiling, —

"Who is it? Is it Mrs. Rouncewell's grandson?"

"Yes, if you please, my Lady. But I don't know that I am in love with him — yet."

"Yet, you silly little thing! Do you know that he loves *you*, yet?"

"I think he likes me a little, my Lady." And Rosa bursts into tears.

Is this Lady Dedlock standing beside the village beauty, smoothing her dark hair with that motherly touch, and watching her with eyes so full of musing interest? Ay, indeed it is!

"Listen to me, child. You are young and true, and I believe you are attached to me."

"Indeed I am, my Lady. Indeed there is nothing in the world I wouldn't do, to show how much."

"And I don't think you would wish to leave me just yet, Rosa, even for a lover."

"No, my Lady! Oh, no!" Rosa looks up for the first time, quite frightened at the thought.

"Confide in me, my child. Don't fear me. I wish you to be happy, and will make you so — if I can make anybody happy on this earth."

Rosa, with fresh tears, kneels at her feet and kisses her hand. My Lady takes the hand with which she has caught it, and standing with her eyes fixed on the fire, puts it about and about between her own two hands, and gradually lets it fall. Seeing her so absorbed, Rosa softly withdraws; but still my Lady's eyes are on the fire.

In search of what? Of any hand that is no more, of

any hand that never was, of any touch that might have magically changed her life? Or does she listen to the Ghost's Walk, and think what step does it most resemble? A man's? A woman's? The pattering of a little child's feet, ever coming on — on — on? Some melancholy influence is upon her; or why should so proud a lady close the doors, and sit alone upon the hearth so desolate?

Volumnia is away next day, and all the cousins are scattered before dinner. Not a cousin of the batch but is amazed to hear from Sir Leicester, at breakfast-time, of the obliteration of landmarks, and opening of floodgates, and cracking of the framework of society, manifested through Mrs. Rouncewell's son. Not a cousin of the batch but is really indignant, and connects it with the feebleness of William Buffy when in office, and really does feel deprived of a stake in the country — or the pension list — or something — by fraud and wrong. As to Volumnia, she is handed down the great staircase by Sir Leicester, as eloquent upon the theme, as if there were a general rising in the North of England to obtain her rouge-pot and pearl necklace. And thus, with a clatter of maids and valets — for it is one appurtenance of their cousinship, that, however difficult they may find it to keep themselves, they *must* keep maids and valets — the cousins disperse to the four winds of heaven; and the one wintry wind that blows to-day shakes a shower from the trees near the deserted house, as if all the cousins had been changed into leaves.

CHAPTER XXIX.

THE YOUNG MAN.

CHESNEY WOLD is shut up, carpets are rolled into great scrolls in corners of comfortless rooms, bright damask does penance in brown holland, carving and gilding puts on mortification, and the Dedlock ancestors retire from the light of day again. Around and around the house the leaves fall thick — but never fast, for they come circling down with a dead lightness that is sombre and slow. Let the gardener sweep and sweep the turf as he will, and press the leaves into full barrows, and wheel them off, still they lie ankle-deep. Howls the shrill wind round Chesney Wold; the sharp rain beats, the windows rattle, and the chimneys growl. Mists hide in the avenues, veil the points of view, and move in funeral-wise across the rising grounds. On all the house there is a cold, blank smell, like the smell of the little church, though something drier: suggesting that the dead and buried Dedlocks walk there, in the long nights, and leave the flavor of their graves behind them.

But the house in town, which is rarely in the same mind as Chesney Wold at the same time; seldom rejoicing when it rejoices, or mourning when it mourns, excepting when a Dedlock dies; the house in town shines out awakened. As warm and bright as so much state may be, as delicately redolent of pleasant scents that bear no trace of winter as hothouse flowers can make it; soft and hushed, so that the ticking of the clocks and the crisp burning of the fires alone disturb the stillness in the rooms; it seems to wrap those chilled bones of Sir Leicester's in rainbow-colored wool. And Sir Leicester is glad to repose in dignified contentment before the great fire in the library, condescendingly perusing the backs of his books, or honoring the fine arts with a glance of approbation. For he has his pictures, ancient and modern. Some, of the Fancy Ball School in which Art occasionally condescends to become a master, which would be best catalogued like the miscellaneous articles in a sale. As, "Three high-backed chairs, a table and cover, long-necked bottle (containing wine), one flask, one Spanish female's costume, three-quarter face portrait of Miss Jogg the model, and a suit of armor containing Don Quixote." Or, "One stone terrace (cracked), one gondola in distance, one Venetian senator's dress complete, richly embroidered white satin costume with profile portrait of Miss Jogg the model, one cimeter superbly mounted in gold with jewelled handle, elaborate Moorish dress (very rare), and Othello."

Mr. Tulkinghorn comes and goes pretty often; there being estate business to do, leases to be renewed, and so on. He sees my Lady pretty often, too; and he and she are as composed, and as indifferent, and take as little heed of one another, as ever. Yet it may be that my Lady fears this Mr. Tulkinghorn, and that he knows it. It may be that he pursues her doggedly and steadily, with no touch of compunction, remorse, or pity. It may be that her beauty, and all the state and brilliancy surrounding her, only gives him the greater zest for what he is set upon, and make him the more inflexible in it.

Whether he be cold and cruel, whether immovable in what he has made his duty, whether absorbed in love of power, whether determined to have nothing hidden from him in ground where he has burrowed among secrets all his life, whether he in his heart despises the splendor of which he is a distant beam, whether he is always treasuring up slights and offences in the affability of his gorgeous clients, — whether he be any of this, or all of this, it may be that my Lady had better have five thousand pairs of fashionable eyes upon her, in distrustful vigilance, than the two eyes of this rusty lawyer, with his wisp of neckcloth and his dull black breeches tied with ribbons at the knees.

Sir Leicester sits in my Lady's room — that room in which Mr. Tulkinghorn read the affidavit in Jarndyce and Jarndyce — particularly complacent. My Lady — as on that day — sits before the fire with her screen in her hand. Sir Leicester is particularly complacent, because he has found in his newspaper some congenial remarks bearing directly on the floodgates and the framework of society. They apply so happily to the late case, that Sir Leicester has come from the library to my Lady's room expressly to read them aloud. "The man who wrote this article," he observes by way of preface, nodding at the fire as if he were nodding down at the man from a Mount, "has a well-balanced mind."

The man's mind is not so well-balanced but that he bores my Lady, who, after a languid effort to listen, or rather a languid resignation of herself to a show of listening, becomes distraught, and falls into a contemplation of the fire as if it were her fire at Chesney Wold, and she had never left it. Sir Leicester, quite unconscious, reads on through his double eyeglass, occasionally stopping to remove his glass and express approval, as "Very true indeed," "Very properly put," "I have frequently made the same remark myself;" invariably losing his place after each observation, and going up and down the column to find it again.

Sir Leicester is reading, with infinite gravity and state, when the door opens, and the Mercury in powder makes this strange announcement, —

"The young man, my Lady, of the name of Guppy."

Sir Leicester pauses, stares, repeats, in a killing voice, —

"The young man of the name of Guppy?"

Looking round he beholds the young man of the name of Guppy, much discomfited, and not presenting a very impressive letter of introduction in his manner and appearance.

"Pray," says Sir Leicester to Mercury, "what do you mean by announcing with this abruptness a young man of the name of Guppy?"

"I beg your pardon, Sir Leicester, but my Lady said she would see the young man whenever he called. I was not aware that you were here, Sir Leicester."

With this apology, Mercury directs a scornful and indignant look at the young man of the name of Guppy, which plainly says, "What do you come calling here for, and getting *me* into a row?"

"It's quite right. I gave him those directions," says my Lady. "Let the young man wait."

"By no means, my Lady. Since he has your orders to come, I will not interrupt you." Sir Leicester in his gallantry retires, rather declining to accept a bow from the young man as he goes out, and majestically supposing him to be some shoemaker of intrusive appearance.

Lady Dedlock looks imperiously at her visitor, when the servant has left the room; casting her eyes over him from head to foot. She suffers him to stand by the door, and asks him what he wants?

"That your ladyship would have the kindness to oblige me with a little conversation," returns Mr. Guppy, embarrassed.

"You are, of course, the person who has written me so many letters?"

"Several, your ladyship. Several, before your ladyship condescended to favor me with an answer."

"And could you not take the same means of rendering a conversation unnecessary? Can you not still?"

Mr. Guppy screws his mouth into a silent "No!" and shakes his head.

"You have been strangely importunate. If it should appear, after all, that what you have to say does not concern me — and I don't know how it can, and don't expect that it will — you will allow me to cut you short with but little ceremony. Say what you have to say, if you please."

My Lady, with a careless toss of her screen, turns herself towards the fire again, sitting almost with her back to the young man of the name of Guppy.

"With your ladyship's permission, then," says the young man, "I will now enter on my business. Hem! I am, as I told your ladyship in my first letter, in the law. Being in the law, I have learnt the habit of not committing myself in writing, and therefore I did not mention to your ladyship the name of the firm with which I am connected, and in which my standing — and I may add income — is tolerably good. I may now state to your ladyship, in confidence, that the name of that firm is

Kenge and Carboy, of Lincoln's Inn; which may not be altogether unknown to your ladyship in connection with the case in Chancery of Jarndyce and Jarndyce."

My Lady's figure begins to be expressive of some attention. She has ceased to toss the screen, and holds it as if she were listening.

"Now, I may say to your ladyship at once," says Mr. Guppy, a little emboldened, "it is no matter arising out of Jarndyce and Jarndyce that made me so desirous to speak to your ladyship, which conduct I have no doubt did appear, and does appear, obtrusive — in fact, almost blackguardly." After waiting for a moment to receive some assurance to the contrary, and not receiving any, Mr. Guppy proceeds. "If it had been Jarndyce and Jarndyce, I should have gone at once to your ladyship's solicitor, Mr. Tulkinghorn of the Fields. I have the pleasure of being acquainted with Mr. Tulkinghorn, — at least we move when we meet one another, — and if it had been any business of that sort, I should have gone to him."

My Lady turns a little round, and says "You had better sit down."

"Thank your ladyship." Mr. Guppy does so. "Now, your ladyship;" Mr. Guppy refers to a little slip of paper on which he has made small notes of his line of argument, and which seems to involve him in the densest obscurity whenever he looks at it; "I — oh, yes! — I place myself entirely in your ladyship's hands. If your ladyship was to make any complaint to Kenge and Carboy, or to Mr. Tulkinghorn, of the present visit, I should be placed in a very disagreeable situation. That I openly admit. Consequently, I rely upon your ladyship's honor."

My Lady, with a disdainful gesture of the hand that

holds the screen, assures him of his being worth no complaint from her.

"Thank your ladyship," says Mr. Guppy, "quite satisfactory. Now — I — dash it! — The fact is, that I put down a head or two here of the order of the points I thought of touching upon, and they're written short, and I can't quite make out what they mean. If your ladyship will excuse me taking it to the window half a moment, I " —

Mr. Guppy going to the window tumbles into a pair of love-birds, to whom he says in his confusion, " I beg your pardon, I am sure." This does not tend to the greater legibility of his notes. He murmurs, growing warm and red, and holding the slip of paper now close to his eyes, now a long way off. " C. S. What's C. S. for! Oh! 'E. S.!' Oh, I know! Yes, to be sure!" And comes back enlightened.

"I am not aware," says Mr. Guppy, standing midway between my Lady and his chair, " whether your ladyship ever happened to hear of, or to see, a young lady of the name of Miss Esther Summerson."

My Lady's eyes look at him full. " I saw a young lady of that name not long ago. This past autumn."

"Now, did it strike your ladyship that she was like anybody?" asks Mr. Guppy, crossing his arms, holding his head on one side, and scratching the corner of his mouth with his memoranda.

My Lady removes her eyes from him no more.

"No."

"Not like your ladyship's family?"

"No."

"I think your ladyship," says Mr. Guppy, "can hardly remember Miss Summerson's face?"

"I remember the young lady very well. What has this to do with me?"

"Your ladyship, I do assure you, that having Miss Summerson's image imprinted on my art — which I mention in confidence — I found, when I had the honor of going over your ladyship's mansion of Chesney Wold, while on a short out in the county of Lincolnshire with a friend, such a resemblance between Miss Esther Summerson and your ladyship's own portrait, that it completely knocked me over; so much so, that I didn't at the moment even know what it *was* that knocked me over. And now I have the honor of beholding your ladyship near, (I have often, since that, taken the liberty of looking at your ladyship in your carriage in the park, when I dare say you was not aware of me, but I never saw your ladyship so near,) it's really more surprising than I thought it."

Young man of the name of Guppy! There have been times when ladies lived in strongholds, and had unscrupulous attendants within call, when that poor life of yours would not have been worth a minute's purchase, with those beautiful eyes looking at you as they look at this moment.

My Lady, slowly using her little hand-screen as a fan, asks him again, what he supposes that his taste for likenesses has to do with her?

"Your ladyship," replies Mr. Guppy, again referring to his paper, "I am coming to that. Dash these notes. Oh! 'Mrs. Chadband.' Yes." Mr. Guppy draws his chair a little forward, and seats himself again. My Lady reclines in her chair composedly, though with a trifle less of graceful ease than usual, perhaps; and never falters in her steady gaze. "A — stop a minute, though!" Mr. Guppy refers again. "E. S. twice? Oh, yes! yes, I see my way now, right on."

Rolling up the slip of paper as an instrument to point his speech with, Mr. Guppy proceeds.

"Your ladyship, there is a mystery about Miss Esther Summerson's birth and bringing up. I am informed of that fact, because — which I mention in confidence — I know it in the way of my profession at Kenge and Carboy's. Now, as I have already mentioned to your ladyship, Miss Summerson's image is imprinted on my art. If I could clear this mystery for her, or prove her to be well related, or find that having the honor to be a remote branch of your ladyship's family she had a right to be made a party in Jarndyce and Jarndyce, why, I might make a sort of a claim upon Miss Summerson to look with an eye of more decided favor on my proposals than she has exactly done as yet. In fact, as yet she hasn't favored them at all."

A kind of angry smile just dawns upon my Lady's face.

"Now, it's a very singular circumstance, your ladyship," says Mr. Guppy, "though one of those circumstances that do fall in the way of us professional men, — which I may call myself, for though not admitted, yet I have had a present of my articles made to me by Kenge and Carboy, on my mother's advancing from the principal of her little income the money for the stamp, which comes heavy — that I have encountered the person, who lived as servant with the lady who brought Miss Summerson up, before Mr. Jarndyce took charge of her. That lady was a Miss Barbary, your ladyship."

Is the dead color on my Lady's face, reflected from the screen which has a green-silk ground, and which she holds in her raised hand as if she had forgotten it; or is it a dreadful paleness that has fallen on her?

"Did your ladyship," says Mr. Guppy, "ever happen to hear of Miss Barbary?"

"I don't know. I think so. Yes."

"Was Miss Barbary at all connected with your ladyship's family?"

My Lady's lips move, but they utter nothing. She shakes her head.

"*Not* connected?" says Mr. Guppy. "Oh! Not to your ladyship's knowledge, perhaps? Ah! But might be? Yes." After each of these interrogatories, she has inclined her head. "Very good! Now, this Miss Barbary was extremely close,—seems to have been extraordinarily close for a female, females being generally (in common life at least) rather given to conversation,—and my witness never had an idea whether she possessed a single relative. On one occasion, and only one, she seems to have been confidential to my witness on a single point; and she then told her that the little girl's real name was not Esther Summerson, but Esther Hawdon."

"My God!"

Mr. Guppy stares. Lady Dedlock sits before him, looking him through, with the same dark shade upon her face, in the same attitude even to the holding of the screen, with her lips a little apart, her brow a little contracted, but for the moment dead. He sees her consciousness return, sees a tremor pass across her frame like a ripple over water, sees her lips shake, sees her compose them by a great effort, sees her force herself back to the knowledge of his presence, and of what he has said. All this, so quickly, that her exclamation and her dead condition seem to have passed away like the features of those long-preserved dead bodies sometimes opened up in tombs, which, struck by the air like lightning, vanish in a breath.

"Your ladyship is acquainted with the name of Hawdon?"

"I have heard it before."

"Name of any collateral, or remote branch of your ladyship's family?"

"No."

"Now, your ladyship," says Mr. Guppy, "I come to the last point of the case, so far as I have got it up. It's going on, and I shall gather it up closer and closer as it goes on. Your ladyship must know — if your ladyship don't happen by any chance to know already — that there was found dead at the house of a person named Krook, near Chancery Lane, some time ago, a law-writer in great distress. Upon which law-writer there was an inquest; and which law-writer was an anonymous character, his name being unknown. But, your ladyship, I have discovered, very lately, that that law-writer's name was Hawdon."

"And what is *that* to me?"

"Ay, your ladyship, that's the question! Now, your ladyship, a queer thing happened after that man's death. A lady started up; a disguised lady, your ladyship, who went to look at the scene of action, and went to look at his grave. She hired a crossing-sweeping boy to show it her. If your ladyship would wish to have the boy produced in corroboration of this statement, I can lay my hand upon him at any time."

The wretched boy is nothing to my Lady, and she does *not* wish to have him produced.

"Oh, I assure your ladyship it's a very queer start indeed," says Mr. Guppy. "If you was to hear him tell about the rings that sparkled on her fingers when she took her glove off, you'd think it quite romantic."

There are diamonds glittering on the hand that holds the screen. My Lady trifles with the screen, and makes them glitter more ; again with that expression which in other times might have been so dangerous to the young man of the name of Guppy.

"It was supposed, your ladyship, that he left no rag or scrap behind him by which he could be possibly identified. But he did. He left a bundle of old letters."

The screen still goes, as before. All this time, her eyes never once release him.

"They were taken and secreted. And to-morrow night, your ladyship, they will come into my possession."

" Still, I ask you, what is this to me ? "

" Your ladyship, I conclude with that." Mr. Guppy rises. "If you think there's enough, in this chain of circumstances put together, — in the undoubted strong likeness of this young lady to your ladyship, which is a positive fact for a jury, — in her having been brought up by Miss Barbary, — in Miss Barbary stating Miss Summerson's real name to be Hawdon, — in your ladyship's knowing both these names *very well*, — and in Hawdon's dying as he did, — to give your ladyship a family interest in going further into the case, I will bring those papers here. I don't know what they are, except that they are old letters : I have never had them in my possession yet. I will bring those papers here, as soon as I get them ; and go over them for the first time with your ladyship. I have told your ladyship my object. I have told your ladyship that I should be placed in a very disagreeable situation if any complaint was made ; and all is in strict confidence."

Is this the full purpose of the young man of the name of Guppy, or has he any other? Do his words disclose the length, breadth, depth, of his object and suspicion in coming here; or, if not, what do they hide? He is a match for my Lady there. She may look at him, but he can look at the table, and keep that witness-box face of his from telling anything.

"You may bring the letters," says my Lady, "if you choose."

"Your ladyship is not very encouraging, upon my word and honor," says Mr. Guppy, a little injured.

"You may bring the letters," she repeats, in the same tone, "if you — please."

"It shall be done. I wish your ladyship good-day."

On a table near her is a rich bauble of a casket, barred and clasped like an old strong chest. She, looking at him still, takes it to her and unlocks it.

"Oh! I assure your ladyship I am not actuated by any motives of that sort," says Mr. Guppy; "and I couldn't accept of anything of the kind. I wish your ladyship good-day, and am much obliged to you all the same."

So the young man makes his bow, and goes down-stairs; where the supercilious Mercury does not consider himself called upon to leave his Olympus by the hall-fire, to let the young man out.

As Sir Leicester basks in his library, and dozes over his newspaper, is there no influence in the house to startle him; not to say, to make the very trees at Chesney Wold fling up their knotted arms, the very portraits frown, the very armor stir?

No. Words, sobs, and cries, are but air; and air is so shut in and shut out throughout the house in town, that about the rings that sparkled on her fingers when she took her glove off, you'd think it quite romantic."

There are diamonds glittering on the hand that holds the screen. My Lady trifles with the screen, and makes them glitter more; again with that expression which in other times might have been so dangerous to the young man of the name of Guppy.

"It was supposed, your ladyship, that he left no rag or scrap behind him by which he could be possibly identified. But he did. He left a bundle of old letters."

The screen still goes, as before. All this time, her eyes never once release him.

"They were taken and secreted. And to-morrow night, your ladyship, they will come into my possession."

"Still, I ask you, what is this to me?"

"Your ladyship, I conclude with that." Mr. Guppy rises. "If you think there's enough, in this chain of circumstances put together, — in the undoubted strong likeness of this young lady to your ladyship, which is a positive fact for a jury, — in her having been brought up by Miss Barbary, — in Miss Barbary stating Miss Summerson's real name to be Hawdon, — in your ladyship's knowing both these names *very well*, — and in Hawdon's dying as he did, — to give your ladyship a family interest in going further into the case, I will bring those papers here. I don't know what they are, except that they are old letters: I have never had them in my possession yet. I will bring those papers here, as soon as I get them; and go over them for the first time with your ladyship. I have told your ladyship my object. I have told your ladyship that I should be placed in a very disagreeable situation if any complaint was made; and all is in strict confidence."

Is this the full purpose of the young man of the name of Guppy, or has he any other? Do his words disclose the length, breadth, depth, of his object and suspicion in coming here; or, if not, what do they hide? He is a match for my Lady there. She may look at him, but he can look at the table, and keep that witness-box face of his from telling anything.

"You may bring the letters," says my Lady, "if you choose."

"Your ladyship is not very encouraging, upon my word and honor," says Mr. Guppy, a little injured.

"You may bring the letters," she repeats, in the same tone, "if you — please."

"It shall be done. I wish your ladyship good-day."

On a table near her is a rich bauble of a casket, barred and clasped like an old strong chest. She, looking at him still, takes it to her and unlocks it.

"Oh! I assure your ladyship I am not actuated by any motives of that sort," says Mr. Guppy; "and I couldn't accept of anything of the kind. I wish your ladyship good-day, and am much obliged to you all the same."

So the young man makes his bow, and goes downstairs; where the supercilious Mercury does not consider himself called upon to leave his Olympus by the hall-fire, to let the young man out.

As Sir Leicester basks in his library, and dozes over his newspaper, is there no influence in the house to startle him; not to say, to make the very trees at Chesney Wold fling up their knotted arms, the very portraits frown, the very armor stir?

No. Words, sobs, and cries, are but air; and air is so shut in and shut out throughout the house in town, that sounds need be uttered trumpet-tongued indeed by my Lady in her chamber, to carry any faint vibration to Sir Leicester's ears; and yet this cry is in the house, going upward from a wild figure on its knees.

"O my child, my child! Not dead in the first hours of her life, as my cruel sister told me; but sternly nurtured by her, after she had renounced me and my name! O my child, O my child!"

CHAPTER XXX.

ESTHER'S NARRATIVE.

RICHARD had been gone away some time, when a visitor came to pass a few days with us. It was an elderly lady. It was Mrs. Woodcourt, who, having come from Wales to stay with Mrs. Bayham Badger, and having written to my Guardian, "by her son Allan's desire," to report that she had heard from him and that he was well, "and sent his kind remembrances to all of us," had been invited by my Guardian to make a visit to Bleak House. She stayed with us nearly three weeks. She took very kindly to me, and was extremely confidential; so much so that sometimes she almost made me uncomfortable. I had no right, I knew very well, to be uncomfortable because she confided in me, and I felt it was unreasonable; still, with all I could do, I could not quite help it.

She was such a sharp little lady, and used to sit with her hands folded in each other, looking so very watchful while she talked to me, that perhaps I found that rather irksome. Or perhaps it was her being so upright and trim; though I don't think it was that, because I thought that quaintly pleasant. Nor can it have been the general expression of her face, which was very sparkling and pretty for an old lady. I don't know what it was. Or at least if I do, now, I thought I did not then. Or at least — but it don't matter.

Of a night when I was going up-stairs to bed, she would invite me into her room, where she sat before the fire in a great chair; and, dear me, she would tell me about Morgan ap Kerrig until I was quite low-spirited! Sometimes she recited a few verses from Crumlinwallinwer and the Mewlinwillinwodd (if those are the right names, which I dare say they are not), and would become quite fiery with the sentiments they expressed. Though I never knew what they were (being in Welsh), further than that they were highly eulogistic of the lineage of Morgan ap Kerrig.

"So, Miss Summerson," she would say to me with stately triumph, "this, you see, is the fortune inherited by my son. Wherever my son goes, he can claim kindred with Ap Kerrig. He may not have money, but he always has what is much better — family, my dear."

I had my doubts of their caring so very much for Morgan ap Kerrig, in India and China; but of course I never expressed them. I used to say it was a great thing to be so highly connected.

"It *is*, my dear, a great thing," Mrs. Woodcourt would reply. "It has its disadvantages; my son's choice of a wife, for instance, is limited by it; but the matrimonial choice of the Royal family is limited in much the same manner."

Then she would pat me on the arm and smooth my dress, as much as to assure me that she had a good opinion of me, the distance between us notwithstanding.

"Poor Mr. Woodcourt, my dear," she would say, and always with some emotion, for with her lofty pedigree she had a very affectionate heart, "was descended from a great Highland family, the Mac Coorts of Mac Coort. He served his king and country as an officer in the

Royal Highlanders, and he died on the field. My son is one of the last representatives of two old families. With the blessing of Heaven he will set them up again, and unite them with another old family."

It was in vain for me to try to change the subject, as I used to try — only for the sake of novelty — or perhaps because — but I need not be so particular. Mrs. Woodcourt never would let me change it.

"My dear," she said one night, "you have so much sense, and you look at the world in a quiet manner so superior to your time of life, that it is a comfort to me to talk to you about these family matters of mine. You don't know much of my son, my dear; but you know enough of him, I dare say, to recollect him?"

"Yes, ma'am. I recollect him."

"Yes, my dear. Now, my dear, I think you are a judge of character, and I should like to have your opinion of him?"

"O, Mrs. Woodcourt!" said I, "that is so difficult."

"Why is it so difficult, my dear?" she returned. "I don't see it myself."

"To give an opinion —"

"On so slight an acquaintance, my dear. *That's* true."

I didn't mean that; because Mr. Woodcourt had been at our house a good deal altogether, and had become quite intimate with my Guardian. I said so, and added that he seemed to be very clever in his profession — we thought — and that his kindness and gentleness to Miss Flite were above all praise.

"You do him justice!" said Mrs. Woodcourt, pressing my hand. "You define him exactly. Allan is a dear fellow, and in his profession faultless. I say it, though I am his mother. Still, I must confess he is not without faults, love."

"None of us are," said I.

"Ah! But his really are faults that he might correct, and ought to correct," returned the sharp old lady, sharply shaking her head. "I am so much attached to you, that I may confide in you, my dear, as a third party wholly disinterested, that he is fickleness itself."

I said, I should have thought it hardly possible that he could have been otherwise than constant in his profession, and zealous in the pursuit of it, judging from the reputation he had earned.

"You are right again, my dear," the old lady retorted; "but I don't refer to his profession, look you."

"O!" said I.

"No," said she. "I refer, my dear, to his social conduct. He is always paying trivial attentions to young ladies, and always has been, ever since he was eighteen. Now, my dear, he has never really cared for any one of them, and has never meant in doing this to do any harm, or to express anything but politeness and good nature. Still, it's not right, you know; is it?"

"No," said I, as she seemed to wait for me.

"And it might lead to mistaken notions, you see, my dear."

I supposed it might.

"Therefore I have told him, many times, that he really should be more careful, both in justice to himself and in justice to others. And he has always said, 'Mother, I will be; but you know me better than anybody else does, and you know I mean no harm — in short, mean nothing.' All of which is very true, my dear, but is no justification. However, as he is now gone so far away, and for an indefinite time, and as he will have good opportunities and introductions, we may consider this past and gone. And you, my dear," said the old lady, who was now all nods and smiles; "regarding your dear self, my love?"

"Me, Mrs. Woodcourt?"

"Not to be always selfish, talking of my son, who has gone to seek his fortune, and to find a wife — when do you mean to seek *your* fortune, and to find a husband, Miss Summerson? Hey, look you! Now you blush!"

I don't think I did blush — at all events, it was not important if I did — and I said, my present fortune perfectly contented me, and I had no wish to change it.

"Shall I tell you what I always think of you, and the fortune yet to come for you, my love?" said Mrs. Woodcourt.

"If you believe you are a good prophet," said I.

"Why, then, it is that you will marry some one, very rich and very worthy, much older — five-and-twenty years, perhaps — than yourself. And you will be an excellent wife, and much beloved, and very happy."

"That is a good fortune," said I. "But, why is it to be mine?"

"My dear," she returned, "there's suitability in it, — you are so busy, and so neat, and so peculiarly situated altogether, that there's suitability in it, and it will come to pass. And nobody, my love, will congratulate you more sincerely on such a marriage than I shall."

It was curious that this should make me uncomfortable, but I think it did. I know it did. It made me for some part of that night quite uncomfortable. I was so ashamed of my folly, that I did not like to confess it even to Ada; and that made me more uncomfortable still. I would have given anything not to have been so much in the bright old lady's confidence, if I could have possibly declined it. It gave me the most inconsistent opinions of her. At one time I thought she was a story-teller, and at another time that she was the pink of truth. Now, I suspected that she was very cunning; next moment, I believed her honest Welsh heart to be perfectly innocent and simple. And, after all, what did it matter to me, and why did it matter to me? Why could not I, going up to bed with my basket of keys, stop to sit down by her fire, and accommodate myself for a little while to her, at least as well as to anybody else; and not trouble myself about the harmless things she said to me? Impelled towards her, as I certainly was, for I was very anxious that she should like me, and was very glad indeed that she did, why should I harp afterwards, with actual distress and pain, on every word she said, and weigh it over and over again in twenty scales? Why was it so worrying to me to have her in our house, and confidential to me every night, when I yet felt that it was better and safer, somehow, that she should be there than anywhere else? These were perplexities and contradictions that I could not account for. At least, if I could — but I shall come to all that by and by, and it is mere idleness to go on about it now.

So, when Mrs. Woodcourt went away, I was sorry to lose her, but was relieved too. And then Caddy Jellyby came down; and Caddy brought such a packet of domestic news, that it gave us abundant occupation.

First, Caddy declared (and would at first declare nothing else) that I was the best adviser that ever was known. This, my pet said, was no news at all; and this, *I* said, of course, was nonsense. Then Caddy told us that she was going to be married in a month; and that if Ada and I would be her bridesmaids, she was the happiest girl in the world. To be sure, this was news indeed; and I thought we never should have done talking about it, we had so much to say to Caddy, and Caddy had so much to say to us.

It seemed that Caddy's unfortunate papa had got over his bankruptcy — "gone through the Gazette," was the expression Caddy used, as if it were a tunnel, — with the general clemency and commiseration of his creditors; and had got rid of his affairs in some blessed manner, without succeeding in understanding them; and had given up everything he possessed (which was not worth much I should think, to judge from the state of the furniture), and had satisfied every one concerned that he could do no more, poor man. So, he had been honorably dismissed to "the office," to begin the world again. What he did at the office, I never knew: Caddy said he was a "Custom-House and General Agent," and the only thing I ever understood about that business was, that when he wanted money more than usual, he went to the Docks to look for it, and hardly ever found it.

As soon as her papa had tranquillized his mind by becoming this shorn lamb, and they had removed to a furnished lodging in Hatton Garden (where I found the children, when I afterwards went there, cutting the horsehair out of the seats of the chairs, and choking themselves with it), Caddy had brought about a meeting between him and old Mr. Turveydrop; and poor Mr. Jellyby, being very humble and meek, had deferred to Mr. Turveydrop's Deportment so submissively, that they had become excellent friends. By degrees, old Mr. Turveydrop, thus familiarized with the idea of his son's marriage, had worked up his parental feelings to the height of contemplating that event as being near at hand; and had given his gracious consent to the young couple commencing housekeeping at the Academy in Newman Street, when they would.

"And your papa, Caddy. What did he say?"

"Oh! poor Pa," said Caddy, "only cried, and said he hoped we might get on better than he and Ma had got on. He didn't say so before Prince; he only said so to me. And he said, 'My poor girl, you have not been very well taught how to make a home for your husband; but unless you mean with all your heart to strive to do it, you had better murder him than marry him — if you really love him.'"

"And how did you reassure him, Caddy?"

"Why, it was very distressing, you know, to see poor Pa so low, and hear him say such terrible things, and I couldn't help crying myself. But I told him that I *did* mean it with all my heart; and that I hoped our house would be a place for him to come and find some comfort in, of an evening; and that I hoped and thought I could be a better daughter to him there, than at home. Then I mentioned Peepy's coming to stay with me; and then Pa began to cry again, and said the children were Indians."

"Indians, Caddy?"

"Yes," said Caddy, "Wild Indians. And Pa said," — (here she began to sob, poor girl, not at all like the happiest girl in the world) — "that he was sensible the best thing that could happen to them was, their being all Tomahawked together."

Ada suggested that it was comfortable to know that Mr. Jellyby did not mean these destructive sentiments.

"No, of course I know Pa wouldn't like his family to be weltering in their blood," said Caddy; "but he means that they are very unfortunate in being Ma's children, and that he is very unfortunate in being Ma's husband; and I am sure that's true, though it seems unnatural to say so."

I asked Caddy if Mrs. Jellyby knew that her wedding-day was fixed.

"Oh! you know what Ma is, Esther," she returned. "It's impossible to say whether she knows it or not. She has been told it often enough; and when she *is* told it, she only gives me a placid look, as if I was I don't know what — a steeple in the distance," said Caddy, with a sudden idea; "and then she shakes her head, and says 'Oh, Caddy, Caddy, what a tease you are!' and goes on with the Borrioboola letters."

"And about your wardrobe, Caddy?" said I. For she was under no restraint with us.

"Well, my dear Esther," she returned, drying her eyes, "I must do the best I can, and trust to my dear Prince never to have an unkind remembrance of my coming so shabbily to him. If the question concerned an outfit for Borrioboola, Ma would know all about it, and would be quite excited. Being what it is, she neither knows nor cares."

Caddy was not at all deficient in natural affection for her mother, but mentioned this with tears, as an undeniable fact: which I am afraid it was. We were so sorry for the poor dear girl, and found so much to admire in the good disposition which had survived under such discouragement, that we both at once (I mean Ada and I) proposed a little scheme, that made her perfectly joyful. This was, her staying with us for three weeks; my staying with her for one; and our all three contriving and cutting out, and repairing, and sewing, and saving, and doing the very best we could think of, to make the most of her stock. My Guardian being as pleased with the idea as Caddy was, we took her home next day to arrange the matter; and brought her out again in triumph, with her boxes, and all the purchases that could be squeezed out of a ten-pound note, which Mr. Jellyby had found in the Docks I suppose, but which he at all events gave her. What my Guardian would not have given her, if we had encouraged him, it would be difficult to say; but we thought it right to compound for no more than her wedding-dress and bonnet. He agreed to this compromise; and if Caddy had ever been happy in her life, she was happy when we sat down to work.

She was clumsy enough with her needle, poor girl, and pricked her fingers as much as she had been used to ink them. She could not help reddening a little, now and then; partly with the smart, and partly with vexation at being able to do no better; but she soon got over that, and began to improve rapidly. So, day after day, she, and my darling, and my little maid Charley, and a milliner out of the town, and I, sat hard at work, as pleasantly as possible.

Over and above this, Caddy was very anxious " to learn housekeeping," as she said. Now, Mercy upon us! the idea of her learning housekeeping of a person of my vast experience was such a joke, that I laughed, and colored up, and fell into a comical confusion when she proposed it. However, I said, " Caddy, I am sure you are very welcome to learn anything that you can learn of *me*, my dear;" and I showed her all my books and methods, and all my fidgety ways. You would have supposed that I was showing her some wonderful inventions by her study of them; and if you had seen her, whenever I jingled my housekeeping keys, get up and attend me, certainly you might have thought that there never was a greater impostor than I, with a blinder follower than Caddy Jellyby.

So, what with working and housekeeping, and lessons to Charley, and backgammon in the evening with my Guardian, and duets with Ada, the three weeks slipped fast away. Then I went home with Caddy, to see what could be done there ; and Ada and Charley remained behind, to take care of my Guardian.

When I say I went home with Caddy, I mean to the furnished lodging in Hatton Garden. We went to Newman Street two or three times, where preparations were in progress too; a good many, I observed, for enhancing the comforts of old Mr. Turveydrop, and a few for putting the newly married couple away cheaply at the top of the house ; but our great point was to make the furnished lodging decent for the wedding breakfast, and to imbue Mrs. Jellyby beforehand with some faint sense of the occasion.

The latter was the more difficult thing of the two, because Mrs. Jellyby and an unwholesome boy occupied the front sitting-room (the back one was a mere closet), and it was littered down with waste paper and Borrioboolan documents, as an untidy stable might be littered with straw. Mrs. Jellyby sat there all day, drinking strong coffee, dictating, and holding Borrioboolan interviews by appointment. The unwholesome boy, who seemed to me to be going into a decline, took his meals out of the house. When Mr. Jellyby came home, he usually groaned and went down into the kitchen. There he got something to eat, if the servant would give him anything ; and then, feeling that he was in the way, went out and walked about

Hatten Garden in the wet. The poor children scrambled up and tumbled down the house, as they had always been accustomed to do.

The production of these devoted little sacrifices, in any presentable condition, being quite out of the question at a week's notice, I proposed to Caddy that we should make them as happy as we could, on her marriage morning, in the attic where they all slept; and should confine our greatest efforts to her mamma and her mamma's room, and a clean breakfast. In truth, Mrs. Jellyby required a good deal of attention, the lattice-work up her back having widened considerably since I first knew her, and her hair looking like the mane of a dustman's horse.

Thinking that the display of Caddy's wardrobe would be the best means of approaching the subject, I invited Mrs. Jellyby to come and look at it spread out on Caddy's bed, in the evening, after the unwholesome boy was gone.

"My dear Miss Summerson," said she, rising from her desk, with her usual sweetness of temper, "these are really ridiculous preparations, though your assisting them is a proof of your kindness. There is something so inexpressibly absurd to me, in the idea of Caddy being married! Oh, Caddy, you silly, silly, silly puss!"

She came up-stairs with us notwithstanding, and looked at the clothes in her customary far-off manner. They suggested one distinct idea to her; for she said, with her placid smile, and shaking her head, "My good Miss Summerson, at half the cost, this weak child might have been equipped for Africa!"

On our going down-stairs again, Mrs. Jellyby asked me whether this troublesome business was really to take place next Wednesday? And on my replying yes, she said, "Will my room be required, my dear Miss Summerson? For it's quite impossible that I can put my papers away."

I took the liberty of saying that the room would certainly be wanted, and that I thought we must put the papers away somewhere. "Well, my dear Miss Summerson," said Mrs. Jellyby, "you know best, I dare say. But by obliging me to employ a boy, Caddy has embarrassed me to that extent, overwhelmed as I am with public business, that I don't know which way to turn. We have a Ramification meeting, too, on Wednesday afternoon, and the inconvenience is very serious."

"It is not likely to occur again," said I, smiling. "Caddy will be married but once, probably."

"That's true," Mrs. Jellyby replied, "that's true, my dear. I suppose we must make the best of it!"

The next question was, how Mrs. Jellyby should be dressed on the occasion. I thought it very curious to see her looking on serenely from her writing-table, while Caddy and I discussed it; occasionally shaking her head at us with a half reproachful smile, like a superior spirit who could just bear with our trifling.

The state in which her dresses were, and the extraordinary confusion in which she kept them, added not a little to our difficulty; but at length we devised something not very unlike what a common place mother might wear on such an occasion. The abstracted manner in which Mrs. Jellyby would deliver herself up to having this attire tried on by the dressmaker, and the sweetness with which she would then observe to me how sorry she was that I had not turned my thoughts to Africa, were consistent with the rest of her behavior.

The lodging was rather confined as to space, but I fancied that if Mrs. Jellyby's household had been the only lodgers in Saint Paul's or Saint Peter's, the sole advantage they would have found in the size of the building would have been its affording a great deal of room to be dirty in. I believe that nothing belonging to the family, which it had been possible to break, was unbroken at the time of those preparations for Caddy's marriage; that nothing which it had been possible to spoil in any way, was unspoilt; and that no domestic object which was capable of collecting dirt, from a dear child's knee to the door-plate, was without as much dirt as could well accumulate upon it.

Poor Mr. Jellyby, who very seldom spoke, and almost always sat when he was at home with his head against the wall, became interested when he saw that Caddy and I were attempting to establish some order among all this waste and ruin, and took off his coat to help. But such wonderful things came tumbling out of the closets when they were opened — bits of mouldy pie, sour bottles, Mrs. Jellyby's caps, letters, tea, forks, odd boots and shoes of children, firewood, wafers, saucepan-lids, damp sugar in odds and ends of paper bags, footstools, black-lead brushes, bread, Mrs. Jellyby's bonnets, books with butter sticking to the binding, guttered candle-ends put out by being turned upside down in broken candlesticks, nutshells, heads and tails of shrimps, dinner-mats, gloves, coffee-grounds, umbrellas — that he looked frightened, and left off again. But he came in regularly every evening, and sat without his coat, with his head against the wall; as though he would have helped us, if he had known how.

"Poor Pa;" said Caddy to me, on the night before the great day, when we really had got things a little to rights.

"It seems unkind to leave him, Esther; but what could I do if I stayed! Since I first knew you, I have tidied and tidied over and over again; but it's useless. Ma and Africa, together, upset the whole house directly. We never have a servant who don't drink. Ma's ruinous to everything."

Mr. Jellyby could not hear what she said, but he seemed very low indeed, and shed tears, I thought.

"My heart aches for him; that it does!" sobbed Caddy. "I can't help thinking, to-night, Esther, how dearly I hope to be happy with Prince, and how dearly Pa hoped, I dare say, to be happy with Ma. What a disappointed life!"

"My dear Caddy!" said Mr. Jellyby, looking slowly round from the wall. It was the first time, I think, I ever heard him say three words together.

"Yes, Pa," cried Caddy, going to him and embracing him affectionately.

"My dear Caddy," said Mr. Jellyby. "Never have"—

"Not Prince, Pa?" faltered Caddy. "Not have Prince?"

"Yes, my dear," said Mr. Jellyby. "Have him, certainly. But, never have —"

I mentioned, in my account of our first visit in Thavies' Inn, that Richard described Mr. Jellyby as frequently opening his mouth after dinner without saying anything. It was a habit of his. He opened his mouth now a great many times, and shook his head in a melancholy manner.

"What do you wish me not to have? Don't have what, dear Pa?" asked Caddy, coaxing him, with her arms round his neck.

"Never have a mission, my dear child."

Mr. Jellyby groaned, and laid his head against the wall again; and this was the only time I ever heard him make any approach to expressing his sentiments on the Borrioboolan question. I suppose he had been more talkative and lively, once; but he seemed to have been completely exhausted long before I knew him.

I thought Mrs. Jellyby never would have left off serenely looking over her papers, and drinking coffee, that night. It was twelve o'clock before we could obtain possession of the room; and the clearance it required then was so discouraging, that Caddy, who was almost tired out, sat down in the middle of the dust and cried. But she soon cheered up, and we did wonders with it before we went to bed.

In the morning it looked, by the aid of a few flowers and a quantity of soap and water, and a little arrangement, quite gay. The plain breakfast made a cheerful show, and Caddy was perfectly charming. But when my darling came, I thought — and I think now — that I never had seen such a dear face as my beautiful pet's.

We made a little feast for the children up-stairs, and we put Peepy at the head of the table, and we showed them Caddy in her bridal dress, and they clapped their hands and hurrahed, and Caddy cried to think that she was going away from them, and hugged them over and over again, until we brought Prince up to fetch her away — when, I am sorry to say, Peepy bit him. Then, there was old Mr. Turveydrop down-stairs, in a state of Deportment not to be expressed, benignly blessing Caddy, and giving my Guardian to understand, that his son's happiness was his own parental work, and that he sacrificed personal considerations to ensure it. "My dear sir," said Mr. Turveydrop, "these young people will live with me; my house is large enough for their accommodation, and they shall not want the shelter of my roof. I could have wished, you will understand the allusion, Mr. Jarndyce, for you remember my illustrious patron the Prince Regent, — I could have wished that my son had married into a family where there was more Deportment; but the will of Heaven be done!"

Mr. and Mrs. Pardiggle were of the party; Mr. Pardiggle, an obstinate-looking man with a large waistcoat and stubbly hair, who was always talking in a loud bass voice about his mite, or Mrs. Pardiggle's mite, or their five boys' mites. Mr. Quale, with his hair brushed back as usual, and his knobs of temples shining very much, was also there; not in the character of a disappointed lover, but as the Accepted of a young — at least, an unmarried — lady, a Miss Wisk, who was also there. Miss Wisk's mission, my Guardian said, was to show the world that woman's mission was man's mission; and that the only genuine mission, of both man and woman, was to be always moving declaratory resolutions about things in general at public meetings. The guests were few; but were, as one might expect at Mrs. Jellyby's, all devoted to public objects only. Besides those I have mentioned, there was an extremely dirty lady, with her bonnet all awry, and the ticketed price of her dress still sticking on it, whose neglected home, Caddy told me, was like a filthy wilderness, but whose church was like a fancy fair. A very contentious gentleman, who said it was his mission to be everybody's brother, but who appeared to be on terms of coolness with the whole of his large family, completed the party.

A party, having less in common with such an occasion, could hardly have been got together by any ingenuity.

Such a mean mission as the domestic mission, was the very last thing to be endured among them; indeed, Miss Wisk informed us, with great indignation, before we sat down to breakfast, that the idea of woman's mission lying chiefly in the narrow sphere of Home was an outrageous slander on the part of her Tyrant, Man. One other singularity was, that nobody with a mission — except Mr. Quale, whose mission, as I think I have formerly said, was to be in ecstasies with everybody's mission — cared at all for anybody's mission. Mrs. Pardiggle being as clear that the only one infallible course was her course of pouncing upon the poor, and applying benevolence to them like a strait waistcoat; as Miss Wisk was that the only practical thing for the world was the emancipation of Woman from the thraldom of her Tyrant, Man. Mrs. Jellyby, all the while, sat smiling at the limited vision that could see anything but Borrioboola-Gha.

But I am anticipating now the purport of our conversation on the ride home, instead of first marrying Caddy. We all went to church, and Mr. Jellyby gave her away. Of the air with which old Mr. Turveydrop, with his hat under his left arm, (the inside presented at the clergyman like a cannon,) and his eyes creasing themselves up into his wig, stood, stiff and high-shouldered, behind us bridesmaids during the ceremony, and afterwards saluted us, I could never say enough to do it justice. Miss Wisk, whom I cannot report as prepossessing in appearance, and whose manner was grim, listened to the proceedings, as part of Woman's wrongs, with a disdainful face. Mrs. Jellyby, with her calm smile and her bright eyes, looked the least concerned of all the company.

We duly came back to breakfast, and Mrs. Jellyby sat

at the head of the table, and Mr. Jellyby at the foot. Caddy had previously stolen up-stairs, to hug the children again, and tell them that her name was Turveydrop. But this piece of information, instead of being an agreeable surprise to Peepy, threw him on his back in such transports of kicking grief, that I could do nothing on being sent for, but accede to the proposal that he should be admitted to the breakfast-table. So he came down, and sat in my lap; and Mrs. Jellyby, after saying, in reference to the state of his pinafore, "O you naughty Peepy, what a shocking little pig you are!" was not at all discomposed. He was very good, except that he brought down Noah with him (out of an ark I had given him before we went to church), and *would* dip him head first into the wine-glasses, and then put him in his mouth.

My Guardian, with his sweet temper and his quick perception and his amiable face, made something agreeable even out of the ungenial company. None of them seemed able to talk about anything but his or her own one subject, and none of them seemed able to talk about even that, as part of a world in which there was anything else; but my Guardian turned it all to the merry encouragement of Caddy, and the honor of the occasion, and brought us through the breakfast nobly. What we should have done without him, I am afraid to think; for, all the company despising the bride and bridegroom, and old Mr. Turveydrop, — and old Mr. Turveydrop, in virtue of his Deportment, considering himself vastly superior to all the company, — it was a very unpromising case.

At last the time came when poor Caddy was to go, and when all her property was packed on the hired coach and pair that was to take her and her husband to

Gravesend. It affected us to see Caddy clinging, then, to her deplorable home, and hanging on her mother's neck with the greatest tenderness.

"I am very sorry I couldn't go on writing from dictation, Ma," sobbed Caddy. "I hope you forgive me now?"

"O Caddy, Caddy!" said Mrs. Jellyby, "I have told you over and over again that I have engaged a boy, and there's an end of it."

"You are sure you are not the least angry with me, Ma? Say you are sure before I go away, Ma?"

"You foolish Caddy," returned Mrs. Jellyby, "do I look angry, or have I inclination to be angry, or time to be angry? How *can* you?"

"Take a little care of Pa while I am gone, mamma!"

Mrs. Jellyby positively laughed at the fancy. "You romantic child," said she, lightly patting Caddy's back. "Go along. I am excellent friends with you. Now, good-by, Caddy, and be very happy!"

Then Caddy hung upon her father, and nursed his cheek against hers as if he were some poor, dull child in pain. All this took place in the hall. Her father released her, took out his pocket-handkerchief, and sat down on the stairs with his head against the wall. I hope he found some consolation in walls. I almost think he did.

And then Prince took her arm in his, and turned with great emotion and respect to his father, whose Deportment at that moment was overwhelming.

"Thank you over and over again, father!" said Prince, kissing his hand. "I am very grateful for all your kindness and consideration regarding our marriage, and so, I can assure you, is Caddy."

"Very," sobbed Caddy. "Ve-ry!"

"My dear son," said Mr. Turveydrop, "and dear daughter, I have done my duty. If the spirit of a sainted Wooman hovers above us, and looks down on the occasion, that, and your constant affection, will be my recompense. You will not fail in *your* duty, my son and daughter, I believe?"

"Dear father, never!" cried Prince.

"Never, never, dear Mr. Turveydrop!" said Caddy.

"This," returned Mr. Turveydrop, "is as it should be. My children, my home is yours, my heart is yours, my all is yours. I will never leave you; nothing but Death shall part us. My dear son, you contemplate an absence of a week, I think?"

"A week, dear father. We shall return home this day week."

"My dear child," said Mr. Turveydrop, "let me, even under the present exceptional circumstances, recommend strict punctuality. It is highly important to keep the connection together; and schools, if at all neglected, are apt to take offence."

"This day week, father, we shall be sure to be home to dinner."

"Good!" said Mr. Turveydrop. "You will find fires, my dear Caroline, in your own room, and dinner prepared in my apartment. Yes, yes, Prince!" anticipating some self-denying objection on his son's part with a great air. "You and our Caroline will be strange in the upper part of the premises, and will, therefore, dine that day in my apartment. Now, bless ye!"

They drove away; and whether I wondered most at Mrs. Jellyby, or at Mr. Turveydrop, I did not know. Ada and my Guardian were in the same condition when we came to talk it over. But before we drove away, too, I received a most unexpected and eloquent compliment from Mr. Jellyby. He came up to me in the hall, took both my hands, pressed them earnestly, and opened his mouth twice. I was so sure of his meaning, that I said, quite flurried, " You are very welcome, sir. Pray don't mention it!"

"I hope this marriage is for the best, Guardian?" said I, when we three were on our road home.

"I hope it is, little woman. Patience. We shall see."

"Is the wind in the East to-day?" I ventured to ask him.

He laughed heartily, and answered "No."

"But it must have been this morning, I think," said I.

He answered "No," again; and this time my dear girl confidently answered "No," too, and shook the lovely head which, with its blooming flowers against the golden hair, was like the very Spring. "Much *you* know of East winds, my ugly darling," said I, kissing her in my admiration — I couldn't help it.

Well! It was only their love for me, I know very well, and it is a long time ago. I must write it, even if I rub it out again, because it gives me so much pleasure. They said there could be no East wind where Somebody was; they said that wherever Dame Durden went, there was sunshine and summer air.

CHAPTER XXXI.

NURSE AND PATIENT.

I HAD not been at home again many days, when one evening I went up-stairs into my own room to take a peep over Charley's shoulder, and see how she was getting on with her copy-book. Writing was a trying business to Charley, who seemed to have no natural power over a pen, but in whose hand every pen appeared to become perversely animated, and to go wrong and crooked, and to stop, and splash, and sidle into corners, like a saddle-donkey. It was very odd, to see what old letters Charley's young hand made; they, so wrinkled, and shrivelled, and tottering; it, so plump and round. Yet Charley was uncommonly expert at other things, and had as nimble little fingers as I ever watched.

"Well, Charley," said I, looking over a copy of the letter O in which it was represented as square, triangular, pear-shaped, and collapsed in all kinds of ways, "we are improving. If we only get to make it round, we shall be perfect, Charley."

Then I made one, and Charley made one, and the pen wouldn't join Charley's neatly, but twisted it up into a knot.

"Never mind, Charley. We shall do it in time."

Charley laid down her pen, the copy being finished; opened and shut her cramped little hand; looked gravely at the page, half in pride and half in doubt; and got up, and dropped me a courtesy.

"Thank you, miss. If you please, miss, did you know a poor person of the name of Jenny?"

"A brickmaker's wife, Charley? Yes."

"She came and spoke to me when I was out a little while ago, and said you knew her, miss. She asked me if I wasn't the young lady's little maid — meaning you for the young lady, miss — and I said yes, miss."

"I thought she had left this neighborhood altogether, Charley."

"So she had, miss, but she's come back again to where she used to live — she and Liz. Did you know another poor person of the name of Liz, miss?"

"I think I do, Charley, though not by name."

"That's what she said!" returned Charley. "They have both come back, miss, and have been tramping high and low."

"Tramping high and low, have they, Charley?"

"Yes, miss." If Charley could only have made the letters in her copy as round as the eyes with which she looked into my face, they would have been excellent. "And this poor person came about the house three or four days, hoping to get a glimpse of you, miss — all she wanted, she said — but you were away. That was when she saw me. She saw me a going about, miss," said Charley, with a short laugh of the greatest delight and pride, "and she thought I looked like your maid!"

"Did she though, really, Charley?"

"Yes, miss!" said Charley, "really and truly." And Charley, with another short laugh of the purest glee, made her eyes very round again, and looked as serious as became my maid. I was never tired of seeing Charley in the full enjoyment of that great dignity, standing before me with her youthful face and figure, and her steady manner, and her childish exultation breaking through it now and then in the pleasantest way.

"And where did you see her, Charley?" said I.

My little maid's countenance fell, as she replied, " By the doctor's shop, miss." For Charley wore her black frock yet.

I asked if the brickmaker's wife were ill, but Charley said No. It was some one else. Some one in her cottage who had tramped down to Saint Alban's, and was tramping he didn't know where. A poor boy, Charley said. No father, no mother, no any one. "Like as Tom might have been, miss, if Emma and me had died after father," said Charley, her round eyes filling with tears.

"And she was getting medicine for him, Charley?"

"She said, miss," returned Charley, "how that he had once done as much for her."

My little maid's face was so eager, and her quiet hands were folded so closely in one another as she stood looking at me, that I had no great difficulty in reading her thoughts. "Well, Charley," said I, "it appears to me that you and I can do no better than go round to Jenny's, and see what's the matter."

The alacrity with which Charley brought my bonnet and veil, and, having dressed me, quaintly pinned herself into her warm shawl and made herself look like a little old woman, sufficiently expressed her readiness. So Charley and I, without saying anything to any one, went out.

It was a cold, wild night, and the trees shuddered in the wind. The rain had been thick and heavy all day, and with little intermission for many days. None was falling just then, however. The sky had partly cleared, but was very gloomy — even above us, where a few stars were shining. In the north and northwest, where the sun had set three hours before, there was a pale, dead light both beautiful and awful; and into it long sullen lines of cloud waved up, like a sea stricken immovable as it was heaving. Towards London, a lurid glare overhung the whole dark waste; and the contrast between these two lights, and the fancy which the redder light engendered of an unearthly fire, gleaming on all the unseen buildings of the city, and on all the faces of its many thousands of wondering inhabitants, was as solemn as might be.

I had no thought, that night — none, I am quite sure — of what was soon to happen to me. But I have always remembered since, that when we had stopped at the garden-gate to look up at the sky, and when we went upon our way, I had for a moment an undefinable impression of myself as being something different from what I then was. I know it was then, and there, that I had it. I have ever since connected the feeling with that spot and time, and with everything associated with that spot and time, to the distant voices in the town, the barking of a dog, and the sound of wheels coming down the miry hill.

It was Saturday night; and most of the people belonging to the place where we were going, were drinking elsewhere. We found it quieter than I had previously seen it, though quite as miserable. The kilns were burning, and a stifling vapor set towards us with a pale blue glare.

We came to the cottage, where there was a feeble

candle in the patched window. We tapped at the door and went in. The mother of the little child who had died, was sitting in a chair on one side of the poor fire by the bed; and opposite to her, a wretched boy, supported by the chimney-piece, was cowering on the floor. He held under his arm, like a little bundle, a fragment of a fur cap; and as he tried to warm himself, he shook until the crazy door and window shook. The place was closer than before, and had an unhealthy, and a very peculiar smell.

I had not lifted my veil when I first spoke to the woman, which was at the moment of our going in. The boy staggered up instantly, and stared at me with a remarkable expression of surprise and terror.

His action was so quick, and my being the cause of it was so evident, that I stood still, instead of advancing nearer.

"I won't go no more to the berryin ground," muttered the boy; "I a'n't agoing there, so I tell you!"

I lifted my veil and spoke to the woman. She said to me in a low voice, "Don't mind him, ma'am. He'll soon come back to his head;" and said to him, "Jo, Jo, what's the matter?"

"I know wot she's come for!" cried the boy.

"Who?"

"The lady there. She's come to get me to go along with her to the berryin ground. I won't go to the berryin ground. I don't like the name of it. She might go a-berryin *me!*"

His shivering came on again, and as he leaned against the wall, he shook the hovel.

"He has been talking off and on about such like, all day, ma'am," said Jenny, softly. "Why, how you stare! This is *my* lady, Jo."

"Is it?" returned the boy, doubtfully, and surveying me with his arm held out above his burning eyes. " She looks to me the t'other one. It a'n't the bonnet, nor yet it a'n't the gownd, but she looks to me the t'other one."

My little Charley, with her premature experience of illness and trouble, had pulled off her bonnet and shawl, and now went quietly up to him with a chair, and sat him down in it, like an old sick-nurse. Except that no such attendant could have shown him Charley's youthful face, which seemed to engage his confidence.

" I say!" said the boy. " *You* tell me. A'n't the lady the t'other lady?"

Charley shook her head, as she methodically drew his rags about him and made him as warm as she could.

" O!" the boy muttered. " Then I 'spose she a'n't."

" I came to see if I could do you any good," said I. " What is the matter with you?"

" I'm a-being froze," returned the boy hoarsely, with his haggard gaze wandering about me, "and then burnt up, and then froze, and then burnt up, ever so many times in a hour. And my head's all sleepy, and all a-going mad-like — and I'm so dry — and my bones isn't half so much bones as pain."

" When did he come here?" I asked the woman.

" This morning, ma'am, I found him at the corner of the town. I had known him up in London yonder. Hadn't I, Jo?"

" Tom-all-Alone's," the boy replied.

Whenever he fixed his attention or his eyes, it was only for a very little while. He soon began to droop his head again, and roll it heavily, and speak as if he were half awake.

" When did he come from London?" I asked.

"I come from London yes'day," said the boy himself, now flushed and hot. "I'm a-going somewheres."

"Where is he going?" I asked.

"Somewheres," repeated the boy, in a louder tone. "I have been moved on, and moved on, more nor ever I was afore, since the t'other one giv' me the sov'ring. Mrs. Snagsby, she's always a-watching, and a-driving of me — what have I done to her? — and they're all a-watching and a-driving of me. Every one of 'em's doing of it, from the time when I don't get up, to the time when I don't go to bed. And I'm a-going somewheres. That's where I'm a-going. She told me, down in Tom-all-Alone's, as she come from Stolbuns, and so I took the Stolbuns Road. It's as good as another."

He always concluded by addressing Charley.

"What is to be done with him?" said I, taking the woman aside. "He could not travel in this state, even if he had a purpose, and knew where he was going."

"I know no more, ma'am, than the dead," she replied, glancing compassionately at him. "Perhaps the dead know better if they could only tell us. I've kept him here all day for pity's sake, and I've given him broth and physic, and Liz has gone to try if any one will take him in (here's my pretty in the bed — her child, but I call it mine); but I can't keep him long, for if my husband was to come home and find him here, he'd be rough in putting him out, and might do him a hurt. Hark! Here comes Liz back!"

The other woman came hurriedly in as she spoke, and the boy got up with a half obscured sense that he was expected to be going. When the little child awoke, and when and how Charley got at it, took it out of bed, and began to walk about hushing it, I don't know. There she was, doing all this, in a quiet motherly manner, as if she were living in Mrs. Blinder's attic with Tom and Emma again.

The friend had been here and there, and had been played about from hand to hand, and had come back as she went. At first it was too early for the boy to be received into the proper refuge, and at last it was too late. One official sent her to another, and the other sent her back again to the first, and so backward and forward; until it appeared to me as if both must have been appointed for their skill in evading their duties, instead of performing them. And now, after all, she said, breathing quickly, for she had been running, and was frightened too, "Jenny, your master's on the road home, and mine's not far behind, and the Lord help the boy, for we can do no more for him!" They put a few halfpence together, and hurried them into his hand, and so, in an oblivious, half-thankful, half-insensible way, he shuffled out of the house.

"Give me the child, my dear?" said its mother to Charley, "and thank you kindly, too! Jenny, woman dear, good-night! Young lady, if my master don't fall out with me, I'll look down by the kiln by and by, where the boy will be most like, and again in the morning!" She hurried off; and presently we passed her hushing and singing to her child at her own door, and looking anxiously along the road for her drunken husband.

I was afraid of staying then to speak to either woman, lest I should bring her into trouble. But I said to Charley that we must not leave the boy to die. Charley, who knew what to do much better than I did, and whose quickness equalled her presence of mind, glided on before me, and presently we came up with Jo, just short of the brickkiln.

I think he must have begun his journey with some small bundle under his arm, and must have had it stolen or lost it. For he still carried his wretched fragment of fur cap like a bundle, though he went bareheaded through the rain, which now fell fast. He stopped when we called to him, and again showed a dread of me when I came up; standing with his lustrous eyes fixed upon me, and even arrested in his shivering fit.

I asked him to come with us, and we would take care that he had some shelter for the night.

"I don't want no shelter," he said; "I can lay amongst the warm bricks."

"But don't you know that people die there?" returned Charley.

"They dies everywheres," said the boy. "They dies in their lodgings — she knows where; I showed her — and they dies down in Tom-all-Alone's in heaps. They dies more than they lives, according to what I see." Then he hoarsely whispered Charley. "If she a'n't the t'other one, she a'n't the forrenner. Is there *three* of 'em then?"

Charley looked at me a little frightened. I felt half frightened at myself when the boy glared on me so.

But he turned and followed when I beckoned to him; and finding that he acknowledged that influence in me, I led the way straight home. It was not far; only at the summit of the hill. We passed but one man. I doubted if we should have got home without assistance; the boy's steps were so uncertain and tremulous. He made no complaint, however, and was strangely unconcerned about himself, if I may say so strange a thing.

Leaving him in the hall for a moment, shrunk into a corner of the window-seat, and staring with an indifference that could scarcely be called wonder, at the comfort and brightness about him, I went into the drawing-room to speak to my Guardian. There I found Mr. Skimpole, who had come down by the coach, as he frequently did without notice, and never bringing any clothes with him, but always borrowing everything he wanted.

They came out with me directly, to look at the boy. The servants had gathered in the hall, too; and he shivered in the window-seat with Charley standing by him, like some wounded animal that had been found in a ditch.

"This is a sorrowful case," said my Guardian, after asking him a question or two, and touching him, and examining his eyes. "What do you say, Harold?"

"You had better turn him out," said Mr. Skimpole?

"What do you mean?" inquired my Guardian, almost sternly.

"My dear Jarndyce," said Mr. Skimpole, "you know what I am: I am a child. Be cross to me, if I deserve it. But I have a constitutional objection to this sort of thing. I always had, when I was a medical man. He's not safe, you know. There's a very bad sort of fever about him."

Mr. Skimpole had retreated from the hall to the drawing-room again, and said this in his airy way, seated on the music-stool as we stood by.

"You'll say it's childish," observed Mr. Skimpole, looking gayly at us. "Well, I dare say it may be; but I *am* a child, and I never pretend to be anything else. If you put him out in the road, you only put him where he was before. He will be no worse off than he was, you know. Even make him better off, if you like. Give him sixpence, or five shillings, or five pound ten — you are arithmeticians, and I am not — and get rid of him!"

"And what is he to do then?" asked my Guardian.

"Upon my life," said Mr. Skimpole, shrugging his shoulders with his engaging smile, "I have not the least idea what he is to do then. But I have no doubt he'll do it."

"Now, is it not a horrible reflection," said my Guardian, to whom I had hastily explained the unavailing efforts of the two women, "is it not a horrible reflection," walking up and down and rumpling his hair, "that if this wretched creature were a convicted prisoner, his hospital would be wide open to him, and he would be as well taken care of as any sick boy in the kingdom."

"My dear Jarndyce," returned Mr. Skimpole, "you'll pardon the simplicity of the question, coming as it does from a creature who is perfectly simple in worldly matters — but, why *isn't* he a prisoner then?"

My Guardian stopped and looked at him with a whimsical mixture of amusement and indignation in his face.

"Our young friend is not to be suspected of any delicacy, I should imagine," said Mr. Skimpole, unabashed and candid. "It seems to me that it would be wiser, as well as in a certain kind of way more respectable, if he showed some misdirected energy that got him into prison. There would be more of an adventurous spirit in it, and consequently more of a certain sort of poetry."

"I believe," returned my Guardian, resuming his uneasy walk, "that there is not such another child on earth as yourself."

"Do you really?" said Mr. Skimpole; "I dare say! But, I confess I don't see why our young friend, in his degree, should not seek to invest himself with such poetry as is open to him. He is no doubt born with an appetite — probably, when he is in a safer state of health, he has an excellent appetite. Very well. At our young friend's natural dinner hour, most likely about noon, our young friend says in effect to society, 'I am hungry; will you have the goodness to produce your spoon, and feed me?' Society, which has taken upon itself the general arrangement of the whole system of spoons, and professes to have a spoon for our young friend, does *not* produce that spoon; and our young friend, therefore, says 'You really must excuse me if I seize it.' Now, this appears to me a case of misdirected energy, which has a certain amount of reason in it, and a certain amount of romance; and I don't know but what I should be more interested in our young friend, as an illustration of such a case, than merely as a poor vagabond — which any one can be."

"In the mean time," I ventured to observe, "he is getting worse."

"In the mean time," said Mr. Skimpole, cheerfully, "as Miss Summerson, with her practical good sense, observes, he is getting worse. Therefore I recommend your turning him out before he gets still worse."

The amiable face with which he said it, I think I shall never forget.

"Of course, little woman," observed my Guardian, turning to me, "I can ensure his admission into the proper place by merely going there to enforce it, though it's a bad state of things when, in his condition, that is necessary. But it's growing late, and is a very bad night, and the boy is worn out already. There is a bed in the wholesome loft-room by the stable; we had better keep him there till morning, when he can be wrapped up and removed. We'll do that."

"O!" said Mr. Skimpole, with his hands upon the keys of the piano, as we moved away. "Are you going back to our young friend?"

"Yes," said my Guardian.

"How I envy you your constitution, Jarndyce!" returned Mr. Skimpole, with playful admiration. "You don't mind these things, neither does Miss Summerson. You are ready at all times to go anywhere, and do anything. Such is Will! I have no Will at all — and no Won't — simply Can't."

"You can't recommend anything for the boy, I suppose?" said my Guardian, looking back over his shoulder, half angrily; only half angrily, for he never seemed to consider Mr. Skimpole an accountable being.

"My dear Jarndyce, I observed a bottle of cooling medicine in his pocket, and it's impossible for him to do better than take it. You can tell them to sprinkle a little vinegar about the place where he sleeps, and to keep it moderately cool, and him moderately warm. But it's mere impertinence in me to offer any recommendation. Miss Summerson has such a knowledge of detail, and such a capacity for the administration of detail, that she knows all about it."

We went back into the hall, and explained to Jo what we proposed to do, which Charley explained to him again, and which he received with the languid unconcern I had already noticed, wearily looking on at what was done, as if it were for somebody else. The servants compassionating his miserable state, and being very anxious to help, we soon got the loft-room ready; and some of the men about the house carried him across the wet yard, well wrapped up. It was pleasant to observe how kind they were to him, and how there appeared to be a general impression among them, that frequently calling him "Old Chap," was likely to revive his spirits. Charley directed the operations, and went to and fro between the loft-room and the house with such little stimulants and comforts as we thought it safe to give him. My Guardian himself saw him before he was left for the night, and reported to me when he returned to the Growlery to write a letter on the boy's behalf, which a messenger was charged to deliver at daylight in the morning, that he seemed easier, and inclined to sleep. They had fastened his door on the outside, he said, in case of his being delirious; but had so arranged that he could not make any noise without being heard.

Ada being in our room with a cold, Mr. Skimpole was left alone all this time, and entertained himself by playing snatches of pathetic airs, and sometimes singing to them (as we heard at a distance) with great expression and feeling. When we rejoined him in the drawing-room, he said he would give us a little ballad, which had come into his head, "apropos of our young friend;" and he sang one about a Peasant boy —

"Thrown on the wide world, doom'd to wander and roam,
Bereft of his parents, bereft of a home,"

— quite exquisitely. It was a song that always made him cry, he told us.

He was extremely gay all the rest of the evening: "for he absolutely chirped," those were his delighted words, "when he thought by what a happy talent for business he was surrounded." He gave us, in his glass of negus, "Better health to our young friend!" and supposed, and gayly pursued, the case of his being reserved like Whittington to become Lord Mayor of London. In that event, no doubt, he would establish the Jarndyce Institution and the Summerson Almshouses, and a little annual Corporation Pilgrimage to St. Alban's. He had no doubt, he said, that our young friend was an excellent boy in his way, but his way was not the Harold Skimpole way; what Harold Skimpole was, Harold Skimpole had found himself, to his considerable surprise, when he first made his own acquaintance; he had accepted himself with all his failings, and had thought it sound philosophy to make the best of the bargain; and he hoped we would do the same.

Charley's last report was, that the boy was quiet. I could see, from my window, the lantern they had left him burning quietly; and I went to bed very happy to think that he was sheltered.

There was more movement and more talking than usual a little before daybreak, and it awoke me. As I was dressing, I looked out of my window, and asked one of our men who had been among the active sympathizers last night, whether there was anything wrong about the house. The lantern was still burning in the loft-window.

"It's the boy, miss," said he.

"Is he worse?" I inquired.

"Gone, miss."

"Dead!"

"Dead, miss? No. Gone clean off."

At what time of the night he had gone, or how, or why, it seemed hopeless ever to divine. The door remaining as it had been left, and the lantern standing in the window, it could only be supposed that he had got out by a trap in the floor which communicated with an empty cart-house below. But he had shut it down again, if that were so; and it looked as if it had not been raised.

Nothing of any kind was missing. On this fact being clearly ascertained, we all yielded to the painful belief that delirium had come upon him in the night, and that, allured by some imaginary object, or pursued by some imaginary horror, he had strayed away in that worse than helpless state ; — all of us, that is to say, but Mr. Skimpole, who repeatedly suggested, in his usual easy light style, that it had occurred to our young friend that he was not a safe inmate, having a bad kind of fever upon him ; and that he had, with great natural politeness, taken himself off.

Every possible inquiry was made, and every place was searched. The brick-kilns were examined, the cottages were visited, the two women were particularly questioned, but they knew nothing of him, and nobody could doubt that their wonder was genuine. The weather had for some time been too wet, and the night itself had been too wet, to admit of any tracing by footsteps. Hedge and ditch, and wall, and rick and stack, were examined by our men for a long distance round, lest the boy should be lying in such a place insensible or dead ; but nothing was seen to indicate that he had ever been near. From the time when he was left in the loft-room, he vanished.

The search continued for five days. I do not mean that it ceased, even then ; but that my attention was then diverted into a current very memorable to me.

As Charley was at her writing again in my room in the evening, and as I sat opposite to her at work, I felt the table tremble. Looking up I saw my little maid shivering from head to foot.

"Charley," said I, "are you so cold?"

"I think I am, miss," she replied. "I don't know what it is. I can't hold myself still. I felt so yesterday; at about this same time, miss. Don't be uneasy, I think I'm ill."

I heard Ada's voice outside, and I hurried to the door of communication between my room and our pretty sitting-room, and locked it. Just in time, for she tapped at it while my hand was yet upon the key.

Ada called to me to let her in; but I said, "Not now, my dearest. Go away. There's nothing the matter; I will come to you presently." Ah! it was a long, long time, before my darling girl and I were companions again.

Charley fell ill. In twelve hours she was very ill. I moved her to my room, and laid her in my bed, and sat down quietly to nurse her. I told my Guardian all about it, and why I felt it was necessary that I should seclude myself, and my reason for not seeing my darling above all. At first she came very often to the door, and called to me, and even reproached me with sobs and tears; but I wrote her a long letter, saying that she made me anxious and unhappy, and imploring her, as she loved me, and wished my mind to be at peace, to come no nearer than the garden. After that, she came beneath the window, even oftener than she had come to the door; and, if I had learnt to love her dear sweet voice before when we were hardly ever apart, how did I learn to love it then, when I stood behind the window-curtain listening and replying, but not so much as looking out! How did I learn to love it afterwards, when the harder time came!

They put a bed for me in our sitting-room; and by keeping the door wide open, I turned the two rooms into one, now that Ada had vacated that part of the house, and kept them always fresh and airy. There was not a servant, in or about the house, but was so good that they would all most gladly have come to me at any hour of the day or night, without the least fear or unwillingness; but I thought it best to choose one worthy woman who was never to see Ada, and whom I could trust to come and go with all precaution. Through her means, I got out to take the air with my Guardian, when there was no fear of meeting Ada; and wanted for nothing in the way of attendance, any more than in any other respect.

And thus poor Charley sickened and grew worse, and fell into heavy danger of death, and lay severely ill for many a long round of day and night. So patient she was, so uncomplaining, and inspired by such a gentle fortitude, that very often as I sat by Charley, holding her head in my arms — repose would come to her, so, when it would come to her in no other attitude — I silently prayed to our Father in heaven that I might not forget the lesson which this little sister taught me.

I was very sorrowful to think that Charley's pretty looks would change and be disfigured, even if she recovered — she was such a child with her dimpled face — but that thought was, for the greater part, lost in her greater peril. When she was at the worst, and her mind rambled again to the cares of her father's sick-bed, and the little children, she still knew me so far as that she would be quiet in my arms when she could lie quiet nowhere else, and murmur out the wanderings of her mind less restlessly. At those times I used to think, how should I ever tell the two remaining babies that the baby who had learned of her faithful heart to be a mother to them in their need, was dead!

There were other times when Charley knew me well,

and talked to me; telling me that she sent her love to Tom and Emma, and that she was sure Tom would grow up to be a good man. At those times, Charley would speak to me of what she had read to her father as well as she could, to comfort him; of that young man carried out to be buried, who was the only son of his mother and she was a widow; of the ruler's daughter raised up by the gracious hand upon her bed of death. And Charley told me that when her father died, she had kneeled down and prayed in her first sorrow that he likewise might be raised up, and given back to his poor children; and that if she should never get better, and should die too, she thought it likely that it might come into Tom's mind to offer the same prayer for her. Then would I show Tom how those people of old days had been brought back to life on earth, only that we might know our hope to be restored in Heaven!

But of all the various times there were in Charley's illness, there was not one when she lost the gentle qualities I have spoken of. And there were many, many, when I thought in the night of the last high belief in the watching Angel, and the last higher trust in God, on the part of her poor despised father.

And Charley did not die. She flutteringly and slowly turned the dangerous point, after long lingering there, and then began to mend. The hope that never had been given, from the first, of Charley being in outward appearance Charley any more, soon began to be encouraged; and even that prospered, and I saw her growing into her old childish likeness again.

It was a great morning, when I could tell Ada all this as she stood out in the garden; and it was a great evening, when Charley and I at last took tea together in the next room. But, on that same evening, I felt that I was stricken cold.

Happily for both of us, it was not until Charley was safe in bed again and placidly asleep, that I began to think the contagion of her illness was upon me. I had been able easily to hide that I had felt at tea-time, but I was past that already now, and I knew that I was rapidly following in Charley's steps.

I was well enough, however, to be up early in the morning, and to return my darling's cheerful blessing from the garden, and to talk with her as long as usual. But I was not free from an impression that I had been walking about the two rooms in the night, a little beside myself, though knowing where I was; and I felt confused at times — with a curious sense of fulness, as if I were becoming too large altogether.

In the evening I was so much worse that I resolved to prepare Charley; with which view, I said, "You're getting quite strong, Charley, are you not?"

"Oh, quite!" said Charley.

"Strong enough to be told a secret, I think, Charley?"

"Quite strong enough for that, miss!" cried Charley. But Charley's face fell in the height of her delight, for she saw the secret in *my* face; and she came out of the great chair, and fell upon my bosom, and said, "Oh, miss, it's my doing! It's my doing!" and a great deal more, out of the fulness of her grateful heart.

"Now, Charley," said I, after letting her go on for a little while, "if I am to be ill, my great trust, humanly speaking, is in you. And unless you are as quiet and composed for me, as you always were for yourself, you can never fulfil it, Charley."

"If you'll let me cry a little longer, miss," said Charley. "Oh, my dear, my dear! if you'll only let me cry a little longer, oh, my dear!" — how affectionately and devotedly she poured this out, as she clung to my neck, I never can remember without tears — "I'll be good."

So I let Charley cry a little longer, and it did us both good.

"Trust in me now, if you please, miss," said Charley, quietly. "I am listening to everything you say."

"It is very little at present, Charley. I shall tell your doctor to-night that I don't think I am well, and that you are going to nurse me."

For that the poor child thanked me with her whole heart.

"And in the morning, when you hear Miss Ada in the garden, if I should not be quite able to go to the window-curtain as usual, do you go, Charley, and say I am asleep — that I have rather tired myself, and am asleep. At all times keep the room as I have kept it, Charley, and let no one come."

Charley promised, and I lay down, for I was very heavy. I saw the doctor that night, and asked the favor of him that I wished to ask, relative to his saying nothing of my illness in the house as yet. I have a very indistinct remembrance of that night melting into day, and of day melting into night again; but I was just able, on the first morning, to get to the window, and speak to my darling.

On the second morning I heard her dear voice — Oh, how dear now! — outside; and I asked Charley, with some difficulty (speech being painful to me), to go and say I was asleep. I heard her answer softly, "Don't disturb her, Charley, for the world!"

"How does my own Pride look, Charley?" I inquired.

"Disappointed, miss," said Charley, peeping through the curtain.

"But I know she is very beautiful this morning."

"She is indeed, miss," answered Charley, peeping. "Still looking up at the window."

With her blue clear eyes, God bless them, always loveliest when raised like that!

I called Charley to me, and gave her her last charge.

"Now, Charley, when she knows I am ill, she will try to make her way into the room. Keep her out, Charley, if you love me truly, to the last! Charley, if you let her in but once, only to look upon me for one moment as I lie here, I shall die."

"I never will! I never will!" she promised me.

"I believe it, my dear Charley. And now come and sit beside me for a little while, and touch me with your hand. For I cannot see you, Charley; I am blind."

END OF VOL. II.

www.ingramcontent.com/pod-product-compliance
Lightning Source LLC
Chambersburg PA
CBHW022018240426
43667CB00042B/936